A Gold Edition Compendium of Jabez Stories

Stories in North Staffordshire Dialect

by A Scott

(Wilfred Alan Bloor)

Keele University

First Paperback Printing, 2015
Paperback Second Edition 2017
Hardback Gold Edition 2022

ISBN-13: 978-1-739800765

Published by
Clayhanger Press
for
A.S., I.K., R.N. & D.M. Bloor

Clayhanger Press

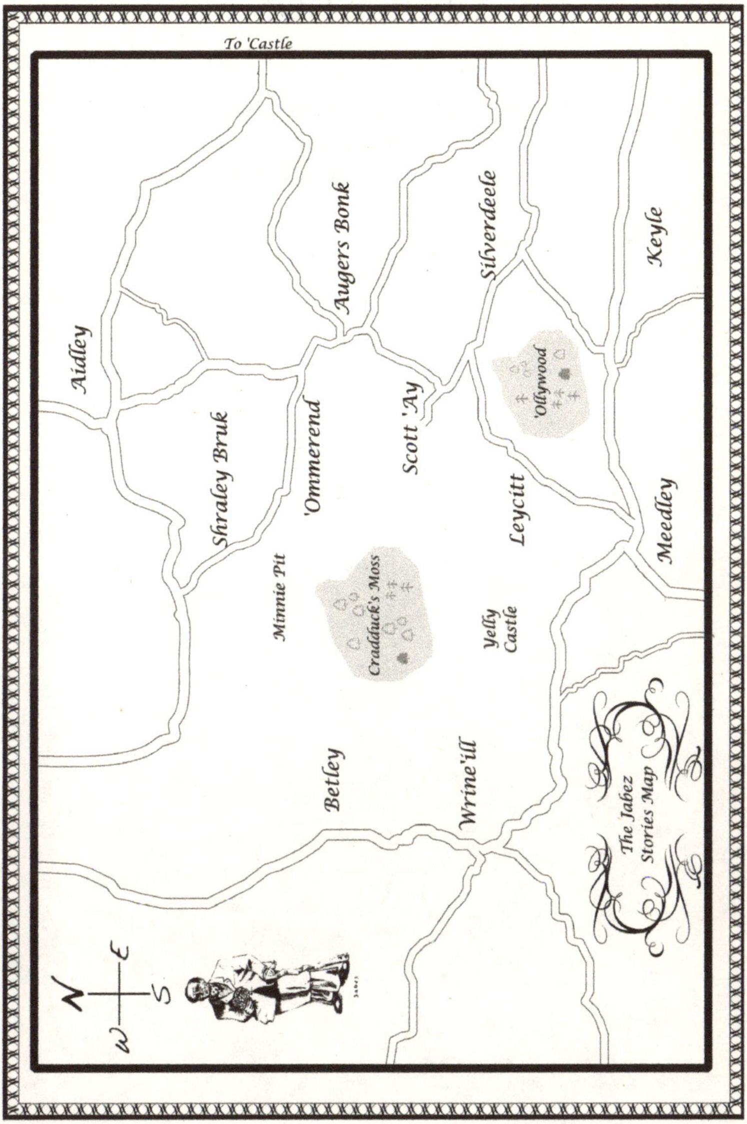
The Jabez
Stories Map
To 'Castle
Aidley
Augers Bonk
Silverdeele
Keyle
Shraley Bruk
'Ommerend
Scott 'Ay
'Ollywood
Leycitt
Meedley
Minnie Pit
Cradduck's Moss
Yelly
Castle
Betley
Wrine'ill
N
E
S
W

DEDICATION

To our parents Wilfred and Irene Bloor
from
Alan, Ian, Roger & David

Jabez

Wilfred Bloor working on a Jabez story

The launch of the first Jabez Book, Wilfred and Irene Bloor with the Lord Mayor and Lady Mayoress of Stoke on Trent, October 1972

CONTENTS

Illustrations

Foreword to the compendium edition

The centenary compendium edition has been produced by the author's sons to commemorate the 100th anniversary of the birth of Wilfred Bloor the author of the Jabez North Staffordshire dialect stories who wrote under the pen name of A Scott.

The book has been compiled from the original three Jabez books published in the 1970's. The original typeset script in the books has been scanned using an optical character reader and converted to a digital file.

The complexities of North Staffordshire dialect have proved a challenge for modern spell checkers and a separate North Staffs Dialect spell checker was developed. This however merely served to prove that a human spell checker was more efficient and the final scanned document was hand proof checked and corrected using the original books and the author's manuscripts at Keele when there was any confusion as to the correct spelling or use of vocabulary.

We were fortunate to have access to many original photographs taken by the author which portray many of the events and scenes which he used as a background for his stories. These photographs and his stories provide a unique social record of life in a North Staffordshire rural mining village in the period between the two World Wars.

Alan, Ian, Roger & David Bloor
July 2015

Forward to the 'Gold' Hardback Edition

This hardback edition is to commemorate the 50th anniversary of the publication of The First Book of Jabez in August 1972. To mark the anniversary Keele University are making some of the recordings performed by Wilfred Bloor, in North Staffordshire dialect, in the character of 'Jabez' freely available online.

In the words of J. S. Tupholme the then editor of the Sentinel – "Carry on, Jabez! May you live for ever!"

Alan, Ian, Roger & David Bloor
December 2022

Wilfred Alan Bloor (A.Scott) 1915 – 1993

The author of the Jabez stories

With a short break in the 1980's Wilf Bloor produced a 'Jabez' story for the Sentinel – the local evening newspaper of North Staffordshire – every week from 1968 until his death in 1993. During that time he also wrote a series of Bible stories, retold in 'dialect'.

Three collections of his stories were published between 1972 and 1978, and each sold several thousand copies.

Over the years he also made many personal appearances at local venues, reading his stories and explaining about the local dialect. One of these was professionally recorded and had great success as an audio cassette. He also read his stories on BBC Radio Stoke and, in collaboration with them, made a second audio tape. He also recorded many of his stories for the local talking newspaper for the blind .

To ensure that his work in producing a lasting record of village life and the local dialect was not lost, his sons established an archive of his manuscripts and studies at Keele University, who now hold the copyright to the stories and the audio tapes. Copies of the tapes, as an audio CD, are available for sale at the Local Studies Library at Keele.

What often amazed people who came to meet him was that all this was only one of his interests, and that in 'real life' he was a scientist working in research to prevent occupational diseases in the pottery industry.

After studying Ceramics at the North Staffordshire Technical College, Wilf was appointed the British Pottery Manufacturers' Federation Research Scholar from 1936 to 1938. This was a post created and funded by the BPMF who were concerned about the incidence of dust related diseases in their industries. His job was to investigate dust conditions in the industry.

The work was carried out by a team of three, including a Factory Inspector. The measurements were made using some of the first commercially available thermal precipitators for collecting personal samples for particle counting. Salicylic acid filters were used to collect static samples and analysed by petrological and chemical methods to determine silica content. The results of this work were published in 1939 in the Transactions of the British Ceramic Society.

From 1938 until the end of the war he worked at the Worksop plant of General Refractories, who were engaged in producing refractories for the then vital iron and steel industry.

After the war he moved to the British Iron and Steel Research Association in Sheffield, and there went back to work in Occupational Hygiene. He was co-author of 5 papers on dust measurement in foundries and the evaluation of local exhaust ventilation systems, which appeared in the 1951 HMSO publication 'Dust in Steel Foundries', and he wrote a paper on dust reduction methods for the Institute of British Foundrymen.

In 1951 he returned to his roots and took up a post at the British Ceramic Research Association at Penkhull, where he was responsible for setting up and leading a research unit specifically to investigate dust control in the Pottery Industry. At this time, each year, there were over 200 newly-diagnosed cases of pneumoconiosis in Stoke-on-Trent. When he retired in 1980, this had been reduced to single figures, an achievement of which he was he was proud to have been part.

Despite the large number of measurements he and his team made over the years he considered that the introduction of the Tyndall Beam, as a tool in visualising dust particles, was a break-through in the development of control measures. One of the most important observations was that, despite the use of early designs of exhaust hoods, much of the dust entering the breathing zone of pottery workers was being generated from their cotton clothing. At BCRA he and his team tested many fabrics and clothing designs to provide protective clothing which did not increase exposure. Together with fabric manufacturers they developed what is still known as 'Ceramic Surface Terylene'. This had a surface texture and weave which did not retain dust or allow dust to penetrate it, while still allowing sufficient 'breathability' to be comfortable to wear. The material was combined with well-thought-out designs which minimised seams and other dust retaining features on the front of the garments. The material and designs were still in use in potteries world-wide until very recently when research on some new fabrics showed ones with even better performance.

The Tyndall Beam also showed up the inefficiency of the local exhaust systems and of the general ventilation systems then available and lead to the development of standards for these by BCRA. Together with the other advances made in the ceramic industry, there followed a dramatic reduction in the number of cases of dust- related diseases.

He was involved in numerous committees, both of Trade Associations and professional bodies. As chairman of the Section of Occupational Health and Preventative Medicine of the North Staffs Medical Institute, he was the first non-physician to hold that post.

He was committed to the furthering of the profession of Occupational Hygiene and was for many years a visiting lecturer in Occupational Hygiene to the London School of Hygiene and Tropical Medicine.

Wilf was an early member of both British Occupational Hygiene Society and the Institute of Occupational Hygienists. He was one of the early Fellows of the Institute and the first Honorary Fellow, as well serving a term as vice-president.

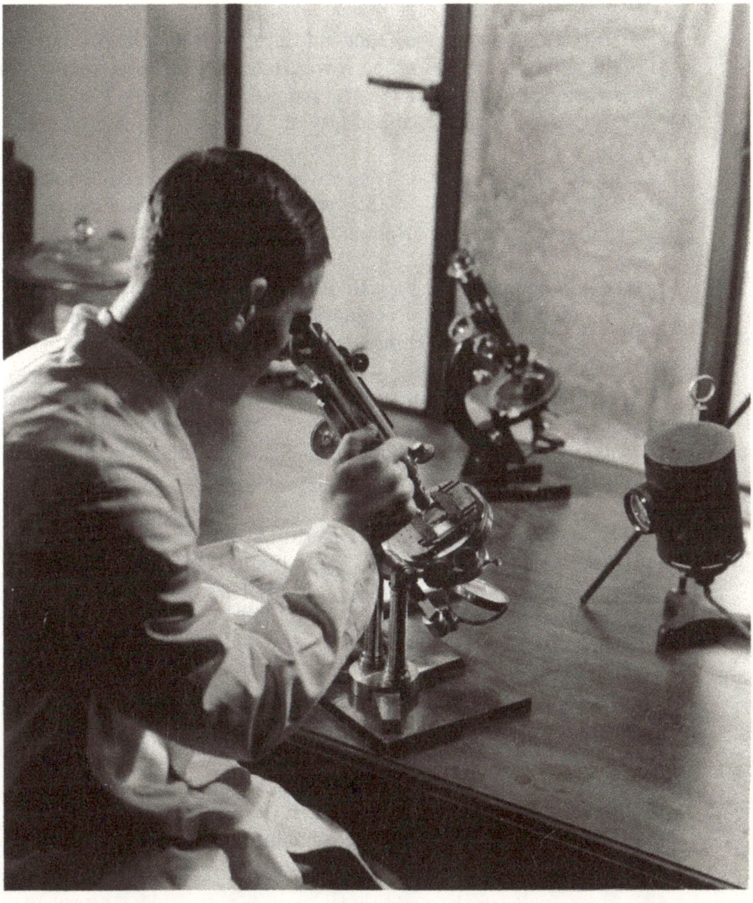

Wilfred Bloor in his research laboratory circa 1940

Acknowledgments for the Compendium Edition

The photographs on the Front and Back cover and the photograph of the author at work on page *vi* were taken by Mr John Tipping for an article published in "Yours" magazine in January 1989. The images are used courtesy of "Yours" Magazine.

The drawing of Jabez on page *v* was used in the original books by kind permission of W. Walker and published here courtesy of the Evening Sentinel. Copyright Staffordshire Sentinel News & Media

The photograph of the First Book of Jabez book launch on page *vi* is used courtesy of the Evening Sentinel. Copyright Staffordshire Sentinel News & Media.

The mural of Jabez from the Hanley Shopping Centre seen in the front cover photograph was created by local artist David Light and was situated alongside those of Sir Stanley Mathews and Captain Smith of the Titanic.

The image of the Bliss Native Herbs advertisement on page 95 is courtesy of Duke University. Copyright R.C. Maxwell Company Digital Collection – XXX0586. John W. Hartman Center for Sales, Advertising, and Marketing History. David M. Rubenstein Rare Book and Manuscript Library, Duke University.

The copyright of all the Jabez stories is held by Keele University and we thank the University for the use of the material in this compendium.

The copyright of photographs which were taken either by Wilfred Bloor or a family member remains with the publishers .

Acknowledgements

With a few exceptions the stories are essentially true, many of them being reminiscences of my early life in the village of Scott Hay. Some of the stories were told to me by relatives and friends, and I am indebted to them. My thanks are due to Mr. Tupholme, the Editor of the Sentinel, for his Foreword and for much help and advice; and to Mr. W. Walker, the Sentinel artist, for permission to reproduce his drawing of Jabez.

I am also grateful to those North Staffordshire exiles living in many different parts of the country who have written letters of appreciation and encouragement.

Finally, this book might never have been published had it not been for the enthusiasm and persistence of Mr. N. J. Bramhall, B.A.

W. A. BLOOR

August, 1972

16, Wilbrahams Walk,
Audley,
Stoke-on-Trent ST7 8HL

Foreword to the First Book of Jabez

Jabez needs no introduction to North Staffordshire people. His down-to-earth philosophy has been part of their staple diet in the Sentinel since he was introduced to them in September, 1968.

I remember that when the author came to see me in that year and showed me the first specimen articles I marveled at his ability to do what so many other people have tried to do without success – to write the North Staffordshire dialect which is so beloved of all who have lived or settled in these parts and so maddeningly incomprehensible to the "foreigner". Not surprisingly the printers to whom he first sent his manuscript wanted to be paid the premium rate which is customary for articles written in a foreign language.

Closer acquaintance with Jabez convinced me that the author had created a lovable character whose counterparts many of us have been privileged to know during a long sojourn in this fascinating part of the Midlands.

Jabez is a real person and, though perhaps born within sight and sound of the Potteries, a countryman at heart. And he has all the genuine "pott'ry" man's contempt for snobbery and artificiality. Without the benefit of a superior education he carries within his head the wisdom of the ages.

Perhaps his breed is dying out with the increasing pace of modern life in which even the village pub, conventional resort of "characters", is tending to succumb to romantic music, "keg" beer and fried scampi. I sincerely hope not. In any case the author has done the district a real service by providing us with a permanent record of his Jabez cameos.

It was high time, too, that he revealed his own identity. Many people will be interested to learn that "A. Scott" is the pen-name of Mr. W. A. Bloor, a principal scientific officer of the British Ceramic Research Association. They will be less surprised to know that he is a native of Scott Hay and now lives at Audley which seems to me an eminently suitable environment for a 'Jabez".

I commend this book to everybody with an affection for local character.

Carry on, Jabez! May you live for ever!

August, 1972. J. H. S. TUPHOLME

Foreword to Second book of Jabez

I have not so far had the pleasure of meeting Mr. Wilfred Bloor though I feel that I have known his Jabez all my life. To some extent my rapport with this intriguing character springs from our common membership of the North Staffordshire brotherhood, but essentially it is Mr. Bloor's creative skill that enables me to number Jabez among my intimate acquaintances.

Because he speaks in the old local patois it may be thought that Jabez' appeal is restricted to the senior inhabitants of his zone of operations. It is my view, however, that the stories are so lively, so full of humour and humanity and above all so well written that they could shed their dialect without suffering too much damage and delight a wider readership.

All the same, there can be no doubt that the sounds conjured up by the printed record of the spoken word, as mouthed by Jabez and his associates, are extraordinarily evocative to readers with a close knowledge of the region. These quixotically mutilated vowel sounds and harsh consonants are not for export. Arnold Bennett, a writer who understood the commerce of literature better than most, used them sparingly even in his Five Towns novels and then only as occasional reminders of the potter's uniqueness. The writing of dialect is always difficult. The writing of comprehensible "pottery" presents the story-teller with almost insuperable problems. Yet Mr. Bloor manages the verbal alchemy with such sleight of hand that the native reader is never, or very seldom, aware of the work involved. And it is, I suppose, this aspect of the Jabez achievement that persuaded the perceptive editor of the Evening Sentinel, the late Mr. J. H. S. Tupholme, to give the stories his blessing and a large circulation. My guess would be that over the years hundreds of aspiring authors have tried to write in the North Staffordshire dialect and have puzzled editors with manuscripts as tough to decipher as the Dead Sea Scrolls.

Jabez is a character, not a card. He is a "potter" at heart because like all inhabitants of the upper Trent valley he thinks of himself as a countryman living in the shadow of the great wen that is the industrial Potteries. Stoke people, I find, do not see themselves as townies comparable with the denizens of Brum, Manchester and Leeds: give them half a chance and they will tell you, especially the stranger or "foreigner", that though the Five Towns are full of factories, foundries and mines "You can be out of them in five or ten minutes". And "out of them" means to be deep in the moorlands to the north and east, the woodlands of the south or the grasslands of Cheshire.

So Jabez is a jack-of-all-trades, by Dickens out of Hardy as it were, and with a homespun philosophy on such maxims as "Theer's nowt like people" and "Money is the root of all evil", and inspired by Wordsworth's

One impulse from a vernal wood
May teach you more of man,
Of moral evil and of good,
Than all the sages can.

I enjoyed The First Book of Jabez enormously, and I have not the slightest doubt that this second ration will prove equally delightful.

Jabez is a minor masterpiece and my only regret concerning him is that his creator has so far neglected to involve him in stories long enough to enchant the reader for hours rather than minutes.

BERNARD HOLLOWOOD

June, 1973

Acknowledgments

The stories first appeared in the Evening Sentinel. Most of them are essentially true, many of them being reminiscences of my early life in the village of Scott Hay. Some of the stories were told to me by relatives and friends to whom I am grateful.

I am indebted to Mr. Bernard Hollowood, (ex-editor of Punch) for his Foreword, and to Mr. W. Walker (the Sentinel artist) for permission to reproduce his drawing of Jabez.

W. A. BLOOR

August, 1973

16 Wilbraham's Walk,
Audley,
Stoke-on-Trent ST7

Jabez was one of those characters one comes across in village life. He was sturdily built, had a face best described as craggy, eyebrows which were distinctly bushy, and small but bright blue eyes that betrayed his roguish sense of humour.

His normal clothes, Sunday excepted, were a nondescript jacket, a "union" shirt and a pair of "moleskin" trousers, the legs of which were tied just below the knees with string or pieces of old bootlace.

I never knew why he did this, but it was common practice among the miners in the village at that time. He often wore a spotted neckerchief which, in exceptionally cold weather, would be replaced or supplemented by a muffler.

It was said that in his youth he had worked in the pit, but for as long as I knew him he never had what you might call a regular job.

He was seldom short of work though. He was much in demand by local farmers for seasonal work, and could lay a hedge or plough a field as neatly as any in the district. He was also a competent bricklayer and carpenter, and I have seen him wipe a lead-pipe joint that would do credit to any plumber.

He could also give you a passable haircut, or sole and heel your shoes. In a village such a man had no need to go looking for jobs.

It was suspected however, that he had gypsy blood in his veins. This was partly because of his intimate knowledge of nature and her ways, and partly because of his habit of disappearing for several days at a time.

This wander-lust could be very exasperating. In the middle of tiling a roof, or plastering a wall, or ploughing a field, he would be up and away without warning. He would turn up again in his own good time and carry on where he left off.

On his return he would often call at our cottage at the end of the village. In spring and summer he would be carrying a posy of wild flowers. These were delightful arrangements, about six inches or so across, having the general shape of a large mushroom. The different coloured flowers, arranged in tight concentric circles, or other regular patterns, must have taken hours to collect and arrange.

Depending on the season he would produce, from his capacious pockets, a bag of mushrooms or hazel nuts, or wild strawberries, or green walnuts for pickling. Invariably he had something to amuse the children; a "penny" whistle made from a piece of elder, a bubble pipe made from an acorn and a piece of straw, or a small animal delightfully carved from a scrap of wood.

Occasionally he would be carrying a new walking stick cut from a blackthorn or holly bush. Some years before he would have pruned and tied the young branches to produce a straight stick with a curved or knobbly handle.

Next day, at first light, he would be back on whatever job he had left unfinished, offering no explanation or excuse for his absence. As you can imagine there was no lack of rumours in the village as to where he went or what he did. But Jabez kept his secret.

A row o' peys

One of the things I value about village life is that the people are real people. A man is known for what he is, rather that for what he thinks he is. Jabez was, above all, a real person, detesting snobbery or insincerity in any form. He could quickly puncture an inflated ego with a few well-chosen words.

I recall the time when I was getting a somewhat neglected garden into shape and was more than a little proud of what I had already accomplished. I suppose that in a town an over-polite neighbour would have said:

"Your garden is looking delightful already. What a lot of work you have put into it." And would have then gone about his business.

Jabez, leaning on the garden wall, his short-stemmed pipe well charged with thick twist, watched me for a full five minutes without speaking and then came up with the observation:

"A reyght owd mess theyt meekin' o' that. 'Ast ever thowght o' settin' some concreyte seyds?" But having said that, he popped over the wall and put in a couple of hours of rough digging during which time he made derogatory remarks about the origin of my favourite pipe tobacco, treated with contempt my offer of payment for his work and said as he left:

"They wants plant that lot wi' taters fer clear th'grind."

He was a keen gardener himself and excelled in growing peas and carnations. His rows of peas were a joy to see; strong, dark green, luscious growth even in the driest of seasons. One year I made a point of watching his preparations for a row of peas. At first I thought he must be putting in a main drain or getting out the foundations of a substantial building. The trench he was excavating was all of two feet deep and nearly as wide.

Out of the garden shed he brought bundles of old clothes and newspapers which he placed in the bottom of the trench. These were followed by alternate layers of soil and old straw. The seeds saved from last year's crop, were rolled in paraffin with the remark: "Them chapel sparrers are 'ungrier than church meyce."

Finally he covered the peas in the trench with a mixture of soil and ashes accumulated from his many garden bonfires. The trench was not completely filled in, the excess soil being piled up on each side. Later on he would go down into the woods with his ancient horn-handled knife and cut down bundles of brushwood and branches to support the peas.

All this hard work to grow a row of peas, but you should have seen that row towards the end of June; fully six feet tall and heavy with long tight pods.

Carnations an' mowles

Among the gardeners of the village Jabez was the acknowledged expert on carnations, and could count on being in the first three in the carnation class at any of the flower shows in the district. To his fellow enthusiasts the talk was of picotees, selfs, fancies, bizarres and flakes, terms which meant little to me at the time.

One of the things which *did* interest me was his unusual method of increasing his stock of plants. While he used the well known method of "layering" for most of his varieties, he had a different method for others.

This consisted of cutting off a young shoot just below a joint and then inserting a radish seed into the bit of hollow stem left below the joint. These cuttings were then planted in pots and kept in the shade. His explanation was that "th'redish seyd 'ull throw ite roots wot'll feyd th'cuttin' 'till it's gotten roots o' its own."

It seemed to work, and the interesting thing is that many years later an article appeared in a scientific journal which appeared to justify Jabez's method. Research work had shown that a growing seedling produces a chemical substance in the soil which encourages root formation in adjacent plants. Just one more example of how subsequent research has found a good reason for practices which, sometimes, for many generations have been a part of the folk wisdom of simple people.

Jabez's carnation plants were well decorated with partly open matchboxes suspended by pieces of thread from the flower stalks or from the supporting stakes. These were his earwig traps whose occupants would otherwise damage his prize blooms. He was also troubled with moles which invaded his garden from an adjoining field. He had methods for dealing with these furry gentlemen, too.

"Mowles" he said, "ave fer 'ave weyter, so if thee cost find ite wheer thee go fer it they cost ketch 'em."

Their source of "weyter" was a ditch on the lane side of his garden hedge. The trick was to find the tunnel leading to the ditch and put a trap in it. The trap was made of wood in the form of a cylinder in which the mole was caught alive. The trap was handled with gloves because, as he put it: "If ey smells thee scent on it ey wunna come anywheer near it."

For moles which were creating havoc in his flower beds he had another method of discouraging them. He would plunge a dibber into the heart of the molehill, drop a piece of "carbide" in to the exposed tunnel and cover it up. The "carbide" was, of course, calcium carbide which reacts with water to give acetylene gas. It was a substance in common use in those days for bicycle lamps.

Voles and mice were caught by sinking a jam jar into the ground with its rim flush with the surface, the mouth of the jar being smeared with mutton fat or bacon fat. Such was his love of nature that I think he regretted the necessity of depriving these little creatures of their freedom. It was significant that none of his devices killed the animals that were caught.

I often wonder what he did with them.

Reen or Shine

So much of the life and work of country folk is governed by the weather that it is small wonder that they become weather wise.

They have the advantage over town folk that they are often able to see the distant sky as well as that overhead. What they see there, in conjunction with wind direction and such local indications as the visibility of prominent landmarks, is often sufficient for them to make a reliable weather forecast.

But Jabez could tell you of other and more interesting weather signs. How that, long before the arrival of the "weather", many of nature's little creatures and lowly plants have had advance warning. At the approach of rain "that poor man's weather glass", the scarlet pimpernel, will have closed tight its petals, the rooks will be "trembling", overhead, the swallows will be skimming low over the water, and the toad will come crawling out at dusk.

With a wind coming up the spider will tighten its web; before a hot spell the gnats will play up and down in the open rather than in the shade, and if the cockchafer beetle bumps into you at night you won't need your raincoat 'till morning.

Jabez's weather forecasts were not infallible. But then, who's are?

In his later years he had some arthritis – "screws in me jynts" he called it. In common with other arthritics it provided a further, if unwelcome, indication of deteriorating weather. I told him of an American doctor who carried out a rather expensive experiment on arthritic patients. He enclosed them in a chamber in which the temperature, humidity and pressure could be controlled.

The experiments showed that in conditions of rising humidity and a falling barometer the patients' symptoms became progressively worse. These, of course, are the two prevailing factors in nature before a rainstorm, the time when most arthritics feel increasing discomfort.

Jabez's comment was: "Dust meyn fer see as yon mon spent aw that money fer find that ite? Ar coulda towd 'im that fer nowt yeers ago."

During a particularly wet summer I had called to see Jabez at his cottage to ask for his help in replacing the staging of a greenhouse. I found him in the garden surveying the rain-soaked earth and his drowning plants.

"Ar was just thinkin' "he said, "as wey could do with Elias fer a bit."

I didn't see the connection and said so. "Dustna they reyd thee Bible?" he asked. "They 'ave a luk in James when thee getst wom. It's somewheer near th'end. Ey preed it wouldna reen on th'earth, an' dust know, sirree, it didna reen fer threy yeer an' six months."

As we sat down on his garden seat he took out his tobacco, carved some flakes into the palm of his hand, rubbed it and slowly filled his pipe. As he lit it he said, in between puffs:

"Mind thee, ar reckon owd Elias owerdid th'preein' a bit."

Home remedies

Jabez couldn't remember the last occasion on which he visited the doctor. The nearest he could get to it was that it was "donkey's yeers since."

Like many country folk of his generation he had more confidence in the home-made remedy than in the doctor's "bottle" or the chemist's pills. Most of these folk had their first acquaintance with a home remedy when only a few hours old. This was the well-known "cinder tea" for wind and colic, made by dropping a red-hot cinder into a cup of water.

A great variety of other remedies were made from plants and barks gathered from field and wood. Jabez was not a fanatic about herbs but he had great faith in the curative powers of a few of them. Some he grew in the garden, and he knew exactly where to find the others.

Comfrey from his garden was in great demand by the villagers for the treatment of wounds and sores and sprains. They would vouch for the effectiveness of peppermint tea for "sweatin' ite a cowd i' th'yed", raspberry vinegar for easing a wheezy chest or a sore throat, feverfew for bringing a temperature down, houseleek for soothing inflamed eyes, a brew of blackberry shoots for diarrhoea, and the familiar brimstone and treacle to "clear th'blood".

It should not be forgotten that many medicinal drugs in common use, such as strychnine, quinine, and cascara are of plant origin. Their use dates back centuries to when, by a painful process of trial and error, man learnt the properties of various plants.

Aspirin, of course, originated from a family of herbal remedies used in many parts of the world as far back as the Stone Age. It is fortunate that there are doctors and scientists who do not lightly dismiss the folk wisdom of simple people and who are prepared to investigate what broad experience suggests might be true.

Had William Wittering, for example, not listened to his patients telling him of how an old Shropshire woman had cured their "dropsy", we might have waited decades for digitalis from the foxglove.

I found one of Jabez's home remedies very interesting and very effective. I had the misfortune to cut my right thumb rather deeply. It was very sore and slow to heal.

" Wots bin up ter nar?" asked Jabez when he saw the bandage. "Let's 'ave a luk at it."

He poked it a bit, smiled and said: "If theyts do that ter thar thumb wot wouldst do ter marn? Come dine wom wi' mey, ar've got summat as'll put that reyght."

The "summat" was an unpleasant smelling liquid which I was to apply to the wound on a thick wad of cotton wool.

"But what is it?" I asked.

"Th'trouble with they is they akses t'many questions. Dust remember what th'Samaritan did when ey funt th'wounded mon at side o' th'road?"

"Yes," I said, "he bound up his wounds, poured in oil and wine and put him on his beast."

"That's reyght," said Jabez. "They atna queyte such a 'eathen as ar thowght thee wost. That's what's in yon bottle, oil and weyn, moer or less."

As I turned to go he said: "Ar anna got a 'oss fer put thee on but theyt no dite manage fer get wom, an' they wutna lose thee thumb."

And I didn't. In fact in a few days the soreness had gone and it was healing rapidly.

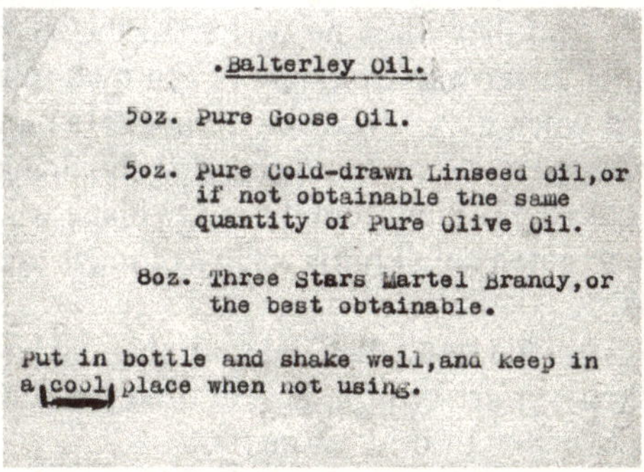

Balterley Oil.

5oz. Pure Goose Oil.

5oz. Pure Cold-drawn Linseed Oil, or if not obtainable the same quantity of Pure Olive Oil.

8oz. Three Stars Martel Brandy, or the best obtainable.

Put in bottle and shake well, and keep in a cool place when not using.

One of Fanny's Home Remedies

Brids an' Bessie

I was telling Jabez about a pair of swallows who were building a nest under the eaves of my cottage.

"Them anna swallers mon," he said, "them are 'ice martins. Ar seyd 'em t'other dee when ar were up yoer road."

He went on to say that a swallow's nest was more like a little bowl, and that they preferred to nest on a beam or ledge inside a farm building where there were animals.

"Ar once seyd a swaller's neyst built inside an owd throstle's neyst on a beym in a shippon. Swallers an' martins are full o' fleys thee knowst. Thee used reckon as thee carried 'em arind fer food when thee were migratin'."

After a pause he chuckled and said:"Ar reckon theen gorra get some snappin' from somewheer anna thee?"

The talk turned to other birds; of the disappearance of the corncrake whose grating call was once a common sound in meadow and cornfield, and of the great increase in the magpie population.

"Thirty or foty yeer sin' ther wonna many maggies rind 'ere. Nar theer aw ower th'pleece. Do a lot o' damage thee knowst ter other brids' neysts."

We reminded one another of the old rhyme about magpies: "One for sorrow, two for joy, three for a wedding, four for a boy, five for silver, six for gold, seven for a secret never to be told."

Jabez said that when he was a lad the rhyme was said about rooks rather than magpies. Some of "th'owd folk" raised their hats or curtsied when they saw a single rook. He thought that by doing this they hoped to avoid the sorrow that should have followed.

He talked of a man from the next village who used to put down bird-lime to catch small birds such as linnets and finches to sell as cagebirds.

"Ar couldna stand that" he said, shaking his head in disgust.

"Whenever ar seyd 'im at it ar used fer mak as much noise as ar could fer fritten th'brids awee.

We sauntered round his garden, lit our pipes and enjoyed the May sunshine. Presently he stopped, inclined his head to one side, obviously listening intently.

"Get thee dine quick" he said, "and bey queyet."

I imagined that he was about to show me some rare bird or some unusual occurrence in the bird world. I looked around the garden but could see nothing to warrant this urgent order from Jabez.

'It's owd Bessie comin' dine th'road," he whispered. "Ar con tell 'er footsteps. 'Ers a reyght owd bletherer, an' if 'er spots us wey shall bey stuck 'ere aw dee."

We crouched down behind the hedge like a couple of miscreants until Bessie was out of earshot. As we straightened up he said:

"Er inna a bad sort, 'er 'earts in th'reyght pleece. Thouble is 'er tungue's 'inged in th'middle an' it wags both ends."

Blackberries an' elderfowers

Jabez and I had been blackberrying. I enjoyed going with him because of the interesting things he could show me which otherwise I would have missed, and because he knew exactly where to find the largest, juiciest berries, the "sugars" or "plums" as they were called. I just wanted a few berries for a pie and a little jam but Jabez needed several pounds for his wine-making.

It had been a rather cool afternoon in early September but the sun had shone during the morning and the berries were dry, as they should be for wine and jam.

On the way back, Jabez invited me into his cottage for a glass of wine. The fire had been "banked-up" before he went out and a few jabs with the poker brought it to life.

The fire was in the centre of an old kitchen range with an oven at one side and a water boiler with a large brass tap on the other side. It was in beautiful condition, being black-leaded and polished each Friday by Hannah, who "did" for him.

A monster of a kettle, suspended over the fire by a pot-hook, began to sing pleasantly, and the brass spill-cups on the hobs reflected the glow of the fire. Opposite the high-backed settle on which I was sitting was a rocking-chair, a family heirloom that was Jabez's usual seat.

In one corner was a bow-fronted cupboard with a rush-bottomed chair standing beneath it. On the wall opposite the range was the pride of his cottage – a Welsh dresser, well decorated with odd pieces of vintage pottery.

The floor was of large red quarries, the hearth being covered by a multi-coloured cloth rug, hand-pegged by Jabez with strips cut from cast-off clothing gleaned from the village. In the alcove formed by the chimney-breast stood his grandfather clock unhurriedly measuring out the time. Here in this room was peace and a pleasant feeling of warmth and security.

We had walked far for our blackberries and perhaps I "nodded off" for a moment or two. I was jolted back to reality by Jabez's voice from the scullery where he kept his wine.

"Ast gone jed or summat in theer? Ar'm esking thee wot sort o' weyn thee wants, but ar mit as well be talkin' ter mesel'."

I was very fond of his elderflower wine and said so.

"Ar mitta known," he said, as he came in carrying a bottle which he set down on the oval table under the window. He filled two small tumblers taken from the corner cupboard and we sat on either side of the fire sipping the wine and appreciating its distinctive bouquet.

"Dust know," he said presently, "it's a funny thing but as soon as th'elder comes into flower th'weyn meede th'year afoer starts workin' a bit aggen."

"Yes," I said, "the wine-makers on the Continent know about this, they call it the malo-lactic ferment."

"Theyt be gettin' thee tungue in a wrobble wi' mithefuls larke that. Thee dunna mak weyn wi' elder-flowers ower theer, do thee?"

"I don't know ' I said, "but they fry them." "Thee what?" asked Jabez. "Thee't 'avin' me on."

So I told him how they held the flower-heads by the stalk, dipped them into a kind of pancake batter and cooked them in oil. "Fancy that nar," he said.

After he had thought about this for a while, he drained his glass and said:

"Ar tell thee wot, sirree, ar'd as leif 'ave me elderflowers ite o' bottle as ite o' a fryin'-pon."

I agree with him. I have his recipe for the wine and make a gallon or two each year. A friend who knows about these things tells me it is very like a Frontenac. Perhaps it is, but to use a Jabez expression "ar'd as lief" drink elder-flower as any wine I have come across.

Th'thrashin' macheyne

Jabez and I were leaning on the field gate watching the combine harvester at work. Inevitably the conversation turned to how this and other machines had taken much of the hard, slogging work out of farming.

All the same, we could not help but feel a pang of regret at the passing of the old threshing machine. We recalled the excitement and pleasure it gave to the children (and to a lot of adults) during its visits to the village.

The children would learn of its imminent arrival from the farmer and there would be a great exodus towards the next village to meet the "thrasher" and to escort it back to the farm. The children aimed to get to the low bridge over the lane before it arrived there. Here the steam traction-engine had to suffer the indignity of having its tall smoke-stack removed to enable it to pass under the bridge.

This great gleaming monster with its polished brasswork, its maroon paintwork, and its delicious smell of hot oil and steam waited impatiently, snorting from its safety-valve and shedding hot cinders from its firebars.

At last it would be on its way again with one or two lucky children riding on the traction-engine whilst others hung on to the back of the "thrasher" or ran up and down the lane, becoming more excited and noisier as they neared the farm.

Casual labour from the village was set on, and the men who travelled around with the threshing machine were fed and accommodated overnight in the farmhouse.

Few were the children who lay abed next morning but, even so, many would awake to find that the work had begun and that the delightful "hum" of the "thrasher" could already by heard from one end of the village to the other.

The farmer was very tolerant towards the children although they often got in the way. Some of the older ones armed themselves with sticks with which to attack the rats and mice as they evacuated the barn.

Jabez in his capacity as an experienced seasonal worker on the farm acted as general supervisor of the farmyard operations. He went around encouraging, chiding and "chuntering."

“Nar yo childer, dunna get aimer tote yon thrasher. It’ll thrash yer inter little peyces an’ pop yer inter th’bag, an’ Jabez conna put yer together aggen.”

To the men on top of the thresher, feeding its hungry mouth:

“An yer gone sleyp up theer or summat? Thers next ter nowt comin’ ite dine ‘ere. Wey shan be thrashin’ aw neyght. “

And to the undersized youth struggling with the sacks of grain to make a shilling or two: “Dunna owerfill them bags lad. Theyt bey rawngin’ theesen.”

Threshing-time was frumenty-time or “firmatree” as Jabez called it. Stew-pots or stone jars, half-filled with wheat, a few raisins and some water would be put into many cottage ovens that night.

Next morning, when all the grains had burst, the frumenty would be eaten hot or cold with sugar and milk. It was good food but very “filling”, and as Jabez used to say:

“When it comes ter eatin’ firmatree most folk’s eyes are a lot bigger than ther bellies.”

Village cricket

Jabez was a regular supporter of the local cricket club and was well versed in the art and science of village cricket.

In these games the weaknesses in technique and temperament of the regular players in both the home and visiting teams are well known to each other and are fully exploited.

A particular player, for example, is known to dislike balls pitched on the leg side, another is terrified of a fast bowler, while another lacks the patience necessary to deal effectively with a slow bowler, and so on.

These facets of the game are not apparent to the casual observer, but should any of them be forgotten or overlooked there is no lack of reminders and free advice from experienced spectators like Jabez.

He always sat by the pavilion where, if need be, he could counsel the ingoing batsmen, make comments about their performance to returning batsmen, and give general advice to the home team when they were fielding. I remember his remarks to a youngster who rather fancied himself as a batsman but who never quite "came off"

He it was who always had the only unplayable ball of the match, or the bad decision from the umpire to excuse his poor performance. As he approached the pavilion after yet another short sojourn at the wicket Jabez said to him:

"Ar reckon ther must bey a lot o' cricket in they."

The youth, obviously flattered by this remark, said, "Do you think so, Jabez?" "Ther must bey" was the reply, "Ther anna come any ite on thee yet."

Advice to the captain of the village team comes thick and fast when two of the visiting batsmen appear to be "getting set". In terms of village cricket this position has been reached when no wicket has fallen for four or five overs. Jabez had a remedy for this situation.

"Put owd Charlie on with 'is uptychucked uns," he would call out to the captain.

Charlie wasn't particularly old but the prefix "owd" served to distinguish him from his son, young Charlie, who also played with the team.

"Owd" Charlie was the slowest slow bowler I ever saw. On leaving his hand the ball soared heavenwards making it difficult for the batsman to see it against the bright sky. If he went out of his crease to hit it before it dropped he was likely to mistime it and get caught, or miss it altogether and get stumped.

If he had enough patience to wait for it to drop it was still a difficult ball to deal with because on a hard wicket it would bounce up chest high and on a soft one it would stop almost where it dropped. After an over or so "owd" Charlie often succeeded in separating the two batsmen. If not, there were several other legitimate tactics aimed at upsetting the batsman:

"Didst sey owd Charlie meeke that signal to th'wicket-keyper?" asked Jabez. I did and I wondered what it meant. "It dunna meyn anythin' but ey meede sure th'batsman seyd it an' nar ey'll bey thinkin' th'pair on 'em are up ter summat." The result of this strategy was that the batsman often became overcautious and made mistakes that cost him his wicket.

Another ruse was to bring in all the fielders near to the wicket to encourage the batsman to hit "owd" Charlie out of the field. Part way through the over, however, he would come ambling up to the bowling crease at his usual pace but at the last moment his arm would whip over and instead of one of his "uptychucked uns" the ball would hurtle down the pitch to the great surprise and discomfiture of the batsman.

As soon as the partnership was broken "owd" Charlie would be taken off and rested. Of course his bowling was sometimes punished by one of the "old hands". On one such occasion, as the third six in succession soared over the boundary, Jabez called out:

"It sarves thee reyght Charlie. Thee wutna ketch an owd brid wi' chaff. Mind thee, ar think theydst got 'im guessin' with that last un, ey didna know whether 'it thee fer a foer or a six."

A slow bowler at Scott Hay Cricket Field

The Miners' Institute at Scott Hay Cricket Field circa 1927

Wilfred with the farm horses

Wilfred harrowing at Scott Hay

Th'big ginger mare

The thing that Jabez regretted most of all about the mechanisation of farming was the redundancy of the horse.

Anyone who has done a day's ploughing with horses on a rough field couldn't fail to appreciate the comparative ease with which the job can be done with a tractor. But Jabez had no affection for tractors and, although he learned to drive them, he used them with what amounted to an air of detachment.

"Thee feydst 'em wi' oil and fuel an' aw thee getst ite at t'other end is smoke, an' thee costna put that on thee rhubub."

His deep love of horses was evident from his many reminiscences of them, although not all his experiences with them had been pleasant ones.

"Thee wutsna remember that big ginger mare," he said. " 'Er was a top-notcher when it come ter workin' in th'feyld, but 'er 'adna 'afe got a temper. 'Er once meede th'gaffer tak ter 'is bed thee knowst."

Apparently the mare had a superfluous hair problem and grew a lot of facial hair including a sort of shaggy beard that made her look untidy. Before taking her to the market in the town, or to the next village to be shod, the farmer first groomed her and then trimmed the superfluous hair from her face, with a pair of scissors.

She liked the grooming but hated the haircut. One day Jabez was sawing some logs in the yard when he heard a yell from the direction of the stable.

"Th'greet foo' 'ad bin at 'er aggen with 'is scissors and 'er'd stamped on 'is foot. Not ony that, sirree, but when ar got theer 'er was 'owdin' 'is foot dine on th'floor with 'ers! Ite o' action fer threy wik ey were wi' crushed toes. It sarved 'im rate ar reckon. Mind thee, 'er welly kilt mey once, tho' it wonna 'er fawt exactly."

It appeared that Jabez had been out all day harrowing and rolling. He left the implements in the fields ready for the next day and was riding the mare back to the farm. Unfortunately they met a steam-wagon coming through the village and the mare took fright and bolted.

" 'Er went up in th'air larke a circus 'oss, an' then belted 'ell fer leather for th'farm."

Somehow he managed to stay on her great wide back as she galloped through the village. He was hoping that the farm gate would be closed, as it usually was, and that she would go straight on up the lane. He would then have a chance of calming her down.

But as they neared the farm he could see that the gate was, open and, worse still, that the stable door was open as well. The mare saw the open gate and, still very frightened, made a bee-line for the stable.

"Ar thowght me number were up. Ar knew th'mare's back ony cleared th'stable lintel be a two-threy inches an' if ar stopped on 'er back somebody were goin' 'ave th'job o' scrapin' Jabez off th'stable wo."

As they went through the gate he managed to swivel round on her back and make a jump for it. He fell flat on his face in the farmyard mud and felt the bruises for many a day.

The mare lived to a good age but when at last the knacker's cart came for her Jabez admitted that he "went wom an' blarted."

A pair o' pidgins

I was showing Jabez a letter I received from a pigeon fancier. During the previous week I had found a dead racing pigeon in the garden.

In addition to its racing ring it had the owner's name and address stamped on the underside of the wing. In his reply to my letter the owner said that fanciers were losing more and more young pigeons and that only occasionally did they get to know what happened to them.

I asked Jabez if he had ever kept pigeons. He laughed heartily and said: "Not sin' ar were a lad. Ar meythered one o' th'pidgin men that much'till ey gimme a pair fer shut me up. "

He told young Jabez to keep them "prisoners" until they had had one brood of youngsters in their new home. To a lad this was a long time to wait and was the more irksome to him because the main reason for wanting the pigeons was to experience the wonder and thrill of having them return to his very own loft from some distant place.

In an attempt to speed things up a bit he provided them with a second-hand bird's nest. He looked in the nest several times a day and after a whole eggless week had gone slowly by he could wait no longer – he just had to give them their trial flight.

He took them in his mother's shopping-bag to the top of a hill overlooking the village.

"It wonna moer than 'afe a mile awee. Ar tuk 'em ite o' th'bag one at a tarme an' afoer ar let 'em go ar pointed ther' yeds at th'village so as th'pidgin-cote were straight in front on 'em. Aw thee 'ad fer do were foller ther noses an' thee'da bin wom in now time. But ar never seyd 'em aggen."

He went to the "pidgin-mon" to ask if they had gone back to their old loft, but he said he hadn't seen them. Jabez went back day after day. In the end, in an attempt to console the lad, the fancier said that perhaps they had turned into woodpigeons.

"So ar tuk some corn an' went dine into th'wood. Ar went aw ower it rattlin' me corn-tin. Ther' were plenty o' woodpidgins abite but none on 'em 'ud come ter mey. It were a lung tarme afoer ar cottoned-on as ey were pullin' me leg."

Both scientists and fanciers have put forward many theories to explain how a pigeon can find its way home from a strange place hundreds of miles from its loft.

It has been variously attributed to the common "bird instinct", to its sense of smell, to its keen eyesight, to its memory, to its ability to navigate by the sun, and to the effects of the earth's magnetic fields. Much of the mystery, however, remains.

"Thee costna 'elp but bey interested in wot them science blokes con find ite," said Jabez, "but nar an' aggen ar think ter mesel' it'll bey a pity if th'tarme ever comes when ther' inna any moer mysteries. Ar larke fer think ther'll always bey summat wey dunna know.

Village customs

Bonfire night in the village had come and gone without serious incident. From about the end of September the children had been gathering material for the fire.

All manner of discarded furniture and furnishings, together with wooden and cardboard boxes, branches, hedge-cuttings, tyres and a drum or two of old oil were carried, dragged or rolled to the accustomed place.

On several occasions I had been invited to "spare a copper for the Guy" by children pushing a wheelbarrow containing a life-size but somewhat deformed effigy. I had the impression that this practice of begging was a fairly recent innovation imported into the village from the town. I asked Jabez about it.

"Now," he said, " wey didna do that when wey were youngsters. Mind thee, wey used ter go beggin' at this tarme o' th'yeer fer summat else. Dustna remember goin' soul-cakin' ?"

I had almost forgotten about this custom which is said to be at least 400 years old. On All Souls' Day (Nov. 2nd) we went round the village from door to door singing:

"A soul-cake, a soul-cake,
Please good missus a soul-cake
One for Peter, two for Paul
And three for Him who made us all."

Sometimes this was followed by:

"If you haven't got a Penny A ha'penny will do.
If you haven't got a ha'penny God bless you."

"Ar remember one owd codger openin' th'doer an' givin' me a paper-bag full o' summat," said Jabez. "In th'dark it felt larke some sort of toffee. But it wonna – it were cinders straight ite o' th'essole. Ar' 'ad me own back on 'im though – ar spread 'em ite aw ower 'is cleyn front-step an' grun em' well in wi' me 'eel. Ar bet 'is missus give 'im some 'ommer next mornin'."

We recalled other customs, some of which are no longer practised to any extent. There is, I suppose, a good reason for discontinuing Empire Day (May 24th). On this day we took flags, or red, white and blue rosettes to school. The assembled children were addressed on the subject of our glorious Empire and sang patriotic songs and hymns.

Hallowe'en is still observed in various ways. One of the customs in the village was to cut a swede or, better still, a pumpkin in half and scoop out the inside. Two eye-holes and a nose-hole were cut in the top-half and a slit for the mouth in the bottom-half. A lighted candle was placed inside the head and the two halves put together again. Its sudden appearance from behind a hedge or a wall could be a frightening thing to young and old alike.

Then there was Royal Oak Day or Oak-apple Day on May 29th. The child who forgot to wear an oak-leaf or an oak-apple on this day would be stung with nettles.

A painful history lesson but an effective reminder of King Charles' escapade at Boscobel. Jabez seemed to think that the persecution ended at noon. After that it was "legging-down" time and anyone running or even walking was likely to be tripped up.

Jabez said that one year he thought up a good scheme. He got up early, about an hour before school time, and went along the hedgerows gathering a bagful of dock leaves.

"Ar tuk 'em schoo' an' when ar seyd anybody get nettled ar swapped 'em a dockleyf fer a sweyt or anythin' else thee 'ad in ther pockets. Ar did a roarin' treede 'cos some o' th'lads nettled the wenches whether thee'd gotten oak leyves or not.

A rogue dog

A well-behaved, obedient dog is an excellent companion. Such a one was Jabez's cocker spaniel.

He had been well-trained – just one word from Jabez or even a hand-movement and the dog knew exactly that was required of him. He had not been beaten into submission. On the contrary he was confident and alert, and had what every dog needs – a firm but kind master to love andrespect.

Most young dogs can be trained to obey simple commands such as "sit", "lie" and "heel" in a matter of days.

There are, however, some nervous, neurotic or hysterical dogs that are more difficult to train, and there are a few that are impossible to train due to mental or physical abnormalities. Jabez had the misfortune to get involved with one of the latter.

It was some years ago now, just before he had the spaniel. He was without a dog at the time but found one wandering around the village looking lost and miserable. It was of mixed ancestry but of pleasing enough appearance.

Jabez managed to coax it back to his cottage where he cleaned him up, fed him, and gave him an old blanket to lie on in the corner of the kitchen by the chimney-breast. In a day or two he was to regret his kindness.

"Theyst 'eerd o' rogue elephants on th'rampage 'astna?" he asked. "Well, this un were a rogue dog. Ey led mey a dance did that youth."

The dog was two or three years old and it soon became evident that he was completely untrained. Jabez set out to remedy this state of affairs and soon had him obeying simple commands. But the dog had a vice – an urge to destroy.

"In th'fost wik ey did fer me doer-mat, ripped up threy cushions and tuk th'backside ite o' me second-best trysers. Thee wutstna beleyve wot a lot o' fithers ther are in threy cushions'till thee seyst 'em spread ite aw ower thee kitchin floer."

Jabez cleaned up the mess, gave him an old slipper to chew and got some bones for him from the butcher. The dog ignored the slipper, buried the bones and carried on with the destruction of Jabez's goods and chattels.

Someone suggested that the dog was not getting enough food or perhaps having the wrong food.

" Ey gets through tweyce as much snappin' as ar do," said Jabez. "Ey's larke a swarm o' locusses, ey eats everythin' in front on 'im. An' ey must bey gettin' th'reyght food 'cos ther inna anythin' ey anna 'ad – they neeme it, ey's eaten it."

This destructive urge in certain dogs is said to be almost impossible to cure by any method of training.

But Jabez was soon to be relieved from his tribulation.

One afternoon he had to go out to do some odd jobs in the village. He tied the dog up in the kitchen by his lead and removed out of range anything that he might destroy. When he opened the door on his return he was appalled by what he saw. The dog had broken loose and the room was a shambles.

"Ar lost me temper," said Jabez, "an' reyched fer me walkingstick. But ar'd fergotten fer close th'doer an' ey musta seyn th'luk in me eye. Ey went through that doer larke a streak o' leyghtnin' an' be th'tarme ar got iteside ey'd crossed one feyld an' were goin' larke a greyhind across th'next. At th'rate ey were goin' ey'd 'it th'coast afoer dark.

"If ever thee comst across 'im in thee travels pretend thee 'astna seyn 'im. Ar anna aw that keen on 'avin' 'im back."

Christmas cheer

I suppose it could be said that Jabez's preparations for Christmas began in the summer and autumn of the previous year when he gathered the flowers and fruit for his wine-making.

And then, a few days before Christmas, there were the apples to be brought down from the spare bedroom. They had been carefully harvested, wrapped individually in paper and stored in a single layer on the bedroom floor. They had now to be unwrapped, inspected and polished.

One of the other preparation jobs in December was to look to his Christmas roses. He put a little clean straw among the plants to prevent the blooms being marked by mud splashes during rain. If he thought that the flowers were going to be late the plants were covered with glass to force them a little.

The main reason for these various preparations by Jabez was that on Christmas Eve he visited some of the old and lonely people in the village. He had done it for so many years that they expected him and would have been keenly disappointed had he not called on them.

Before knocking on the door and handing in his gifts of wine, Christmas roses and apples, he sang a carol for them. He had several humorous stories to tell of his experiences during these Christmas Eve visits.

There was the dear old lady who said that she could no longer manage to eat the apples so could she have an extra bottle of wine instead? On one occasion he was given some advice by three young children coming away from the house to which he was going.

"Thee towd me it wonna woth me goin' ter that 'ice 'cos they'd sung two carols an' ony bin given a penny betweyn threy on em.

One of his stories concerned an encounter with a villager who had celebrated the festive season rather too well and who insisted on singing carols with him.

"Ar towd 'im ey could sing after ar'd finished, but ey said it 'ad got fer bey a duet an' ey were goin' sing th'tenor part. Theyst never 'eerd such a row as that mon kicked up. 'Afe-wee through th'fost voss o' Noel ey stopped me an' said ey didna want fer bey ockerd but, withite mentionin' any neemes, it were 'is opinion as somebody were ite o' tune.

“Ar felt larke clockin’ ‘im one but then ar remembered it were th’seyson o’ peyce an’ goodwill.” When he perceived that Jabez was getting just a little annoyed he agreed to stop singing if he could have a bottle of wine. Reluctantly Jabez gave him a bottle of elderberry on condition that he took it straight home to his wife.

“Th’next dee ar’eerd as when ey walked in th’ice ‘is missus screymed an’ passed ite aw of a ruck on th’kitchin floer. Th’owd bezzler ‘ad opened th’bottle o’ elderberry on th’road wom an’ spilt it aw ower ‘imsel’, an’ ‘is missus thowght ey were covered in blood.

“When ey seyd ‘er lyin’ theer ey were sure er’d gone jed an’ rushed ite fer fetch th’neeghbours. When ‘er come rind thee aw ‘ad a good laugh ite on it, but it musta upset ‘im ‘cos it was a lung wheyle afoer ar seyd ‘im th’woss fer drink aggen.

Jabez thought that perhaps that was the most rewarding bottle of wine he had ever given away.

Keypin' th'fire in

Jabez was sweeping his chimney. He had borrowed a set of rods and brushes and was having, as he put it, "a rattlin' good cleyn ite."

The professional sweep was seldom seen in the village; most chimneys just caught fire or were deliberately set on fire.

"Ar've seyn a chimney cleyned be pokin' a gun up it an lettin' fly," said Jabez. "Thee 'adst fer bey quick else thee gotst thee gun full o' sut. Some o' th'owd folk used fer climb on th'roof an' lower a rope dine th'chimney. Somebody in th'ice tied a bunch o' 'olly or laurel sprigs on thend an' th'mon on th'roof pulled it up through th'chimney."

This talk of chimneys reminded Jabez of an incident in his childhood. The parents of one of his playmates were going out for the afternoon.

The two lads were given a copper or two to spend and told to keep the fire in. When they came to attend to the fire the key of the cottage was not in its usual hiding-place.

They could see that the fire needed attention but all the windows were closed and there appeared to be no way in which the fire could be saved.

It was at this point that Jabez's friend had a bright idea. Why not get the ladder out, climb up to the chimney and drop the coal onto the fire that way? No sooner said than done. The ladder was erected, the lad filled his cap with cobbles of coal and carried it up to the chimney.

Meanwhile young Jabez peered through the window to see if the operation was successful. The cobbles came hurtling down the chimney and bounced out across the room in all directions. And then the soot began to fall.

The other lad joined Jabez and, with their noses flattened against the window-panes, they viewed with dismay the gradual coating of the interior of the room with a thick layer of soot. They could see no escape from the wrath to come.

It was dusk when the couple returned home. The lads hid round the corner of the cottage and listened.

"Th'doers locked an' th'fire's ite," said mother.

"Ar know, " said father. "Ar tuk th'key wi' me be mistake."

"Thar greet foo' ! Wot's th'use o' mey tellin' th'lad fer mend th'fire when theyst got th'key in thee pocket?" said mother.

The door was unlocked and they went inside. The lads crept round to the open door and what they heard went something like this:

"Ar con smell sut," said mother. "Ther's bin a fo' o' sut. Kindle that lamp so wey con sey wot's 'appened."

The lamp-light revealed the full extent of the calamity.

"Ee!" said mother, temporarily bereft of words. "Ee! Oh my lors. Th'place's covered in sut – thers sut everywheer. It's thar fawt, ar towd thee that chimney wanted sweypin."

"Ar wondered ar long it 'ud bey afoer thee sedst it were mar fawt. But it's a funny thing," said father.

"If they cost sey anythin' funny in this lot they must bey goin' soft in th'yed," retorted mother.

"Theest got me wrung aggen," said father. "Wot ar'm tryin' fer tell thee is that ther anna ony bin a fo' o' sut, thers bin a fo' o' coal an' aw. Luk thee at them cobbles under th'dresser an' dine theer be th'teeble. Ar'm thinkin' thers bin an explosion or summat. " At the word "explosion" mother ran towards the door crying "Oh me lad! me poer lad. Summat's 'appened ter 'im – ar know it 'as."

The "poer" lad decided that this was a suitable moment to put in an appearance. Mother clasped him to her and he blurted out the whole sorry story,

Mother's emotions were obviously in a turmoil. She was relieved to see the lad, angry at the thought of all the cleaning she now had to do, and amused by their efforts to keep the fire in. In the end she said, "Yer a pair o' nowty lads. Ar'd a good mind fer give yer both a good 'idin'. Yer mitta kilt yersels gettin' up ter yon chimney."

It was poor old father who once again, got the sharp edge of her tongue for taking the key with him.

Warts an' Boils

Amongst the home remedies for a host of common ailments are the so-called "cures" for warts and boils. Those for warts are innumerable.

In an idle moment Jabez and I tried to recall all the different treatments of which we had heard. A common practice in the country was to tie a horse-hair around each one, although most villages had someone with the ability to charm them away.

There are cures in which the warts are rubbed with one or other of a great variety of substances including washing-soda, mouldy cheese, raw potato, apple, banana, the inside of a broadbean pod, the "milk" from a dandelion stalk, the water found in a cleft of an elm tree, the moistened end of a live match, and so on.

In a slightly different category are those in which it is believed that the affliction is actually transferred to the substance with which they are rubbed. Common amongst these substances are meat and animal fat which are subsequently buried or allowed to rot. There is something very primitive about this practice; it savours of the witch-doctor and the medicine man.

In another category is the touching of each wart with separate small stones, or peas, or beans, which are put into a bag and either thrown away or deliberately left somewhere.

It is implied that whoever finds the bag will acquire the warts, the original sufferer being cured. It is of interest that Pliny the Elder, who perished in the eruption of Vesuvius nearly 1,900 years ago, referred to this practice in one of his writings.

"Ar wonna troubled much with warts," said Jabez, "but ar 'ad one o' Job's afflictions when ar were a youth – ar were smitten wi' boils. Ee! ar 'ad some beauties in th'most ockerd pleeces they cost think on."

He was not short of advice from interested villagers, many of whom had their own certain cures for boils.

"They wutsna beleyve th'different things folk towd me fer tak. 'Ast ever etten cuttle-fish bones or grun-up oyster shells? Some on 'em said yeyst were th'best thing. Ar 'ad baker's yeyst, brewer's yeyst, dried yeyst – it's a wonder ar didna start fermentin'."

A gipsy woman who happened to call at the cottage during the time of his affliction offered him a life-time's immunity from boils in exchange for crossing her palm with silver. She advised him to get a piece of butter the size of a walnut, roll it in the soot as far up the chimney as he could reach and swallow it! He decided he had wasted his money.

There were many methods of bringing boils to a head – "drawing" them. Amongst these were the two tortures of hot cobbler's wax and the neck of a hot empty bottle.

"Me mother were a big beleyver in powlticin'. 'Er'd powltice anythin'. 'Er used linseyd meyl mostly – red hot! Ar remember th'tarme when ar 'ad a crop o' boils on me backside an' 'er got th'powlticin' tackle ite."

He soon learned to squeal loud and long each time she applied a poultice, otherwise she concluded they weren't hot enough and the next one would be a scorcher.

"As soon as 'er'd gotten a powltice ready, me young brother kept runnin' upsteers in front on 'er singin':

" 'Ere comes th'noss with a red-hot powltice, slaps it on quick an' taks now nowtice.'

"It were a good job ar couldna get at 'im. Thee't a bit 'andicapped fer scuftin' anybody when thee't lyin' on thee bally with thee trysers dine."

Slarrin' an' sledgin'

Snow was a beautiful exciting thing when we were young. Trees and hedgerows were suddenly transformed into fairyland.

Familiar outlines disappeared, new shapes and contours took their place. The sheer joy of tramping through deep virgin snow, the excitement of building the snowman, the exhilaration of the sledge-ride, the excruciating tingle of numbed fingers that followed snow-balling, the thrill of the slide on the farm pond; all these are half-remembered memories of childhood winters.

The magic seems to fade with age and we come to regard snow as more and more of a nuisance. Nowadays, because of our increasing dependence on different forms of transport, a few inches of snow play havoc with our normal activities.

Even in the country the effect of a snowstorm is much greater than it used to be because the villagers are more dependent on outside supplies and services. Time was when the essentials for living were virtually on the doorstep. The milk and eggs, potatoes and turnips, butter and cheese were no further away than the farm at the bottom of the lane.

Bread came out of the kitchen oven, the bacon and home-cured ham hung in the cellar, and school and work were within walking distance.

In snowtime, the slopes to the west of the village were a happy playground for the children. It was an ideal place for sledging and "slarrin'." Not every child had a sledge but on such a slope a box, or plank, or even a tea-tray would suffice.

Jabez laughed as he described the antics of a lad hurtling down the slope in a tall-sided box.

"Aw thee couldst sey on 'im ower th'edge o' th'box were top o' 'is yed an' two big eyes poppin' ite larke chapel 'at-pegs.

"Ey went rind an' rind larke a top. When ey got ter th'bottom o' th'bonk ey were that giddy ey couldna stand up an' fell flat on 'is face in th'snow.

He also recalled an experience he had on a sledge made by a local blacksmith for his young son. It was constructed of steel tubing and was long enough to accommodate half a dozen lads.

It had a full crew for its first run and it went down the slope at a fearful speed. At the end of the first slope the ground rose a little and then sloped quickly away again.

Ordinary sledges came to rest on the rising ground but the blacksmith's sledge took the rise in its stride and, to their great dismay, was soon accelerating down the second slope. The ground here was thick with gorse-bushes, and beyond them was a deep pool. The outlook was grim.

"Wey were in a bit of a quandary," said Jabez. "If wey jumped off wey'd likely cripple ersel's, if wey didna jump off wey 'ad th'choice betweyn finishin' up in a gorse-bush or goin' through th'ice on th'poo'. Wey went through two or threy fair-sized bushes an' then wey 'it a big un!

"Th'sledge stopped jed an' wey aw went yed ower 'ales inter th'middle o' th'bush. Ar were pickin' prickles ite on me fer a wik or moer. Wey towd th'lad fer tak th'flippin' thing wom an' tell 'is feyther fer put some breekes on it."

Pig-killin'

Many of the cottages in the village had a pigsty at the bottom of the garden. They were well-used and the killing of a pig was a frequent occurrence, providing a grim but fascinating spectacle for the village children.

"Word soon went rind th'village as ther were goin' fer bey a killin'," said Jabez, "an' wey used fer sit on th'wo' an' wetch."

The actual killing was done by the butcher from a neighhouring village who arrived in a pony and trap, bringing with him some of the tools of his trade and a well-scrubbed bench.

After inspecting the doomed animal he took off his jacket, rolled up his sleeves and donned a large apron.

"Ey were a nice enough bloke," said Jabez, "but ther were one thing ar didna larke abite 'im – ey sharpened 'is kneyves in front o' th'pig. It wonna a very nice thing fer do, was it?"

When the butcher was ready the pig was pushed and dragged from the pigsty by three or four helpers and put onto the slaughtering bench

"Thee said it wonna cruel but, from wot ar remember, th'pig didna synd as though ey were exactly enjoyin' it," said Jabez.

A few days later the owner of the pig would be selling some of the carcase, together with such delicacies as chawl and chitterlings, brawn and savoury ducks.

There was one pig that earned for itself a postponement of the death sentence. It belonged to an old widow and as the men went to get it from the pigsty it eluded them and ran off up the garden path.

It so happened that both the back and front doors of the cottage were open and the pig was able to go straight through into the street.

It was chased through the village, eventually captured and brought back, protesting loudly. But the old lady was touched by the pig's pathetic attempt to prolong its life and she called off the killing.

" 'Er sed it 'ud bey larke murderin' th'poer thing. 'Er sowd it alive ter th'butcher an' ey tuk it awee in th'pony and trap. Wey didna get a pig's bladder fer plee footbo' with that dee," said Jabez.

One of the village families had a prolific sow called Sally Anne. In the intervals between litters she was a good-tempered creature and was treated by the family as a household pet. She wandered in and out of the cottage at will and would flop down in front of the kitchen fire like a large dog.

The village children had to walk about a mile to school and in bad weather they often took sandwiches to eat at lunchtime.

"One dee," said Jabez, "wey sut in th'classroom 'avin' us butties when one o' th'wenches started blartin'. 'Er were that upset 'er could 'ardly speyke. 'Er were tryin' fer tell us 'er couldna eat 'er butties 'cos Sally Anne were on 'em. Thee'd 'ad fer kill th'owd sow but th'lass just couldna stomach th'idea o' eatin' poer owd Sally Anne."

Nickneemes

I was asking Jabez about his somewhat unusual name. He said that although he had a distant relative of that name he didn't think his parents christened him Jabez on that account.

"From wot me mother towd me ar gethered 'er 'ad a rough tarme when ar were born. Ar musta bin a bit backerd at comin' forrerd, if thee seyst wot ar meyn. It wouldna surprise me if 'er cawd me Jabez on accynt o' 'er beyin' a big reyder o' th'Bible. P'raps er'd bin reydin th'fost book o' Chronicles – 'ave a luk at chapter foer when thee getst wom."

In the 9th verse, of Chapter 4 I found these words.,

"And Jabez was more honourable than his brethren; and his mother called his name Jabez saying 'Because I bare him with sorrow'."

It was during religious revivals that it became the fashion to make use of old biblical names and we got Elijah and Elisha, Daniel and Jacob, Jonah and Moses, Rachael and Rebecca, and so on.

One of the interesting features of village life was the use of nicknames. Some of these were mere corruptions of real names such as Watty for Walter, Knocker for Enoch, Johnty for John or John Thomas. Other nicknames were attached to persons because of their job, or appearance, or habits, or because of some unusual behaviour or indiscretion.

Often the person's real Christian names were so seldom used as to be almost forgotten. Clogger was the local cobbler, Tommy Twofoot was "small of stature," Peg-leg had had an unfortunate accident, Puddin' was short and round, Soapy wasn't too bright, Holy Joe was a "ranter"and Toddles had big feet.

But what about such nicknames as Bojum, Simpy, Thumper and Minty? Jabez thought that Thumper may have referred to the size of the man, the word "thumping" often being used to describe something that was unusually large.

In Minty's case Jabez could clearly remember the circumstances in which he acquired his unusual nickname.

It appeared that one Sunday morning the man's wife asked him to go into the village and get a sprig or two of mint to have with the joint of lamb. On the way he met a couple of old drinking pals from another village who persuaded him to go with them for "a walk rind."

Somehow the "walk rind" turned into a pub crawl from village to village with the result that the man was in no fit state to return home that evening or even the following morning. Meanwhile his wife was getting very concerned at his absence.

"Poer woman were welly ite o' 'er mind wi' worry," said Jabez. " 'Er were sure summat 'ad 'appened ter 'im an' 'er'd bey shamed 'cos ey adna got 'is cleyn underclose on. But ey turned up on th'Monday af'noon an' wot dust think ey'd got in 'is 'and?"

"A bunch of mint?" I ventured. "thee't reyght," said Jabez. "Ey walked in th'ice as bowd as brass an' towd 'is missus ey were surry ey'd bin a long tarme but ey'd 'ad fer weet for th'mint grow."

From that day onwards the man was always known as Minty.

"Dust think it's possible fer a cat fer bey ony ninepence ter th'shillin'?" asked Jabez.

I said, "I suppose some cats are more intelligent than others, but I've never heard of a mentally, deficient cat."

"Ar reckon wey 'ad one,," said Jabez. "Ey did th'daftest things. Wey funt 'im dine th'closet one dee. Ee! ey were in a mess! Wey cleyned 'im up a bit an' then weshed 'im. Me mother sprinkled 'im wi' lavender weyter fer try an' freshen 'im up a bit."

"But any cat might accidentally fall into a closet," I said. "It wouldn't mean that he was an idiot." "Ar'd agrey wi' thee," said Jabez, "except fer one thing – ey were dine th'seeme closet aggen th'very next dee. Ar dunna think ey'd got much oil in 'is can fer get into that mess tweyce."

The cat's capacity for taking punishment is proverbial. Boys, for some reason, are notorious cat tormentors.

Jabez remembered a boy who seemed to have a grudge against all cats and who went out of his way to ill-treat them. On one occasion he was supposed to be looking after his young sister whilst his mother was out for a few minutes.

When she returned the lad was missing. The little girl, who was in tears, kept pointing to the fireplace and saying something about "a pussy."

"Th'woman tuk now notice fer a bit an' then 'er 'eerd a cat miaowin'. 'Er could 'ardly beleyve 'er ears – it were comin' from th'oven! 'Er opened th'oven doer an' a cat shot ite larke a cannonbo'. Ey'd put th'poer thing in th'oven an' gone ite."

When father came home the couple discussed at some length a suitable form of punishment for such cruelty. They had tried the usual ones for previous ill-treatment of cats.

The boy eventually returned but, much to his surprise, nothing was said about the cat. His parents sat on either side of the fireplace talking of this and that. Their attitude obviously puzzled the lad and they could sense his growing uneasiness. "It's cowd in 'ere terneyght," said father. "Fetch that bucket o' coal in lad, let's stoke up a bit."

The boy got up, opened his mouth to say something but changed his mind and went for the coal. Soon there was a roaring fire.

"Ar tell thee wot," said mother, "weyn'ave some roasted taters fer us supper. Th'oven's nice a' ot – theen be done in now tarme."

The lad squirmed in his chair, glanced nervously at the oven and brushed back a tear from his eye. He was near to breaking point.

"Good idea!" said father. "Ar fancy a roast tater. Ar'll go an' get a two-threy big uns."

When he returned with the scrubbed potatoes the lad could stand it no longer and broke down completely. "A cat in th'oven?" exclaimed father. "Wot on earth at talkin' abite? A cat wouldna get in th'oven." But before he could open the oven door the lad had fled upstairs. They heard his sobs far into the night.

"Ar never 'eerd tell o' 'im 'avin 'owt do with cats after that," said Jabez.

"Ast ever 'ad beestin' custard?" asked Jabez.

Beestings is the colostrum of the cow, the first milk after the birth of a calf. It makes an excellent custard, but it isn't everyone's "cup of tea."

"Thee dustna 'ear much abite pobs theyse dees," said Jabez. "At one tarme a lot o' folk kept a basin o' pobs on th'ob."

"Pobs" or "soakies" was made by putting pieces of bread or toast into a basin and adding milk and tea.

It was kept warm on the hob and members of the household in need of a snack helped themselves to some of the contents, putting the remainder back on the hob.

The basin was replenished from time to time with more bread and leftover tea. It was this concoction that gave birth to that derisive expression: "Go an' get thee pobs."

I fancy I can still smell that appetising odour of meat or sausages being cooked in front of the fire of an old-fashioned range using a "tin-bonnet." Did it really smell and taste so much better than that cooked on modern grills or is it just imagination?

Lobby, of course, is still a popular food, and excellent stuff it is too. "Get a ballyful o' lobby," said Jabez, "an' thee't ready fer owt."

We talked of "spotted-dick" and bread pudding, "cratchin' " cake and barm-bread, savoury ducks and chitterlings, herb beer and buttermilk. There was nothing quite as good as herb beer for quenching a thirst.

Buttermilk, besides being a refreshing drink, had several uses in the kitchen. It made delicious oatcakes and was often added to potatoes.

"Me mother were a dab 'and at meekin' greevy," said Jabez.

"Ar con taste it nar! 'Er used put some sugar in an owd teeblespoon and pop it under th'bottom fire-bar. Th'sugar melted an' then ketched fire. 'Er let it burn fer a bit an' then stuck it in a cup o' cowd weyter. Better than any o' thee new-fangled greevy brynin', that was."

Jabez said that his mother was very particular about the meat she bought. Not only did she tell the butcher exactly which cut she wanted, she often told him how to cut it!

"Every wik when ey cawd fer th'order ther 'ad fer bey an inquest on th'last wik-end jynt. Mind thee, 'er was jonnuck with 'im. If it were a good un 'er said so, but if it wonna, ey were fer it. Ar used feyl surry fer that butcher.

"Ar remember 'er rindin' on 'im once abite a peyce o' beyf. It were a bit tough an' 'er fetched wot were left on it ite o' the' pantry. Er lapped it up in a peyce o' peeper an' towd 'im tak it wom wi' 'im. 'Er said if ey could eat it 'er'd pee for it; if not, ey could whistle fer 'is money.

"After ey'd gone ar towd 'er ar thowght 'er'd bin a bit 'ard on 'im, but 'er said a butcher were supposed fer sell meyt fer eatin'. If ey wanted sell shoe-leather ey'd come ter th'wrong 'ice; ey shoulda sowd it ter th'cobbler."

A Valentine

There are probably more old sayings about February than any other month of the year. In addition to the familiar "February fill dyke," Jabez and I could recall the following:

"Sunbeams on St. Bridget's Day (February 1st)
Are sure to bring the snow in May."

"If Candlemas (February 2nd) be fair and clear
There'll be two winters in the year."

"St. Dorothea (February 6th) brings the snow."

"St. Matthias (February 24th) breaks the ice."

"Fogs in February, frosts in May."

"If snails come out in February
They'll stay at home in March."

Most of these old sayings infer that a mild February is often followed by a period of severe weather. Traditionally, of course, Spring begins on St. Valentine's Day and the old idea was that on this day the birds chose their mates for the year.

"Did anybody ever send thee a Valentine?" asked Jabez.

"I had a few," I replied, "including one that caused me some trouble. It was sent to me just two months after my marriage."

"Ee!" said Jabez. "Ar bet that caused a bit of a flutter in th'dovecote. Mind thee, it shows they musta bin good-lukkin' at one tarme – ar'd never 'ave guessed it! Didst manage fer smoothe things ite wi' thee missus?"

"It wasn't easy," I said,"and I spent a long time in the doghouse."

"They wost lucky," he said. "Ar neyly went gaol ower a Valentine." This sounded like the start of a good story, so I encouraged him to go on.

"Ar were in me teyns an' ther were a lass ar tuk a fancy ter in Augers Bonk. It wunna do any 'arm fer tell thee nar, 'cos th'family flitted off th'Potteries road soon after it 'appened."

"Soon after what happened?" I asked.

"Ar'm tellin' thee anna ar?" he said. "Dunna fluster me." He paused for a while and then said, a little wistfully:

" 'Er were a tidy lass, an' 'er wonna mashin' as fer as ar'd 'eerd, so ar thowght ar'd send 'er a Valentine. Ar got a card – th'vosses were a bit sloppy but thee knowst wot it's larke when thee't young an' th'Spring's comin' on. Ar wonna certain o' th'number o' th'ice so ar decided fer tak it mesel' an' pop it under th'doer after thee'd aw gone bed."

Late that night he set off with the card safely in his pocket. When he approached the cottage of his ladylove he could see there were still two lights burning, one in a bedroom and one downstairs.

"Ar propped mesel' up on th'gardin' wo' an' weeted fer th'leyghts go ite. After a bit ar 'eerd a bloke walkin' up th'road but ar didna tak much notice. Th'next think ar knew ar were dine on th'floer wi' this bloke on top on me. It were th'lass's feyther!

"Ey started leatherin' inter me an' shytin' summat abite a Peypin' Tom. Ar were frittened stiff but when ey mentioned th'bobby ar threw 'im off pretty quick an' skidaddled afoer ey recognised me. Fancy 'im thinkin' ar were a Peypin Tom. Thee 'ast fer bey careful wot thee getst up to, dustna?"

"At superstitious?" asked Jabez. I said it depended on what he meant by superstition.

"Sometarmes," he said, "they't a aggrivatin' sort o' bloke. Next tarme they givst mey a straight answer ter a straight question it'll bey th'fost."

In my defence I went on to explain that many of our so-called superstitions and "old wives' tales" have been shown to be founded on generations of folk wisdom or sound commonsense or even good solid fact. It was therefore unwise to dismiss any of them too lightly, although undoubtedly there were some that were plain nonsense.

"Ee!" said Jabez. "They dust do some rattlin'. If thee't shut up a bit ar'll tell thee abite owd Joe an' 'is sister. Er'd bin jilted in 'er young dees an' er'd never got ower it – it taks some on 'em larke that. Anyroad, after ey'd buried 'is missus owd Joe got 'er fer come live with 'im but it wonna very lung afoer ey regretted it.

" 'Er was a reyght misery. An' 'er were that superstitious th'mon never 'ad a bit o' peyce.

" 'Er read tey-leyves an' cards an' stars, but accordin' ter owd Joe 'er never seyd anythin' in 'em 'cept death an' disaster – ey cawd 'er a prophet o' doom. 'Er beleyved that rubbish abite things 'appenin' in threys.

"Dust know sirree, if owd Joe brok summat in th'ice er'd meeke 'im breek two match-teels so's ey wouldna breek anythin' else. If somebody deyd in th'village 'er reckoned ther'd bey two moer deaths afoer th'twelve month were up.

"Ther come a tarme when owd Joe 'ad fer tak ter 'is bed with a dicky ticker. Ey couldna fathom whey 'er were meekin' such a fuss on 'im 'till ey remembered ther'd bin two funerals in th'village leetly.

"It began fer dawn on 'im as er'd got 'im dine fer number threy. Ey reckoned 'er were awready thinkin' abite th'funeral arrangements – whether it ought fer bey a kneyfe an' fork do or if thee'd meeke do wi' sandwiches an' curran' bread.

"But when 'er said somethin' abite 'is will ey meede up 'is mind ey'd got fer larn 'er a lesson. So when it went dark ey lit th'lamp at th'side o' th'bed an' turned it dine low. Then ey tuk 'is teyth ite an' put 'em under th'piller an' weeted.

"When ey 'eerd 'er comin' up th'steers ey threw th'bedclose off, dropped 'is bottom jaw as fer as it 'ud go, cocked 'is big toes up an' lee on 'is back starin' up at th'ceylin. Ey'ad a job fer keyp 'is face straight, but it worked – 'er were convinced ey'd gone jed!

" 'Er let ite a screym an' ran fer fetch th'woman from next doer. When ey 'eerd 'em comin' back up th'steers ey got ite o' bed, pulled th'neck o' 'is neyght-shirt up 'till it covered' is yed an' then went dine th'landin' flappin' 'is arms an' moanin'.

"Th'pair on 'em were frittened stiff an' belted dine th'steers quicker than thee'd come up. But when th'pair on 'em tried fer get through th'stair-foot doer two abreast ey couldna stand it any lunger an' bost ite laughin'. It didna do 'is ticker any good but ey lived fer sey 'is sister off, an' ey give 'er a kneyfe an' fork do an' aw."

Bumbers, an' brids' neysts

"It's a funny thing," said Jabez, "but when thee getst owder thee rememberst things wot 'appened foty or fifty yeer sin' as clear as deeleyght, but thee costna remember wot 'appened last wik."

"Some o' th'fost things ar can remember," he said, "were meekin' deesycheens, diggin' fer pig-nuts, an' ketchin' bumbers in a jam jar wi' some clover yeds in it. When thee seydst a bey on a flower thee putst a peyce o' cardboerd on one side o' th'flower an' thee jam jar on th'other an' bringst 'em 'gether quick. Thee 'adst fer bey wary o' them wi' red behinds though – folks said them 'ad 'otter stings than th'others."

He recalled the pleasure derived from his first pair of clogs with which he could kick tin-cans around the village and make sparks fly from the road; of how he became so absorbed in his iron "bowler" that he collided with a cow, and how he was so overcome with excitement at catching his first "asker" that he fell headlong into the pond and lost it.

"Ar wonna very owd when ar 'ad me fost ice-creyme in a cup off th'oky-poky mon. Ey come rind in a pony an' trap an' blew a bugle when ey were comin' up th'leene. Ey sowd wafers an' cornets an' aw, but on'y posh folk 'ad them. Anyroad ar larked it best ite o' a cup – thee couldst get thee cup full fer a penny."

Like most country boys, Jabez started a collection of birds' eggs at an early age. It was usual to take only one egg from a nest, the egg sometimes being replaced by a smooth pebble to deceive the bird.

It was believed that on returning to a nest robbed of all its eggs the bird would lay just one more and then desert or "forsake" the nest. Such a nest containing a single cold egg was called a "sakies". As a result of this egg-collecting hobby, children became very knowledgeable about nesting habits and could recognise most birds and their eggs at a glance.

"Talkin' abite brids' neysts," said Jabez, "Ther were a lot o' gorse-bushes dine th'feylds at one tarme. Th'farmer set fire ter 'em nar an' aggen fer stop 'em spreadin'. One dee, threy or foer on us 'ad bin pleein' rind th'feylds an' wey thowght wey'd 'elp th'farmer ite a bit be settin' fire ter one o' th'bushes.

"Soon as it got goin' a linnet come flyin' rind ower us yeds, kickin' up such a kerry. An' then wey could sey ther were a neyst o' young uns tote th'middle o' th'bush! Wey tried fer put th'fire ite with us jackets but it were now use, it'd got too good a 'owd. Th'neyst ketched aleyght an' th'poer little things were burnt death. Ee, it didna 'afe upset us.

"Th'lad as 'ad put th'match ter it started blartin', an' then one on 'em whose feyther were a local preycher said wey ought fer 'ave a funeral service or summat. But none on us could think o' th'reyght words, so in th'end wey aw knelt dine at th'side o' th'burnin' bush an' said th'Lord's Prayer. Wey felt a bit better after that but wey didna set any moer gorse-bushes aleyght fer a bit."

Messin' abite in weyter

"Didst ever go ketchin' jack-sharps with a worm on a peyce o' string?" asked Jabez. His question reminded me of the many happy boyhood days spent in and around the ponds near the village.

Some of these ponds no longer exist – one or two have been filled in, whilst others have silted up and become overgrown. Time was when these ponds provided all those pleasures associated with "messin' abite in weyter" including bathing in summer and sliding in winter.

Preparations for bathing often included the removal of various items of discarded ironmongery and the occasional drowned cat or dog. Bathing trunks were the exception rather than the rule, and one merely submerged at the approach of passers-by.

The ponds were no more than two or three feet deep so that bathing was safe if somewhat unhygienic, and testing the ice by sending the fattest boy on first was unlikely to end in a winter tragedy.

All the ponds contained "jack-sharps" which, at times, would almost queue up to swallow the worm.

"Thee cudst ketch 'em two at a tarme if thee tiedst thee worm in th'middle," said Jabez. "Wey caught a couple o' big jars full one dee. Wey didna know wot fer do with 'em so wey put 'em in next doer's reen-weyter butt. Thee cudstna expect lads fer know as th'woman used reen-weyter fer do 'er weshin' with, cudst ?

"Th'owd mon used fill th'copper an' kindle th'fire on weshin'-dees afoer ey went work. 'Er didna notice owt 'till 'er come fer do th'manglin'. Ther were peyces o' boiled jack-sharp aw ower th'weshin'. 'Er come runnin' rind fer tell me mother it'd bin reenin' fishes an' th'weyter butt were full on 'em.

"Me mother said er'd 'eerd abite it reenin' frogs but reenin' fishes were summat new. 'Er 'ad a luk in next doer's butt an' then 'er lukked in our butt an' said it was a funny thing but it 'adna reened fishes on our 'ice. An' then 'er lukked at mey an' said: 'Ast they 'ad owt do wi' this, Jabez?' Ar couldna tell 'er a lie. 'Er leed ite o' me ear'ole an' tuk me ter th'butt. 'Er said: 'Get them fishes ite o' theer else ar'll put they in with 'em.'

"Ar could tell 'er meant it, so ar got me peyce o' string ite o' me pocket an' a worm ite o' th'gardin' but th'fishes didna seym fer bey 'ungry anymoer. Ar 'ad fer get most on' 'em ite wi' a culinder. Ar thowght ar'd 'ave a bit o' fun with me mother, so ar tuk 'em ter ‘er in th’culinder an’ eksed ‘er if er’d cook ‘em for me. Quick as a flash ‘er said: ‘Awreyght, they bone ‘em, ar’ll cook ‘em.’ Thee cudstna cod me mother.”

Wilfred and two cousins “messin’ abite in the weyter”

Sundee Schoo'

"Sundee inna wot it used bey," said Jabez. I assumed from this remark that I was about to have a lecture on the virtues of the old-time Sunday. To my surprise, however, he went on to say that he looked back on his early days in Sunday School with mixed feelings.

"Ar didna tak ter it very well," he said. "Mind thee ar 'adna any option in th'matter – ar 'ad fer go tweyce a dee. P'raps it didna do me any 'arm though."

As he looked through the schoolroom windows on a warm afternoon he longed to change out of his uncomfortable blue serge suit and his unyielding boots and be away to the cool woods and streams. On such a day his idea of heaven was to climb into the branches of a tall tree and surround himself with the cool sweet-smelling leaves.

Here, the monotonous drone of the teacher would be replaced by the soothing hum of wasp and bee, and the tedious grown-up hymns by the far sweeter music of bird-song and rippling stream.

There were, of course, such compensations as the annual "treat" held on the village cricket ground, the book given as a prize for regular attendance, and the feeling of importance at being on the stage at the "Charity".

" It were a lot better when ar were owd enough fer go into th'Bible class" he said. "It got moer interestin' then."

It was in this class, taught by the village cobbler, that he acquired his simple faith and his abiding affection for the Bible.

They sat in a screened-off corner of the schoolroom reading, in turn, a verse of the chosen passage of scripture. Some of the younger ones rattled the words off in quick style to demonstrate their superior reading ability, whilst an elderly one with less education and with failing eyesight read with difficulty, following the lines of words with a work-worn finger.

When all the verses had been read, the cobbler in his simple way explained their meaning and their application to the Christian way of life.

Jabez was reminded of a true story which he loved to relate. It concerned a village Sunday School and a class of boys who were so unruly that a succession of teachers had all given them up as uncontrollable. For a while they were without a teacher but, after much persuasion, a man who had recently returned to the village agreed to see what he could do with them.

When he confronted them on the first Sunday morning he found them sprawled on a form, leaning back against the wall.

"Nar lads," he said, "get up an' just bring that form ite abite a couple o' foot frum th'wo." Reluctantly, and a little puzzled, they did as they were told. The man took his chair, placed it in front of them and sat down. He looked at each lad in turn and then raising his fist almost under their noses he said, very firmly:

"Th'fost lad wot's nowghty ar'll knock 'im backerds off that form inter th'wo."

Not, you might think, a good start to a Sunday School class, but the new teacher had been in the Navy and had his own ideas about the meaning of the word discipline. Almost before the lads had recovered from their shock he had captured their attention with stories of his adventures in far-off parts of the world.

"Dust know," said Jabez, "ey tuk that class fer nigh on 30 yeer. When ey deyd 'is owd scholars come from aw ower th'country fer 'is funeral. Two on 'em were parsons an' most on 'em 'ad done well. Thee costna put a price on a mon larke that."

Sundee neyght

"Ar remember th'tarme when th'Chapel were welly full on a Sundee neyght," said Jabez. On a cold night the old coke-stove had a cosy glow and the brass oil-lamps hanging from the ceiling gave out a warm gentle light.

There was a pervading odour of the camphor-balls with which the prudent housewife preserved the family's Sunday clothes from the depredations of the moth. A sensitive nose could detect the peppermints and chlorodynes surreptitiously popped into mouths and quietly sucked as comforters during the sermon.

The harmonium player had little effect on the tempo of the hymns since, no matter how furiously he pedalled, he was unable to get enough volume out of his instrument to be heard above the hearty singing.

"Ey bosted th'bellers one neyght when ey were pleein' 'Onwerd, Christian Sowdjers.' Ey 'adna 'afe bin givin' it some 'ommer but wey didna know ey'd stopped pleein''till wey got ter th'end o' th'voss."

There was a certain amount of what nowadays would be called "audience participation." Shouts of "Amen," "Hallelujah," and "Praise the Lord" were common during the prayers and the sermon.

One old stalwart, a little hard of hearing, sat as near as possible to the pulpit and listened with "cupped" ear to every word. He signified his agreement or disagreement with the preacher by appropriate movements of his head. When deeply stirred he would call out: "Thee't reyght, lad, thee't reyght."

Jabez had many vivid memories of that great body of local preachers who, after a week's hard work, tramped many miles in all weathers to keep appointments at distant village chapels.

Amongst these dedicated Christians were several outstanding "characters".

One, for whom Jabez had a great admiration, was a miner whose face, and hands bore many a blue scar, honourably acquired in the bowels of the black earth. This man was a born orator and had no need of sermon notes. The pulpit was too small a space for his energetic style. He was soon out of it, pacing to and fro across the full width of the Chapel. His descriptive powers were exceptional.

"Ar've 'eerd tell," said Jabez, "as when ey were describin' th'return o' th'Prodigal Son, folks were known fer turn ther yeds rind, 'afe-expectin' fer sey th'lad comin' dine th'aisle."

In his enthusiasm he often lapsed into dialect with dramatic effect.

"Ey were now bigger than threy penn'orth o' copper" is surely a more graphic description of Zacchaeus than the Bible phrase "little of stature."

In describing the Prodigal Son's pitiable state, imagine the impact on a village congregation of changing the words ". . . he fain would have filled his belly with the husks that the swine did eat" to ". . . ey were that clemmed ey got dine on 'is kneys an' eat th'pig-swill."

Hardly a literal translation, but this miner was no literary man – he just preached the simple Gospel with great effect.

"Didst 'ave th'cane much when thee wentst schoo'?" asked Jabez.

"Yes," I said, "but probably no more than I deserved."

"Ar reckon ar 'ad moer than me fair share," he said. "Th'schoolmester were a bit too 'andy wi' th'cane fer mar larkin'. Folks said if thee putst a peyce o' 'oss-'air across thee 'and it'd breek th'cane, but it didna work fer mey. Mind thee it wouldna ave meede much difference 'cos ey'd got plenty o' spares on top o' th'cupboard."

He learned to hold his hand up as high as possible so as to shorten the stroke, and then to move his hand down with the cane to soften the blow.

"Thee 'adst fer keyp thee thumb ite o' th'road an' aw," he said. "If ey ketched thee across thee thumb it didna 'afe give thee some jip."

After the punishment the victim was closely watched by the other boys for any sign of tears; crying was looked upon as an inexcusable weakness. If he passed the test the lad might find a warm sticky sweet on his desk that had been quietly passed from hand to hand by his sympathetic fellows.

For Jabez and his contemporaries going to school involved a long walk through the fields to the next village. There were so many interesting things to see and do on the way that it was easy for a lad to forget the time.

Late marks were entered in the register in red ink and persistent lateness was punished with the cane. A really bad case could mean a visit from the dreaded School Board man.

In those days the headmaster and teachers all travelled to school by train. The railway ran through the valley between the two villages and there was a steep gradient as it approached the station.

"If it were an owd ingin' or a fresh driver ey didna get enough speyd up on th'flat an' got bucked up th'bonk. On th'road schoo' wey could sey th'smoke from th'ingin' as it come through th'woods. Wey got as wey could tell if ey were comin' fast enough fer get up th'bonk. If th'wheyls started spinnin' it were napoo. Ey'd get slower an' slower 'till ey stopped awgether.

"Th'station-mester was a dapper little feller with a billy-goat beard an' ey used come runnin' dine th'track an' climb up on th'footpleete. Th'treen 'ad fer go aw th'wee back inter th'woods an' stop theer 'till thee got steym up aggen ready fer 'ave another go.

"Schoo' couldna start 'till thee managed fer get th'treen inter th'station. So wey pleed arind 'till th'last minute an' then went in schoo' an' sut dine in us desks as though wey'd bin theer aw th'tarme. Wey put th'red ink ite one mornin' so's th'schoolmester could give 'imsel' a leete mark. Ey didna larke that a bit."

Th'toad

"Inna yon youth ugly!" said Jabez. "Ey reminds me o' somebody but ar conna just think who it is."

He was referring to his toad who had waddled towards us as we sat on the garden seat in the gathering dusk.

"Ar funt 'im dine th'leene – it must bey seven or eight yeer ago nar. Ey were lukkin' reyght miserable an' aw covered in dirt. Ar think a dog 'ad 'ad a go at 'im or mebbe some lads 'ad bin pleeguing 'im. Anyroad, ar tuk 'im wom in me pocket an' weshed 'im an' put 'im in th'gardin. Ey's bin knockin' arind ever since."

As the toad came nearer to us Jabez's spaniel got up and walked away down the garden path whimpering a little. Jabez called out to him: "Thar greet babby – ey wunna 'urt thee." But the dog kept his distance.

"Ey larned 'is lesson a lung tarme ago" Jabez went on. "Ey picked th'toad up one dee but ey dropped 'im aggen pretty quick. They shouldsta seyn 'im, sirree, ey were larke a soul in torment. Ar mopped 'is mithe ite wi' a peyce o' rag but ey were offside fer a dee or two. Ey keyps well awee from 'im nar."

The "old wives' tale" that toads are venomous is substantially true. They secrete a poison in the glands of the skin which serves to protect them from some of their enemies. Dogs who pick them up may suffer greatly from this poison and a dog that swallows one is likely to die.

Jabez turned over a spit of soil with his spade and picked out a couple of earthworms. The toad sat there, its throat dilating and its liquid eyes unblinking.

"Just wetch 'im," he said. "Ey larkes theyse."

He dropped the worms one at a time in front of the toad and they disappeared almost as soon as they hit the ground. That quick flick of the toad's tongue takes only a fraction of a second.

" 'Andy gadgits them eyeballs o' 'is," said Jabez. "Ey draws 'em inter 'is yed an' squashes th'worms aggen 'em with 'is tungue – cunnin' int it?"

The toad waddled away across the garden and the dog came trotting back to sit in his accustomed place by his master's feet.

"When ar were a lad me feyther kept a toad in th'greyn-'ice an' ey used talk ter it. Ar were very partial ter them little red tomaters – sweyt as a nut thee were. When ar went in th'greyn-'ice fer pinch one or two th'owd toad 'ud bey sittin' theer wetchin' me. Me feyther could allees tell when ar'd bin in – ar couldna' understand it. Ar began fer think th'toad 'ad summat do with it, so ar used cover 'im up with me cap."

Old superstitions die hard. The past association of the toad with witchcraft and other unnatural practices have endowed it with a legacy of suspicion that still lingers on.

"Yeers after, when ar towd me feyther abite th'toad wetchin' me, ey laughed 'is yed off an' said: 'They couldstna shut th'greynice doer proper – that's th'ony road ar could tell when theedst bin in'."

"Ee!" said Jabez, "Ar spent some 'appy dees in yon valley. It were a grand spot fer a lad. In th'olidees ar tuk a bit o' snappin in me pocket an' ar didna bother a soul fer th'rest o' th'dee."

The valley of which he spoke lay about a mile to the west of the village where the dark soil of Staffordshire begins to give way to the red earth of neighbouring Cheshire.

It had much to interest a lad – clumps of gorse and grassy slopes, tall trees and thick bushes, a stream, a swamp, and an outcrop of sand. Sheltered on three sides from the elements it attracted animals, birds, and insects in profusion.

The rough pasture or "moss" at the open end of the valley was the habitat of peewit and snipe, rabbit and hare, mole and shrew.

In early spring there was the excitement of wandering across the "moss" in search of peewits' nests. The birds rose from the ground with urgent cries and swept passed at head height to lure you away from their eggs.

"It were now use lukkin' fer th'neyst wheer th'peewit flew up from," said Jabez. "Thee wonna as daft as that. Thee'd run across th'grind fer many a wee afoer thee tuk ter th'wing. Thee meede fawse neysts an' aw, wey cawd 'em cock's neysts."

In the nest, which was little more than a depression in the ground, the brown, green and fawn-marked eggs blended so well with their background that they were well-nigh invisible. On the softer, marshy ground the startled snipe erupted into zigzag flight and climbed high into the sky to produce that delightful drumming sound with its tail-feathers.

The willow-fringed stream was barely four feet wide but to an imaginative lad it became a mighty untamed river where his home-made boats with matchstick masts and paper sails negotiated fearsome rapids and cruel rocks, only to founder in a vicious whirlpool.

Tired of his boats he could play in the loose sand at the bottom of the outcrop in whose vertical face the sand-martins had their nesting burrows; or he could stir up the marshy ground and listen to the gas bubbling its way through.

A mighty thirst could be slaked in the cool clear water of the spring that gushed from the hillside and then, face down on the grassy slope chewing a stalk of grass, he could listen to the great chorus of nature's voices echoing around the valley.

Towards evening on a spring day a dog-fox would call to his vixen across the valley and a nearby farm-dog tethered to his kennel would start a chain of barking that spread to farm-dogs for miles around.

"Ar once seyd a fox meeke a pack o' 'ounds luk silly dine that valley," recalled Jabez. "Ar could 'ear th'unt in th'distance an' just nar th'fox come beltin' ower th'top o' th'bonk an' meede fer that swamp dine th'bottom end. Th'cunnin' beggar knew 'is road across that swamp but th'ounds didna. Thee aw went lommerin' inter th'black mud up ter ther necks. That was th'end o' th'unt. Ar bet that owd fox were backside o' a bush somewheer laughin' 'is yed off"

That happy boyhood playground no longer exists. It was decreed that the common good would be better served by obliterating the valley and replacing it by a motorway. Such is progress. In the words of Jabez: "Thee wanted ther yeds lukkin'."

"Ar tell thee wot," said Jabez, "thee dustna sey kids pleein' geemes in th'road larke thee used fer do. It's many a wheyle since ar seyd wenches pleein' 'opscotch, an' ar anna seyn a lad wi' a whip an' top fer yeers."

There was a time when the village street seemed to be completely taken over by children playing games of one kind or another. Many of these games were seasonal.

For a few weeks the street would be full of cracking whips and flying tops, and then, almost overnight, the boys turned to marbles, or to bodger, or to peggy, and the girls were playing hopscotch, or ball-bouncing, or the many different skipping games.

Some of the girls' games were played to the singing or chanting of verses and rhymes that had been handed down from one generation to another.

The various games of marbles, and rinkers and nunk had their own strict rules and a specialised vocabulary. There were taws, alleys, pugs, spotties, shotties, glassies, duckers and iron bobbers.

"Ar never did figure ite whether th'owd woman in th'shop seyd us pleein' marbles an' then ordered some, or whether wey seyd th'marbles in th'shop-winder an' that started us pleein," said Jabez. "It were a case o' th'chicken an' th'egg if thee seyst wot ar meyn. Thee couldst get a lot o' marbles wi' thee Satdee penny – aw different colours.

"When ar were skint ar used meeke me own. Ar knew wheer ther was some red clee wot meede reyght good uns. Ar rowled it up into little bo's in me 'ands an' put 'em on th'ob fer dry.

"Then ar put 'em on a peyce o' brick an' beeked 'em in th'kitchin fire. Thee wonna as good as bought 'uns but thee 'adst fer do summat when thee wast skint."

It was in the long dark evenings of autumn and winter that the game known in the village as "leave-o" was played.

This was a superior form of hide and seek. The full width of the street in front of the village shop was the "den" and the two "sides" of equal numbers of boys were the hunters and the hunted.

The latter were allowed to hide themselves and were then under an obligation to call out "leave-o" loud enough to be heard by the hunters back in the den.

After that, the chase was on – the only restriction being that no-one must enter a house. A lad was considered to be caught when he could be held long enough for his captor to spit over his head.

He then had to return to the den and could only be released by someone from his own side running right through the guarded den. One game could last for a week or more.

In the fields and along the unlit roads in and around the village there was ample scope for the exercise of initiative and ingenuity.

"One o' me feevourite tricks was fer climb up inter th'top o' th'entry betweyn two 'ises," said Jabez. "Thee putst thee back aggenst one wo' and thee feyt aggenst th'other an' workst theesel' up wi' thee 'ands an' thee feyt 'till thee wast reyght up at th'ceylin' o' th'entry.

"Thee tukst a bit o' findin' when thee wast spragged up theer. Ar come a cropper one neyght though – a lad got 'owd o' a line-prop an' went dine aw th'entries pokin' 'em. Ey got th'wost on it mind thee – ar dropped straight on top on 'im."

Th'elder bush

"Just luk at that!" said Jabez. "Ar'll give yon farmer a peyce o' mar meynd next tarme ar sey 'im. Fancy cuttin' a elder bush dine larke that – ey wants lukkin' at! Ar've 'ad enough flowers and berries off that theer bush in one yeer fer meeke threy or foer gallons o' weyn."

Jabez was visibly upset. It was difficult to see what possible reason there could be for cutting the bush down. It had occupied an otherwise useless corner in a field of rough pasture and for years its fragrant flowers and rich berries had given pleasure to many people.

Jabez had a great regard for the elder and in this respect he was carrying on a tradition that goes back for many centuries. The roots, pith, bark, buds, flowers, leaves and berries have all been used from time to time for their medicinal properties.

"Me mother used meeke elderberry syrup an' elderflower ointment" said Jabez. "Th'syrup were meede be boilin' th'elderberry juice wi' sugar – larke thee meekst jam ony not queyte as thick. Come th'winter 'er'd fetch it ite an' dose us with it fer cowds in th'yed an' bad throats.

"Th'ointment was good stuff an' aw. 'Er boiled th'flowers wi' lard wot 'er'd rendered dine 'ersel', an' then streened it inter jars. Rattlin' good stuff it were fer chapped 'ands an' soers."

The wood of the elder has been used to make flutes and paper, skewers and clothes-pegs. Its roots were thought to cure snake-bite and hydrophobia, its berries boiled with honey cured earache, and tea made from its flowers cleared away freckles and relieved headaches.

A fragrant white wine can be made from its flowers in July and a rich red wine from its berries in September. No doubt some of the old herbalists exaggerated its curative powers but its imposing list of medicinal properties accumulated over centuries must surely have some justification.

"Ar'll never ferget goin' getherin' elderberries with me mother – ar wonna very owd at th'tarme. It were one af'noon at th'back-end o' September, an' wey went dine th'feylds wi' a couple o' baskets – a little un fer mey an' a big un fer 'er.

"It was gettin' tote tea-tarme afoer weyd got enough berries. Ar was feylin' thirsty so wey cawd at a farm-'ice fer a drink o' weyter. But thee knowst wot it's larke when a couple o' women get 'gether.

Me mother 'ad fer go in fer a cup o' tea an' a chin-wag wi' th'farmer's missus.

"It were goin' dusk when wey set off back wom. Wey 'adna gone moer than 'afewee when ar spotted a little mon perched on top o' a bonk reyght in front on us.

"Ey was now moer than two foot taw! Ar got it inter me yed as ey was one o' them little fellers wot thee reydst abite – wot dust caw 'em?"

I laughed and said: "Well, there are gnomes and pixies and elves and trolls and leprechauns." "They cost laugh," he went on, "but it wonna funny – ar were frittened death. Me mother towd me not fer bey daft but ar could tell 'er wonna aw that sure 'ersel'.

"Theer this little mon was, in th'tweyleyght, on th'skyline, an' th'path went straight passed 'im! Ar got backside o' me mother an' kept peypin' ite fer sey if ey were still theer.

"Theedst never guess wot it was if ar give thee from nar 'till Christmas. It was me feyther lukkin' fer us! 'Ey was a miner thee knowst, an' when a miner squats dine on 'is haunches ey inna much moer than two foot taw. They 'ave a luk next tarme thee seyst one."

Leedybirds an' ants

"Ladybird, ladybird, fly away home, your house is on fire, your children all burned. Ladybird, ladybird, fly away home."

The two of us, Jabez and I, sat at the edge of the little copse and chanted this ditty to a ladybird that was crawling over Jabez's hand.

"It's a good job thers nowbody abite fer listen terus," he said. "Folk's 'ud think wey'd gone soft in th'yed."

He had been collecting ladybirds in a matchbox to put in his greenhouse. Some of his hot-house plants had been attacked by greenfly and this troublesome aphid is a favourite diet of the ladybird.

Presently, the ladybird on his hand raised its smooth neat wing-cases and flew away, just as they used to do when we sang to them on those long summer days of our childhood.

While most other kinds of beetles are disliked or even feared, the ladybird is regarded with a great deal of affection. Neither of us could recall seeing a child deliberately harm one. Bird's don't attack them either – their bright contrasting colours serve as a warning that they are not nice to eat.

"Come on," said Jabez. "Wey conna sit arind aw dee pleein' wi' leedybirds. Ar've got enough on 'em fer bey goin' on with. Let's cut across th'stony feyld, it'll bey quicker."

Amongst old country folk there was a saying that some fields grew stones. The one we were walking across was so littered with them that one could almost believe the old saying to be true.

From time to time attempts had been made to plough it, but it must have been heartbreaking work.

It had been pasture now for many years, and the sight of the stones lying amongst the grass reminded Jabez of a favourite pastime of his childhood – turning over the larger stones to see what was underneath them.

They concealed a great variety of small creatures, but it was under the large flat ones that the nests of the ant were to be found.

Immediately the stone was removed they began to remove their so-called "eggs" and soon they had all disappeared to a lower level.

"Ar once seyd ants stop a cricket match," said Jabez. "Ther come a swarm o' flyin' ants ower an' got aw mixed up wi' th'cricketers. Fost one an' then another started scrattin'.

“Th’ants got dine inside ther shirts an’ up ther tryser legs an’ stung ‘em summat cruel. Th’umpire put ‘is ‘and up fer firk one ite o’ ‘is earhole an’ th’batsman at t’other end thowght ey’d bin given ite!

“Thee tried fer carry on but in th’end thee aw come runnin’ inter th’pavilion as if th’owd lad was after ‘em.

“Wey set leyght ter th’lung gress in th’ite-feyld an’ th’smoke shifted ‘em off. But it were a lung tarme afoer thee could start th’match aggen, an’ nar an’ aggen theedst ‘ear one of th’batsmen shytin’ ter th’bowler: ‘Owd thee whip a bit sirree, ar’ll ‘ave fer ‘ave another scrat’.”

Th'little red apples

I was asking Jabez if he was troubled by children stealing from his garden. He had a few fruit trees and I was remembering some of my own boyhood escapades in that direction.

"Thee dunna trouble mey aw that much," he said. "Theer welcome ter a two-threy apples but ar wish thee'd come an' eks fer 'em instead o' lommerin' up th'treys an' breekin' th'branches dine. Mind thee, ar did mar share o' that when ar were a lad.

"Ther was a big trey in th'owd farm orchard wot used bey smothered wi' little red apples. Sweyt as a nut thee were. Th'owd woman 'ud fill thee cap full o' wind-blown uns fer a penny, but thee 'adst fer wetch ite fer th'grubs.

"One neyght wey were at a bit of a loose-end so wey decided fer 'ave some apples straight off th'trey. Ther were six or seven on us an' wey got behind th'orchard wo' an' weeted 'till it begun fer go dark.

"Th'apple trey were reyght in front o' th'kitchin winda an' th'farmer was nodding-off in 'is arm-cheer, an' 'is missus was doin' a bit o' mendin'.

"Just nar 'er got up an' kindled th'lamp an' dropped th'blind dine. Wey weeted fer it get a bit darker an' then wey 'opped ower th'wo' an' crept up ter th'trey.

"Wey sent Fatty up fer sheeke th'apples dine ter us but wey must 'ave meede a lot o' noise cos th'dog started barkin', an' then th'farmer come runnin' rind from back o' th'ice

"Wey skidaddled ower th'wo' but poer owd Fatty was left stranded up th'trey. Th'farmer stood theer squintin' into th'neyght an' shytin': 'Ar know who y'are. Ar'll 'ave a word wi' yer feythers in th'mornin'.'

"Ey were ony tryin' fer cod us though – ey'd got now moer idea than fly who wey were.

"If Fatty 'ad kept still th'farmer wouldnera known ey was up th'trey. But ey was a bit of a devil was owd Fatty an' when ey seyd th'farmer standin' theer ey couldna resist sheekin' a apple or two on'im.

"One on 'em must 'ave landed on 'is yed 'cos ey swore an' danced arind 'till poer owd Fatty got a fit o' th'giggles wi' wetchin' 'im."

"That give th'show awee 'cos everybody in th'village knowed Fatty's laugh. Th'farmer didna know wot fer do next. Ey meede as if ey were goin' climb th'trey but Fatty give it another bit of a sheeke an' ey soon cheenged 'is mind.

"Ey stormed an' raged an' threatened wot ey'd do fer 'im when ey did come dine. Fatty decided ey was better off stoppin' wheer ey was.

"Then ey said ey was goin' fetch th'gun. As soon as ey'd gone rind th'end o' th'ice, Fatty dropped ite o' th'trey larke a stone an' come beltin' across th'orchard ter th'wo'. Wey leed ite on 'im an' yanked 'im ower just as th'farmer come back with 'is double-barrel, an' th'dog.

"Ey thowght Fatty was still up th'trey but ey soon funt ite ey wonna 'cos Fatty went an' 'ad another bout o' th'giggles behind th'wo. Thee couldstna stop that lad frum laughin'.

"Mind thee, ar dunna expect ey laughed aw that much next dee after th'farmer 'ad bin their 'ice – ey 'ad a reyght good tankin' off 'is feyther.

"Ey didna split on any on us, but wey didna go fer a cap-full o' windblown uns fer a bit."

Dares

One of the pastimes of childhood was the game of "daring" or "doffering", in which children challenged one another to perform some difficult or daring feat.

The game was commendable in the sense that it fostered a competitive spirit and afforded a feeling of achievement.

Many of the "dares", however, were either mischievous or downright dangerous. Although a boy might realise that a particular "dare" was too frightening or beyond his capabilities, he was almost compelled to "have a go".

No-one likes to be thought of as a coward – a boy least of all. That chant of "Cowardy, cowardy custard" from his pals falls hard on the ears of a healthy boy.

"One o' th'dares was fer walk rind th'top o' an owd pit-shaft," recalled Jabez. "Th'shaft 'ad bin built up wi' bricks ter abite eight or nine foot off th'grind, an' then some barbed weyer 'ad bin stretched across th'ole.

"Thee 'adst fer scrawm up th'wo an' balance theesel' on th'top, an' then walk aw rind th'wo. Th'top were ony a brick weyd, thee knowst, an' that rusty owd barbed weyer wouldnera stopped anybody from fo'in' in.

"If thee dropst a brick dine that shaft it was many a wheyle afoer thee 'eerdst it splash in th'weyter at th'bottom. Even nar ar breek ite in a cowd sweat when ar think abite walkin' rind that wo'."

Jabez paused for a while and slowly shook his head as if to rid himself of a nightmare. Then his face creased into a smile and he went on: "Ar got inter a reyght owd mess ower another dare. Ther was a gang on us dine th'feylds pleein' arind th'bruk. Thers a 'awthorn 'edge runs dine one side on it an' th'dare was fer jump ower th'edge an' th'weyter – larke them 'osses do in th'Grand National.

"Two or threy o' th'lads jumped it awreyght an' ar reckoned ar could jump as good as any on 'em. Ar tuk a reyght good run at it but wot dust think sirree? – one o' me boot-leeces ketched in a branch at th'top o' th'edge an' ar went yed fost into th'weyter. Ee, ar was in a mess. Ar lukked larke a drynded rat an' ar was rowelled up wi' mud.

"Ar dostna go wom in that state, so wey meede a wood fire an' ar tuk me close off an' dreyed 'em. But that mud was better than any starch – me trysers were that stiff thee couldst stand 'em up on th'grind.

"So ar 'ad fer walk dine ter th'spring in me nothin's an' wesh me close an' bring 'em back ter th'fire. It seymed fer tak a wik o' Sundees fer dry 'em, an' me shirt lukked as if it 'ad just come ite o' th'ragbag. Ar got some o' th'lads fer sit on it fer get some o' th'ruckles ite on it.

"Aw me close smelt o' burnin' wood an' me gansy 'ad shrunk that much ar couldna get it ower me yed.

"When ar walked in th'ice me mother said: 'Theyst bin pleein' wi' fire aggen – ar con smell it. An' whey 'astna got thee gansy on? – it inna as 'ot as aw that.'

"Ar said nowt, an' 'id me gansy in th'bottom o' me drawer upsteers. Come ter think on it ar never seyd that gansy aggen. Ar wonder wot become on it."

Th'treycycle ride

The main road up the hill to the village is still known as the lane or "th'leene". The lane joins the village street at about its mid-point and it was at this junction that the old village green was situated.

"Reyght wheer ar'm standin' was abite th'middle o' th'greyn," said Jabez. "Thee 'ad fer do awee with it when th'road were weydened. It were just a threy-cornered patch o' gress in th'middle o' th'road.

"Ar spent many a 'appy 'our pleein' nunk an' meekin' mudpies. Mind thee, ther wonna much traffic abite in them dees – thee didstna stand much chance o' gettin' run ower. Ther was th'lamp-oil mon, an' th'bread-cart, an' th'Co-op mon, an' th'Freydee-neyght mon, an' a two-threy moer – that was abite aw 'cept fer th'farmer's tackle an' th'neyght-soil cart.

"In them dees th'leene was ony narrer – ar funt that ite ter me cost one dee. One o' th'lads 'ad some relatives off Manchester road – ar think thee musta bin well-off. Anyroad, theyse relatives sent word thee'd gotten a treycycle thee wanted get rid on. So this lad's feyther 'ad a dee off work, fer 'is eyes, an' off thee went on th'fost treen fer Manchester fer fetch it.

"Wey got fer know wot tarme thee were comin' back, an' aw us lads went dine ter th'steetion fer weet fer 'em. Thee'd put this treycycle in th'guard's-van. Thee shouldsta seyn it sirree – it were a greet big full-sized un! Wey 'ad fer 'elp 'em push it up th'feylds an' lift it ower th'stiles.

"Next dee, wey aw went rind ter th'lad's 'ice fer sey if wey could 'ave a go on it. But it was too big fer a lad – none on us could reych th'pedals. It didna matter though, wey 'ad plenty o' fun pushin' one another abite on it. Th'leene was th'best pleece fer it – it went larke an express treen dine that bonk.

"One dee there was five on us on it – one on th'seyt, one on th'cross-bar, one on th'andlebars an' two standin' up on th'back axle.

"Wey set off dine th'leene an' wey were goin' larke th'wind when aw of a suddin wey seyd a charabang comin' up. Ther wonna room fer us pass one another. Wey put th'breeks on, but wi' five on us on it th'breeks wouldna 'owd, an' wey kept goin' tote this charabang!

"Th'lad on th'cross-bar started blartin', an' th'one on th'andlebars started shytin' fer 'is mother – ey were th'youngest o' th'lot on us. Mind thee, they couldst understand th'little chap werritin' a bit 'cos ey was th'one wot was goin' 'it th'charabang fost. Ther were ony one thing fer it – wey 'ad fer go inter th'edge.

"Th'front wheyl dropped inter th'ditch an' wey aw went yed fost inter th'edge. Folks ite o' th'charabang come runnin' up fer sort us ite but ther were now sign o' th'little mon wot 'ad bin on th'andlebars.

"It was a bit afoer wey funt 'im. Ey'd gone cleyn ower th'edge inter a feyld o' chonnucks. Ey were awreyght though after wey'd got th'dirt off 'im an' rubbed 'im dine a bit."

Scott Hay looking down th'leene circa 1911

Th'Charity

As we walked up the garden path, Jabez looked up at the front of his cottage and said: "Ar reckon ar'll 'ave give th'iteside a coat o' peent afoer th'Charity, an' ar'd better get them curtins weshed ite an' aw."

For more than 90 years the Sunday School Anniversary, or "Charity", has been a very important event in the life of the village. Preparations for this festival begin several months in advance, and traditionally it is the housewives' target-date for the completion of spring-cleaning and redecorating.

It is also the time for buying and wearing new clothes. For this purpose, the Sunday School used to operate a "Clothing Club" to which parents contributed week by week to enable them to provide their children with new "Charity" clothes.

The twice-weekly practices of the special music to be sung by children and choir are the source of much good humour and many headaches.

The "great day" itself is something of a 12-hour marathon which begins with a parade of the children dressed in their new clothes and a tour of the district by the choir, with a break for coffee and buns.

The tour involves the choir in a walk of several miles with innumerable stops for the singing of their special hymns. Nevertheless, on a fine May morning, in a country setting, this outdoor singing is a pleasurable thing for the performers and, it is hoped, for the listeners.

According to Jabez, however, there was one occasion when the music wasn't appreciated by some of the listeners.

"One Charity," he said, "th'choir didna know one o' th'hymns very well, so when thee were goin' through th'wood th'conductor decided fer 'ave a practice under th'treys wheer nowbody could 'ear 'em.

"Th'creytures in th'wood wondered wot on earth was appenin'. Them on foer feyt tuk ter ther 'eels an' yedded fer wom, an' th'brids scattered in aw derections as fast as ther wings 'ud carry 'em.

Th'poer things 'ad never 'eered anythin' larke it at 9 o'clock on a Sundee mornin'! Ar bet ther were any amynt o' deserted neysts that yeer.

After the outdoor singing is over there is just time for a hurried lunch before the afternoon service. Many ex-Sunday School scholars return to the village to attend the services and it is a favourite occasion for family re-unions. Households have often found it necessary to have two "sittings" at tea-time to feed all their guests. Years ago, people wishing to secure a good seat at the evening service had to arrive soon after the afternoon service had ended, and many late-comers were unable to get a seat at all.

"One o' th'owd stewards was a dab 'and at packin' folks in," recalled Jabez. "Ar've seyn 'im tak a fat bloke ite o' a pew an' put 'im on a cheer in th'aisle, an' then put two thin uns wheer ey'd 'ad th'fat un from.

"Ar think it used grieve 'im if ey 'ad fer leyve anybody standin' iteside – ey's 'ad as many as 'afe a dozen packed under th'steege wheer th'children sit! When ey'd finished packin' em in ther were now dite abite it – it was a full 'ice!"

Children's Choir at Scott Hay Methodist Chapel circa 1930

Cravin' fer a donkey

"When ar were a lad," said Jabez, "ar 'ad a cravin' fer a donkey o' me own. Wey couldna afford one, but that didna stop mey meytherin' after one.

"Ar fancied mesel' ridin' rind th'feylds an' th'woods on a donkey, an' goin' schoo' on it an' aw. Ar musta meed a nuisance o' mesel' ower this donkey, 'cos ar remember me mother said: 'Ar wish theedst shut up abite a donkey – wey get donkey at every verse end!'

"Me feyther said even if weyd got a donkey wey adna got a steeble fer put it in. But that didna put me off – ar started collectin' bricks.

"Ther were some owd ruined 'ises dine th'feylds an' ar carted th'bricks wom one at a tarme. Ar knocked th'owd mortar off 'em wi' a 'ommer an' stacked 'em up at th'bottom o' th'gardin ready fer when ar'd got enough fer build th'steeble.

"In th'meyntarme ar meede do wi' other folks's ponies an' osses. On Satdees, th'butcher come rind deliverin' meyt in a pony an' trap. Ar persueeded 'im fer let me go with 'im. Ee, ar thowght ar was cock o' th'middin drivin' that pony an' trap arind. Ar used 'ave walk a mile back wom after wey'd finished deliverin', but ar didna mind.

"In th'wik ar used go dine ter th'farm. Mind thee, them were big cart-'osses an' thee frittened me a bit 'cos ar wonna very owd then. Ar used ride on 'em when ar got th'chance but it wonna aw that comfortable. Ther backs were that weyd ar couldna sit on 'em withite doin' th'splits.

"Th'farm leebourer used plee some tricks on me When ar was groomin' one o' th'osses ey'd sneyk inter th'steeble on t'other side o' th'oss an' shyt: 'Gerower'. Th'oss 'ud come lommerin' ower, an' ar 'ad fer drop dine on th'floer pretty quick an' go under its bally or else bey crushed death against th'wo'

"Another thing ey used do – ey'd snatch me cap off an' put it under th'mare's teele. This mare was a bit 'andy with 'er back legs an' it used tak me a bit fer pluck up enough courage fer lift 'er teele up an' get me cap ite. When ar'd got it ite ar 'ad fer 'eng it up iteside in th'fresh air fer a bit.

“Anyroad, one dee one o’ me uncles seyd an advert in th’Sentinel abite a donkey fer auction in th’Smithfeyld at ‘Castle.

So ‘im an’ ‘is mate went off early on th’Mondee mornin’ fer buy it fer me. When ar come ite o’ schoo’ at neyght ar ran aw th’wee wom expectin’ fer sey this donkey tethered dine th’bottom o’ th’gardin – but it wonna.

“Thee said thee’d bid aw th’money thee’d gotten but it wonna enough fer buy th’donkey.

“But dust know wot thee did, sirree? Thee tuk me on one o’ theyse dee excursions ter Blackpoo’ an’ thee peed fer me ‘ave donkey rides ‘till me backside was soer.

“It were good on ‘em, wonna it? But ar never did get a donkey o’ me own.”

Buildin' a cabin

One of the pleasures of those long summer days of childhood was the building of "cabins".

There were two types – those built among the trees in the wood and those made by excavating a large hole in the ground or in the side of a hill.

A favourite place for a cabin in the wood was in the middle of a clump of young birch trees. The tops of the trees were bent down and tied to each other, or to the ground, to form arches.

These served as the cabin framework on which covering materials could be placed. Discarded or "borrowed" wire-netting was a highly-prized material because, when spread over the arches, it would support a layer of bracken or brushwood or any other covering material that happened to "come to hand".

The hole-in-the-ground cabin involved plenty of hard digging but needed fewer constructional materials. A sheet of corrugated iron covered with clods made an ideal roof for this type of cabin.

No cabin was considered complete unless it had a fire-grate and a chimney. A useful grate could be made from a few iron bars and some bricks bonded with clay mortar. Drain pipes which the local farmer didn't appear to need served as a chimney.

There was no fuel problem for the cabins in the wood but those fire-grates seemed to consume a vast quantity of logs in the course of a day.

A slower-burning fuel was sun-dried "cow-flops" of which there was always a plentiful supply in the surrounding fields. One soon got used to the unusual aroma of the smoke.

"Wey once 'ad a kitchin-range in a cabin dine th'wood," said Jabez. "One o' th'lads 'ad gone up inter th'village fer summat an' ey come runnin back fer tell us as th'rag-an-bone mon 'ad got a range on 'is cart!

"So off wey went fer try an' get it off 'im some road or other. Wey offered fer collect some rags fer 'im if ey'd give us th'range, but ey said ey wanted a tanner fer it as well as some rags.

"It didna tak us many cracks fer get a pile o' rags, an' wey managed fer scrape up a tanner betweyn us. But as soon as th'owd skinflint 'ad gotten th'rags ey went back on 'is word an' said ey didna want sell it after aw.

"Wey towd 'im wot wey thowght abite 'im, but ey ony laughed at us. Anyroad, wey 'ung abite'till ey went rind th'back o' one o' th'ises.

"Be th'tarme ey come back wey'd gotten th'range off th'cart an' 'idden it behind th'edge. Ey pleed holy Moses but ther wonna much ey could do abite it. Wey give 'im 'is tanner an' ey went off chunterin' ter 'imsel'.

"Wey tuk th'range dine th'wood on a barrer an' built it inter th'cabin. It was brokken a bit but it lukked grand when it was blackleaded!

"Th'oven never worked proper though – it tuk aw dee fer roast a few taters. An' then one dee wey 'ad a calamity – th'cabin ketched fire! Wey were frittened lest it should set aw th'wood on fire, but wey managed stop it from spreadin'.

"Th'next dee wey just built another cabin rind th'owd range an' then meede a ponful o' lobby. Well, it lukked a bit larke lobby."

Flirters an' a cockerel

"Ar tell thee wot," said Jabez. "It's a lung tarme since ar seyd a lad with a pair o' flirters. Mind thee, it's perhaps as well – thee couldst do a lot o' damage with a pair o' flirters."

In the hands of an experienced lad a well-made catapult was an accurate weapon. The essential constructional materials for these "flirters", or "catties", or "strags," as they were called, were a Y-shaped piece of wood cut from a growing tree, two lengths of "elastic" and a piece of thin leather to hold the missile.

A lad's first pair of flirters were usually poor things, crudely put together, and often making use of some second-hand knicker elastic.

The more "professional" job, however, was a veritable work of art. Great care was exercised in the selection and assembly of the different materials. The type of wood, the lengths of each of the limbs of the Y-piece, and the angles they made with each other were all important features affecting the balance and the ultimate accuracy of the weapon. The best "elastic" was solid black rubber of square section.

Other essential requirements for the "professional" job were two leather button-hole pieces cut from a pair of trouser-braces. These were firmly bound to each of the top limbs of the Y-piece. The two lengths of rubber were then looped through the buttonholes and tied neatly with strong twine.

The length of the rubbers was supremely important – if they were too short the range and velocity were poor, and if they were too long the weapon would be inaccurate.

Target shooting at tin cans and bottles was the most common use for the flirters, although many birds and even the occasional rabbit fell victim to the well-aimed pebble.

"Ther used fer bey a little farm next doer ter th'school when ar went," said Jabez. "One plee-tarme ther were a gang on us sittin' on th'wo' lukkin' across th'feyld behind th'plee-grind.

"Just nar ther come a cockerel struttin' across th'feyld. Th'farmer's son was with us an' when ey seyd this cockerel ey nipped ower th'wo', got 'is flirters ite o' 'is pocket an' let fly at it.

"Moer be luck than judgment, ey 'it this cockerel side o' th'yed an' it spun rind larke a top an' dropped dine jed!

"Just then th'schoo'-mester come ite with 'is little bell fer ring th'end o' plee-tarme. Ey seyd this jed cockerel an' th'farmer's son tryin' fer stuff 'is flirters back in 'is pocket. So ey leed ite on 'im an' tuk 'im in schoo' an' give 'im a reyght good wollopin' with th'cane.

"Wey thowght now moer abite it but straight after dinner th'farmer come bostin' inter th'schoo'-room larke a mad bull an' threatened wot ey were goin' do ter th'schoo'-mester.

"Ey said if 'is lad wanted kill one o' 'is cockerels it were nowt fer do with th'schoo'-mester an' ey'd better keyp 'is 'ands off th'lad or else."

Jabez laughed and then said : "Dust know sirree, ar've thowght abite th'reyghts an' th'wrungs o' that fer yeers an' ar still anna sure who was in th'reyght. Wot dust *they* think?"

Oatcake Billy an' Lastic Fred

There were many "self-employed" people who used to make a living touring the villages selling their wares or services, collecting for clubs or maxims, or just plain begging. Jabez remembered many of these individualists.

There was "Oatcake Billy" with his clean-scrubbed basket covered by a spotless linen cloth; there was "Lastic Fred" who peddled an astonishing assortment of haberdashery out of a tattered brown suitcase. He acquired his nickname from his pronunciation of the word "thread". On opening the door to him, his first words were always: " Lastic, fred or buttons?"

Then there was the "Freydee-neyght mon" who ran a shilling-a-week club for items of clothing and who very wisely came on the evening of the local colliery's "reckonin' " day.

The "oky-poky mon" sold real ice-cream and announced his arrival in the village with a blast from his bugle; the "lamp-oil mon's" cart was hung about with so many tin-baths, buckets and snappin'-tins that he had need of no other audible warning of approach.

There was the "herb-mon" with his Santa Claus beard who sold pills and potions of herbal origin and gave free advice on all sorts of human ailments. One of his most popular concoctions was for the relief of constipation – it was called "Bliss"!

One character with a speech impediment went round the village singing from door to door – at least it was supposed to be singing. His favourite song was a rather tuneless version of "Grandfather's Clock" which he rendered partly in dialect.

What with his lack of tune, his speech difficulty and the dialect, only the experienced listener knew what the poor fellow was trying to sing. Few people, however, failed to put a copper or two in his cap which he held in front of him during his performances.

"Th'fish-mon used come tweyce a wik – Tuesdees an' Freydees," said Jabez. "Ey awwees shyted 'fish alive-o' but ar never seyd anythin' but jed uns on 'is cart. Ther was an owd tum-cat wot used sit weetin' fer 'im – ar'll swear that cat knew wot dee o' th'wik it was.

"Ey was a wopper an 'a bit of a tyrant. Ey ruled th'roost amongst th'village cats an' ey wonna frittened o' dogs eether. Ey used foller th'fish-cart arind an' th'fish-mon 'ud throw 'im a yed or a teel when ey got ter th'end o' th'village.

"Ey never offered fer get on th'cart 'cept once when th'fishmon fergot aw abite 'im. Th'owd warrior didna intend fer go withite 'is bit o' fresh fish though.

"Th'fish-mon 'appened fer luk rind when ey was well on 'is road ter th'next village an' theer was this tum 'elpin' 'imsel' ter a peyce o' best 'alibut off th'cart. Ey tuk off after 'im with 'is filletin' knife but ey couldna ketch 'im.

"But th'fish-mon 'ad larned 'is lesson. Ever after that ey didna ferget give th'owd tum a good yed or a teel every Tuesdee an' Freydee.

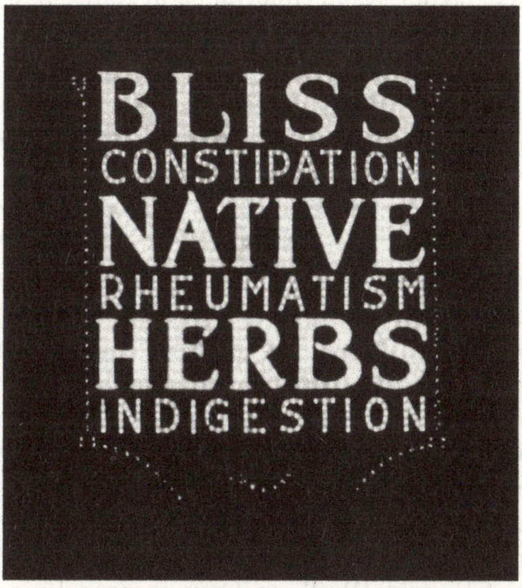

Advertisement for Bliss 1921

Th'wyter-otter

At one time, Staffordshire had a great reputation for the breeding and training of dogs for both sport and pleasure. One of the legacies of this tradition is the county's large fund of stories about dogs and their owners. Whenever the conversation turned to the subject of dogs, Jabez could be relied upon to recount some personal anecdote, or some story he had heard concerning them.

"Ther was a relative o' marn," he said, "wot 'ad a little black pom wot ey'd treened fer pick money up off th'floer. On Satdee neyghts when th'pub were a bit cryded ey used tak this dog with 'im.

"Ey'd sit on one end o' th'settle an' put th'dog underneyth. As soon as this little pom 'eerd any money drop on th'floer ey'd nip ite an' pick it up an' bey back under th'settle afoer anybody seyd 'im.

"Th'pubs wonna very well lit in them dees an' with th'dog beyin' black ey were larke a bit of a shadder flittin' abite. After a wheyle th'bloke 'ud put 'is 'and dine under th'settle an' th'little pom 'ud give 'im th'money. Ey got th'price o' many a pint o' ale that road."

That dainty-looking creature, the whippet, was bred for racing and rabbit-coursing. Years ago they were still very popular in the village, and were commonly seen at the heels of the miner, the pigeon man, and the poacher. Jabez had a story about an unfortunate whippet

"Theyse two blokes were walkin' rind th'basselows with a whippet an' ey put up a rabbit. At that tarme ther was a lot o' owd pitshafts amongst th'basselows an' some on 'em wonna covered up aw that well – a two-threy planks, or summat larke that, put ower 'em.

"Anyroad, when this dog was beltin' after th'rabbit ey wonna lukkin' wheer ey was goin', an' one o' theyse owd shaft-covers 'ad caved-in. That was th'end of th'whippet.

"Th'pair on 'em stood lukkin' dine this shaft an' wot dust think one on 'em said? Ey said: 'Well, ar'll bey jiggered. Ey's never done that afoer."

The bull-terrier and the ratting dog were renowned for their aggressiveness and courage. Long after the dog-pit and the rat-pit became illegal these dogs continued to be bred by many hardworking, hard-living sons of Staffordshire.

It was the habit of some of them to foregather in a particular pub to discuss the merits of their dogs and to enlarge upon their fighting qualities.

"One neyght," said Jabez, "one o' theyse men neemed Sam said ey'd gotten an animal wot none o' th'other blokes' dogs dost tackle. One o' th'blokes said th'animal adna bin invented yet wot 'is dog wouldna 'ave a go at.

"Sam said, 'Awreyght, ar'll tak aw on yer on – a pint o' ale a dog. Ar've gotten 'im in a shed rind th'back.' When thee eksed Sam wot sort o' animal it was, ey said it were an owd weyter-otter.

"One on 'em said 'is dog 'ad etten otters afoer 'is breakfast. Sam said: 'Ey wunna eat this un!'

"So, one be one, theyse blokes tuk ther dogs rind ter th'shed an' then come back inter th'pub sheekin' ther yeds an' tellin' th'other blokes as th'flippin' dog wouldna go anywheer near this otter.

"Dust know wot it was, sirree? It was a paraffin stove with a kettle o' 'ot weyter on it! Owd Sam 'ad persuaded 'em not fer give th'show awee ter th'others when thee went back into th'pub.

"Anyroad, thee aw 'ad a good laugh ite on it, an' Sam 'ad a neyght's beer drinkin' ite o' 'is owd weyter-'otter."

Village Tricks

There are those grown-ups who will tell you that when they were young they wouldn't have dared to do the sort of things that children do nowadays.

There are others, such as Jabez, who, with a twinkle in their eyes, will tell you that children don't have half the fun that they had when *they* were young.

Before the advent of television and of organised activities, village children in particular had perforce to entertain themselves with such games and "tricks" and make-believe as they could devise.

Although many of the "tricks" were not intentionally malicious, they could be extremely annoying to the victims. The mysterious "tap-tap-tap" on the window-pane produced by a button, a length of thread and a stout pin could be very upsetting on a dark night.

The sudden staccato rattle of a notched cotton-spool revolving on the window of a quiet cottage was likely to make the dozing occupants jump out of their chairs with fright.

"Wey used tie two doers 'gether with a peyce o' close-line an' then knock on both on 'em an' wetch 'em pullin' aggenst one another," said Jabez. But th'best un were done with a tin-bath. A lot o' folks used 'eng ther tin-baths up on th'wo' iteside. Thee 'ad iteside taps in them dees an' wey used fill th'tin-bath with weyter an' balance it on summat, an' then tie it ter one o' th'doers. Wot with th'clatter o' th'tin-bath an' th'splashin' o' th'weyter thee didna 'afe 'ave a freyght when thee opened th'doer.

"Me feyther towd me as when ey were a lad ey tied a billy-goat ter one doer. Th'owd bloke wot opened th'doer 'ad bin on th'beer an' when ey seyd this billy-goat's face with 'orns on th'top an' a beard ey thowght th'owd lad 'ad come fer 'im. Ey was off th'beer fer a wik or moer. "

To see a miner groping around in the dark for the cap which had been neatly whipped off his head by a piece of string stretched across the road was amusing – to hear him was an education.

The dear old lady who found the heavy parcel lying in the road suffered agonies of indecision. What should she do with it? Should she open it, or take it home, or leave it where it was, or report it to the police?

She didn't know that it only contained an old brick and that the boys behind the hedge would have been happier if someone else had been the victim.

The village closets were "up th'yard" or "dine th'gardin." To make this journey on a winter's night and then to find much too late that the seat had been removed could result in hard language unfit for the ears of the young perpetrators behind the wall.

"One owd feller wot wey pleed a trick on decided fer 'ave is own back," said Jabez. "Ey musta crept dine th'entry fer slat a jugful o' weyter on us but th'fost thing wey knew abite it was when th'jug come flyin' across th'road. Ey stood theer with 'is mithe open an' th'jug 'andle in 'is 'and. It 'adna bin stuck on very well an' it 'ad come off

"Th'missus come ite, an' when 'er seyd this jug smashed ter smithereyns in th'road 'er started shytin' at 'im. It was th'quart jug wot 'er fetched th'beer in from th'ite-doer licence.

"Wey used sey 'er trottin' off every neyght fer th'beer with this jug under 'er apron. 'Er awwees wore a mon's flat cap 'cept on Sundees. Mind thee, ar reckon 'er wore th'trysers in their 'ice an' aw. Ar often wondered whey 'er used carry th'jug under 'er apron – p'raps it was fer keyp th'flies ite or th'dust.

"Ar dunna know wot 'er fetched th'beer in that neyght though. It didna luk larke a jug wot 'er'd got under 'er apron – it were th'wrung sheepe!"

Leycitt Road Scott Hay circa 1911

Judder the joker

George, or "Judder" as he was called, was an exponent of the gentle art of leg-pulling. Some of the village folk thought him just a clown but most of these were his one-time victims. Others appreciated his dry humour and admired the audacity of some of his practical jokes.

"Judder was dine th'tine doin' a bit o' shoppin' one dee," said Jabez, "an' ey stopped fer 'ave a luk at a trench wot thee were diggin' – it was fer put a sewer pipe in or summat. Anyroad, ey was 'avin' a good luk dine this trench when a bloke come up ter 'im an' eksed 'im if ther were any jobs goin'. Ey musta thowght Judder were th'*gaffer* with 'im 'avin' 'is cap on.

"Th'fellers wot were diggin' th'trench 'ad gone fer ther snappin' so ey says ter this bloke: 'Cost use a shovel?' th'bloke said ey could use a shovel with th'next. So Judder says: 'Awreyght, ar'll set thee on. Get 'owd o' one o' them big shovels from ower theer an' start fillin' this trench in'. Judder weeted 'till th'bloke 'ad got started an' then ey reckoned ey'd better skidaddle afoer th'men come back from ther snappin'. Ey thowght thee mit bey a bit upset at 'avin' this trench filled in afoer thee'd put th'pipe in it.

"An' talkin' abite diggin' 'oles," Jabez went on, "one o' th'lads ite o' th'village was a bit of a lone wolf. Ey didna seym fer plee with th'other lads much – ey were awwees messin' off on 'is own. Judder 'ad ketched 'im a tarme or two 'elpin' imself ter stuff ite o' th'gardin. Ey copped 'im pinchin' goose-gogs one dee, so ey tied 'is 'ands behind 'is back, filled 'is pockets full o' goosegogs an' sent 'im wom. Judder thowght th'lads feyther 'ud tak th'int an' wollop 'im, but ey didna. So th'next tarme ey ketched 'im ey reckoned ey'd 'ave do summat a bit moer drastic.

"Ey meede th'lad sit dine in th'gardin' an' then ey started diggin' a big 'ole in th'grind. When ey'd gotten abite two foot dine ey towd th'lad fer stand up, an' then ey started measurin' 'im up with a peyce o' string. Judder said: 'Ee! they't a lot bigger than ar thowght thee wost. Ar'll 'ave fer weyden th'ole ite a bit!'

That was enough fer th'lad – ey didna stop fer open th'geete, ey went lommerin' ower th'top on it.

"Mind thee, it was ony a salery trench Judder was startin' but ey never seyd th'lad in th'gardin after that.

"Judder didna awwees 'ave things 'is own road though. One dee th'bloke next doer got 'owd o' a length o' timber from somewheer fer meeke a line-prop ite on. Th'missus 'ad bin meytherin' th'poer mon fer wiks abite this line-prop.

"Judder towd 'im ey'd funt ite as th'best road fer put a notch in th'top o' a line-prop was fer rear it up aggenst th'wo' an' lean ite through th'bedroom winda with a saw. So ey got Judder fer 'owd it up an' ey was 'afe-wee upsteers with 'is saw afoer it struck 'im as Judder was 'avin' 'im on. So ey sneyked dine th'steers an, went ite through th'front doer an' rind th'back.

"Ey stood many a wheyle wetchin' Judder 'owdin' this prop up, an 'then ey said: "Ar'll tell thee wot Judder – if thee 'owdst that prop up lung enough it'll most larkly tak root !' Judder spun rind an' went as if ey were goin' slat th'line-prop at 'im, but ey didna. Ey just laughed fer think as somebody 'ad gotten th'better on 'im fer once."

On a fine summer morning, Jabez could often be seen returning to his cottage around 9 o'clock for his "second breakfast". It was his habit on such a morning to set off at the crack of dawn for what he called a "walk rind".

In former days the country around the village was well served by paths which were in constant use. Many of them, alas, have long since disappeared without trace. After years of disuse, stiles and gates have been removed and large areas of countryside have become inaccessible to the ordinary walker.

"Ar got used ter goin' fer walks afoer ar was owd enough go schoo'," said Jabez. "Ther was an owd woman wot used tak us young uns fer walks dine th'feylds an' woods. 'Er'd tak 'afe-a-dozen or moer at a tarme. Ar think 'er larked walkin' but 'er didna relish goin' on 'er own. Ar con sey 'er nar, gettin' ready fer tak us fer a walk.

"'Er'd fetch 'er button-up boots from upsteers an' then get th'ivory-'andled button-hook ite o' th'top drawer o' th'dresser. It tuk 'er many a wheyle fer button 'em up. Then 'er'd go ter th'mirror ower th'mantel-peyce an' put 'er 'at on. 'Er skewered it on 'er yed with a couple o' greet 'at-pins wot 'ad pearl knobs on th'end.

"Then 'er locked th'doer an' put th'key on th'closet seat an' wey'd be off. 'Er was a bit larke an owd 'en with a clutch o' chickens."

They went gathering nuts or blackberries, herbs or wild flowers, sticks or leafmould. Sometimes they visited one of the farms for buttermilk. They stopped frequently for a rest and the old woman showed them how to make daisy chains or to plait and weave little baskets and mats from rushes.

She told them stories of her own childhood and always carried a bag of sweets in the large pocket in the side of her skirt.

"Sometarmes th'sweyts were them little sugar fishes," said Jabez. "Thee were aw different colours but thee aw teested o' peardrops. Wey 'ad fer go up ter 'er one at a tarme an' pick one ite o 'th'bag. Woe betide thee if thee triedst fer tak two.

"Sometarmes thee were them ducks, greyn peys an' new taters – dust remember 'em? 'Er'd let thee tak one duck or one tater or threy peys. Threy peys lasted lunger 'cos thee couldst suck 'em one at a tarme. Thee meede thee tungue as greyn as gress. Nar an' aggen 'er brought some stuff cawed locust. 'Er said it were good fer us, but ar didna larke that – it were some sort o' dreyd-up pods.

"Once, when wey were blackberryin', th'owd woman was pickin' off th'top o' a big bush. 'Er was reychin' up on tiptoe an' 'er was that intent on gettin' some big uns from reyght on top 'er missed 'er footin', owerbalanced an' fell face dynerds into th'bush.

" 'Er wonna one fer mincin' words an' wot 'er towd that blackberry bush afoer 'er managed fer get ite was nowbody's business – an' 'er a big chapel-woman an' aw!

"Mind thee, 'er tuk a bit o' gettin' ite – th'bush 'ad gotten a good 'owd on 'er. 'Er 'at were ower 'er eyes an' 'er skirt were ower er yed. In th'end 'er 'ad fer come ite backerds on 'er 'ands an' kneys. Ar'd never seyn any red-flannel drawers larke them afoer, an' nar ar come think on it ar anna seyn any since."

Th'cat's-whisker twiddlers

During the early 1920s, a great quiet seemed to descend on some of the cottages in the village. These were the homes of the cat's-whisker twiddlers who, with headphones clamped firmly in position, listened intently to their newly-acquired wireless-sets and demanded utter silence.

Other members of the household had to move about on tip-toe or sit staring idly into space. Conversation was forbidden – urgent information had to be imparted to the listeners by sign language. Dummies were stuffed into the mouths of crying babies, and noisy young children were ordered to "go ite an' plee thee." The evening newspaper lay unread because of the intolerable rustle produced by turning its pages.

Grandmothers sat dozing in their chairs because the clickety-clack of their knitting needles could not be endured. From a distance the backs of the cottages began to resemble a large harbour or dockyard as yet another 30-foot aerial mast was put in position.

"Dust remember owd Liza-Jane wot used live with 'er son an' 'is missus?" asked Jabez. "At th'tarme ar'm speykin' abite th'son was in th'Infirmry – ey was at death's doer be aw accynts.

"Anyroad, ar cawed at their 'ice one neyght fer tak a two-threy flowers an' fer sey if ey was any better. Th'doter-in-law wonna in an' Liza-Jane opened th'doer. Ee! th'owd soul was in a reyght pickle.

" 'Er eyes were red-raw with scrykin' an' th'tears were runnin' dine 'er face. 'Er eksed me inside an' ar said ar were reyght surry thee'd 'ad bad news. 'Er said: 'Bad news? Wot at talkin' abite Jabez?'

"So ar towd 'er ar thowght with 'er beyin' upset thee musta ad word from th'Infirmry abite th'lad. "Weyn'ad word as ey's on th'mend,' 'er said. 'An' ar dunna reckon that's bad news.' So ar said: 'Well, wot th'angment at scrykin' fer then?'

"'Er said: 'It was them childer wot went dine in that ship. Ee! it was a terrible thing, wonna it?'

"Ar didna know wot 'er were on abite – ar wonna follerin' er. So ar said: 'Wot ship? Ar anna 'eerd abite any ship goin' dine, an' ar anna seyn anythin' in th'peeper abite it eether.'

" 'Er said: 'It wonna in th'peeper, it was on th'weyless. Thee couldst 'ear th'poer little mites screymin' an' cryin' fer ther mothers.'

"An' off 'er went aggen, blartin' larke a two-yeer owd. So ar said: 'Thar greet foo'. It wonna' appenin' – thee were just pretendin'.

"But 'er wouldna 'ave it. 'Er said: 'Dunna bey daft, mon. Thee couldst 'ear th'wind 'owlin' an th'weeves knockin' th'ship ter peyces, an' aw theyse poer folks dryndin' ter death. Thee costna tell mey it wonna 'appenin'.' "

The crystal-sets were eventually replaced by the valve-sets with their horn-shaped loud-speakers. One local radio-man, with commendable enterprise, arranged for a demonstration of a loud-speaker-set in the village hall. The highlight of the evening was that the assembled villagers were to hear Big Ben striking the hour.

"Ar sut next ter an owd collier," said Jabez. "As soon as ey eerd Big Ben start strikin' ey pulled 'is big wetch ite o' 'is wescot pocket an' said: 'Inna it marvellous fer 'ear that clock as lyde as that aw th'wee frum London. An' luk thee, sirree, ey's ony 'afe a minute slow be Leycitt pit buzzer!' "

"Dust know," said Jabez, "ar wonna even on th'back row when thee dished brains ite. Ar reckon ar musta bin sittin' iteside on th'step. Weyn 'ad some clever lads in th'village though – some on 'em finished up at University, thee knowst. One on 'em won one o' theyse scholarship things.

"Mind thee, ey was just as big a nowt as any on us, but ey did a lot o' book-learnin' an' that. Ey was awwees tellin' us abite things wot ey'd read in theyse books.

"One o' th'ideas ey come up with was fer ketchin' fish withite anybody knowin'. Ther was a poo' near ter one o' th'farms wot'd got plenty o' fish in. Th'farmer didna mind us pleein' rind th'poo' but ey wouldna let us fish in it.

"Ey' reckoned it'd cost 'im a lot o' money fer stock it up. Mind thee, wey'd pulled one or two ite when ey wonna lukkin', but it was a bit ockerd 'cos ey could sey th'poo' from th'farm. Anyroad, wey decided wey'd try ite this idea wot was in this lad's book.

"Wey meede a little boat ite o' some bits o' wood an' then wey put a mast on it an' a peyce o' rag fer a seel. Wey tied fishin' hooks on little peyces o' string an' fastened 'em under th'bottom o' th'boat so's thee'd dangle dine in th'weyter.

"After wey'd put worms on th'ooks wey tethered th'boat with a lung peyce o' string an' set it seelin' across th'poo'. It were a clever idea wonna it? But it wonna lung afoer th'owd farmer spotted us an' come treypsin' across th'feyld fer sey wot wey were up to.

"Ar reckon ey thowght ther were summat a bit funny abite'afe-a-dozen big lads pleein' with a little boat on th'end o' a peyce o' string. Ey stood wetchin' us fer a bit an' then ey spit on th'gress an' said: 'Yo lads get moer larke babbies every dee.' But ey didna twig nowt, an' wey got a couple o' 'is fish.

"Wey neyly got inter 'ot weyter with another o' this lad's ideas. It was a road ey'd read abite fer droppin' chimneys. Yer knocked a 'ole in th'side o' th'chimney big enough fer wedge a peyce o' timber in, an' then yer kept takkin' moer bricks ite 'till th'weight started comin' on ter th'timber. Then aw yer 'ad do was fer set fire ter th'timber an' th'chimney fell dine!

"Ther 'appened fer bey a chimney nice an' 'andy. Thee knowst wheer 'Ollywood is, dustna? Well, at one tarme ther was a little pit up theer. It was a funny thing abite this pit – when it closed dine nowbody bothered fer shift owt. Th'weyndin' injin an' th'boiler 'ice an' th'yed-sticks an' this chimney were just as thee'd left 'em.

It wonna a very big chimney – p'raps fifty or sixty foot or so. On th'Satdee mornin' wey tuk as many 'ommers an' chisels as wey could get 'owd on.

"Wey'd gotten th'idea as wey were goin' 'ave this chimney dine afoer dinner-tarme, but it tuk us aw mornin' fer get threy or foer bricks ite! Ar dunna know who'd built it but, whoever it was, ey knew a thing or two abite meekin' mortar.

After wey'd worked on it fer two Satdees wey'd got enough bricks ite fer put this peyce o' timber in. On th'next Satdee wey'd just started knockin' moer bricks ite when who should come walkin' through th'wood but th'bobby.

"Ey whipped 'is cape off 'is showder an' clouted us reyght well with it an' then ey put aw us neemes an' addresses in 'is little book.

"Wey didna 'ear now moer abite it but a dee or two after ther was an awmighty crash up 'Ollywood. It was th'owd chimney droppin'. Th'bobby musta sent fer some blokes belongin' th'pit an' it was decided as this chimney wonna safe with this 'ole in it. So thee blew it up.

"Ar reckon it was a good job that bobby 'appened fer bey strollin' through th'wood, dustna they? Another brick or two ite o' that chimney an' wey shoulda bin as flat as poncakes."

A bird in th'chimney

Jabez was on the roof of his cottage doing something to a chimney-pot. I called to him to ask if there was anything I could do to help.

"Theytst better stop wheer thee at," he said. "Folks tell me they getst giddy when thee 'ast thee shoes soled an' 'eyled. Ar shoulda done this bit of a job yeers ago, but ar reckon weyer aw th'seeme – wey keyp puttin' things off 'till summat forces us fer do 'em. Ar shanna bey many cracks."

When he had finished I held the ladder while he climbed down and then helped him to put it away.

"Ar were just puttin' a peyce o' weyer-nettin' ower th'top o' th'chimney-pot," he said. "Thers summat funny abite that chimney. Ar conna understand it – brids keyp foin' dine it. Ar've 'ad aw sorts o' brids in that chimney – sparrers an' starlins an' jackdaws, an' ar 'ad a throstle once. But yisterdee capped th'lot. Ar 'eerd this flutterin' an' scrattin' goin' on in th'chimney-breast as soon as ar come dine steers.

"Ar said ter mesel': Jabez lad, it sarves thee reyght. They shouldsta put summat ower that chimney-pot afoer nar – theyst gotten another brid on thee 'ands.'

"Theyse brids get dine on ter a bit of a ledge tote th'chimney-bottom an' ar con put me arm up an' fang 'owd on 'em. But it's a dirty job – thee getst rowelled up. So ar towd 'im ey'd 'ave weet 'till ar'd 'ad me breakfast.

"After ar'd cleared me pots awee ar rowled th'rug up an' shifted th'fender ite o' th'road. Then ar lee dine on th'floer an' put me 'and up th'chimney.

"But ar wished ar 'adna! Instead o' mey fangin' 'owd o' 'im, ey fanged 'owd o' mey. I drew me 'and back pretty quick but ey'd drawn blood. Ar said: 'Ar dunna know wot thee at, but thers one thing for certain, they atna a sparrer or a starlin'.

"So ar lit a candle an' lee dine on th'floer with me yed in th'fire-basket an' lukked up th'chimney. Dust know wot it was, sirree? It was a flippin' owl – a greet big un

"Ey cocked 'is yed on one side an' lukked dine at me with 'is big eyes an' then th'varmint flapped 'is wings an' covered me aw ower with sut. Ar got up off me back a bit sharpish an' banged me yed on th'firepleece. Me eyes were full o' sut, an' ar couldna sey wot ar were doin'. Ar think ar musta 'ad me mythe open an' aw – ar started coughin' an' splutterin'. Ar 'ad sit dine a bit fer get me breath back. Then ar shyted up th'chimney: 'Anymoer o' that an' ar'll leyve thee fer clem death.'

"Dust know, it tuk me best part o' th'dee fer get that youth ite o' th'chimney. Ar tried aw sorts of things. Ar tried firkin' 'im dine with th'andle o' me walkin' stick; ar tried coaxin' 'im dine with a peyce o' raw meyt, an' then ar tried pushin' 'im back up th'chimney with rods an' a brush, but ar were frittened o' squashin' 'im.

'In th'end ar 'ad fer smoke 'im ite. Ar kindled a bit of a fire with a two-threy little sticks an' then put a lot o' damp leyves on it ite o' th'gardin' Ther wonna any flames but it didna 'afe kick up a puther. It wonna lung afoer ey dropped dine th'chimney an ar grabbed 'im be th'feyt.

"Ey didna struggle much, th'smoke'ad knocked aw th'stuffin' ite on 'im. Ey was as black as club ten though. Ar kept 'im in th'back-pleece 'till it began fer go dark an' then ar let 'im go. Ey went flyin' off into th'neyght. So, if thee seyst a big black owl knockin' abite it inna a new sort – it's that youth ite o' mar chimney."

Caged birds

In spite of the great chorus of wild-bird song to be heard in and around the village, there were many families who kept caged birds of one kind or another. Linnets, finches, song-thrushes, canaries, parrots and even the occasional skylark were subjected to solitary confinement.

The district had its specialists in the art of wild-bird trapping. They used several devices, but bird-lime and the "riddle" were the ones most commonly employed. The riddle was a coarse sieve propped up at an angle by a notched stake to which was attached a length of string. The unfortunate birds were enticed onto the bird-lime or under the riddle by decoys and scraps of food.

"Parrots an' canaries were one thing," said Jabez, "but linnets an' finches an' such-like were another. It wonna reyght ter mar wee o' thinkin'. When ar seyd anybody ketchin' 'em, ar used kick up as much row as ar could fer fritten th'brids awee.

"Did ar ever tell thee abite that linnet? A bloke eksed me if ar'd luk after it fer a wik when ey went gallivantin' off ter th'seyside. Th'mon shoulda known better. Anyroad, ar were cleynin' it ite one dee an' wot dust think 'appened, sirree? Ar went an' fergot fer close th'cage-doer. An' it's a funny thing but th'backdoer 'appened fer bey open as well. Th'linnet were off larke a shot ite o' a gun.

"This bloke wonna 'afe vexed when ey come back off 'is 'olidees. But larke ar towd 'im, ar get theyse bouts o' fergettin' things at tarmes."

One of the villagers kept a parrot. In warm weather its cage was put on the wall at the back of the cottage. Whenever the farmer wanted to do any work with a horse in the adjoining field, he had to ask for the parrot to be taken indoors. The horse was unable to distinguish between the orders given by the farmer and those given by the parrot.

"Ey could do now good at aw with th'oss when th'parrot was on th'wo," said Jabez. "One dee, th'farmer come fer tell 'em tak th'parrot in but ey'd left th'oss an' cart just inside th'feyld.

“Ey’d barely got ter th’ice when th’parrot shyted: ‘Ger-up’ an’ th’owd ‘oss started off across th’feyld. Th’farmer shyted: ‘Whoa!’ an’ th’parrot shyted: ‘Ger-up!’ an’ betweyn ‘em thee ‘ad a reyght shytin’ match. Th’poer ‘oss didna know whether ey were comin’ or goin’.

“Another dee, when th’parrot was on th’wo, ther were a lot o’ squawkin’ an’ squeylin’ goin’ off, an’ then a thunderin’ big crash. Thee rushed iteside an’ funt th’cage on th’grind. Th’parrot was awreyght, but a bit dazed larke.

“Then thee noticed th’parrot ‘ad gotten a peyce o’ black fur in ‘is beyk. Thee couldna understand it ‘till th’next-doer’s tum-cat come wom with th’end o’ ‘is teel missin’! Th’cat musta bin nosin’ rind th’cage an’ gotten ‘is wagger betweyn th’bars. Th’owd parrot ‘ad fanged ‘owd on it an’ when th’cat jumped ey’d dragged th’cage off th’wo’.

“This seeme parrot used ‘ave some o’ th’village women on a peyce o’ string. Ey could mimic th’fish-mon’s shyte, an’ th’lamp-oil mon’s, an’ a lot o’ others besides. Th’bread-mon didna shyte – ey blew a whistle. On bread dees, thee ‘ad fer remember fer cover th’cage up or else th’parrot ‘ad theyse women poppin’ in an’ ite o’ th’front-doers larke rabbits in a warren. Ey could imitate that bread-mon’s whistle a treat.”

An ockerd customer

One of the characters of village life in days gone by was that paragon of a woman who acted as unpaid nurse, midwife and "layer-out" of the dead.

These women had no formal training. They combined a natural aptitude for the job with some essential "know-how" handed down by their predecessors.

Over the years they acquired a vast amount of experience in dealing with the expectant mother, the seriously ill and the deceased. In spite of the time and effort involved in these ministrations, many of them managed to rear large families of their own. Such a one was Fanny.

"Ther were tarmes when that woman didna go bed fer neyghts on end," said Jabez. " 'Er'd bey 'elpin' somebody inter th'world or easin' somebody ite on it. An' 'er 'ad some ockerd customers fer deyl with an' aw.

"Ar remember an owd widower wot 'er was lukkin' after. Ar went tak 'im a few flowers an' when Fanny opened th'doer 'er said: 'Ee! Jabez, theyt th'answer ter me prayer. Cost sit with 'im fer an hour or two so's ar con go an' do a thing or two at wom?'

"Ar towd 'er ar'd never done any nossin' but th'woman lukked that done-up ar said ar'd sit with 'im fer a bit. 'Er warned me as ey was a bit of an 'andful. That woman never spok a truer word!

"Talk abite sittin' with 'im – ar was never off me feyt. Ey 'ad me up an' dine them steers larke a bucket in a well. An' when ar'd fetched 'im wot ey wanted ey didna want it anymoer.

"Tote supper-tarme ey wanted 'is teyth in. One o' th'things are conna abide is other folks's fawse-teyth. Theyse teyth were in an owd Jubilee mug on th'wesh-stand. Ar 'eld th'mug so's ey could tak th'teyth ite 'imsel', but ey said ey wonna puttin' 'em in 'till thee'd bin weshed.

Ey 'adna 'ad 'em in moer than a couple o' minutes afoer ey started compleenin' abite 'em 'urtin 'im. Ey said thee wanted a bit fetchin' off th'back o' th'top-set. Ar towd 'im ey'd 'ave weet 'till somebody could tak 'em ter th'dentist. But ey said: 'Dentist me foot – fetch me a file ite o' me tool box.' Ar tried fer talk 'im ite on it but ey was a stubborn mon.

"Ar thowght ter mesel' if ar just bring a file it'll eether bey th'wrung un or else ey'll want summat else – larke a 'ommer an' chisel or summat. So ar mauled th'toolbox up an' dumped it on th'bed an' said: ' 'Ere thee at, 'elp theesel'.'

"Ey filed awee at theyse teyth an' then ey said ey wanted a bit o' sandpeeper fer smoothe it off. Ar give 'im me matchbox but that wouldna do fer 'im. Ar couldna find any sandpeeper anywheer, so ey said some bath-brick 'ud do, or some Brasso. Ar said: 'Thee costna put Brasso on thee teyth, mon!' Ey said ey could put wot ey larked on 'is teyth an' it were none o' mar business.

"Anyroad,when ey'd gotten 'is teyth workin' proper ey wanted summat eat. Ther were nowt in th'pantry bar some tinned-stuff an' a two-threy pittled onions. Ar couldna sey th'owd chap goin' 'ungry, so ar nipped dine wom an' fetched 'im some bread an' cheyse fer go with theyse onions.

"Ey got it dine 'im but ey didna reckon much ter th'cheyse. Mind thee, ar think it was th'Brasso wot spoiled th'teeste o' th'cheyse, 'cos it were a bit o' good Cheshire was that.

"When Fanny come back 'er said 'er'd fergotten tell me abite th'beyf-tea fer 'is supper. Ar said: 'Beyf-tea nothin'! Ey's 'ad bread an' cheyse an' pittled onions!

"Ar thowght 'er was goin' pass ite. 'Er said: 'Ey's 'ad wot? Ee! th'poer soul. Theyst kilt 'im fer sure. Dustna know th'mon' gotten a terrible bad stomach? Ey's bin on slops fer threy wik.'

"But th'owd feller just lee theer with 'is mythe weyd open snorin' larke a little pig. Ey lived fer many a yeer after that."

Larke a fish ite o' weyter

Nowadays, many city-dwellers are able to transport themselves and their families into the countryside at frequent intervals.

This facility has given them the opportunity to become better acquainted with various aspects of country life.

There was a time, however, when the incursions of city-folk into the country were so infrequent that they behaved like the proverbial fish out of water.

Indeed, the city child plunged into a rural environment often presented a picture bordering on the pathetic. Jabez remembered a London boy and his mother who came to stay with relatives in the village.

"Ey was a nice lad but ar dunna think ey'd bin in the country afoer. Th'fost dee when ey come ite fer plee with us wey tuk 'im dine th'feylds.

"That lad's mother shoulda 'ad moer sense than turn 'im ite in a good suit an' a pair o' fancy shoes. It inna exactly th'sort o' thing fer wear when thee't climbin' treys an' messin' abite dine th'feylds.

"Wey 'adna gone very fer afoer ey slipped on a fresh-done cow-flop an' finished up on 'is backside. That didna do 'is trysers any good fer a start.

"Wey scraped some on it off with a peyce o' stick an' then weyped 'im dine with 'andfuls o' gress. Ey didna seym fer bey aw that gain on 'is feyt – p'raps it was with beyin' used ter walkin' on th'level dine London.

"Be th'tarme wey'd climbed a trey or two an' pleed in th'bruk an' rind th'basselows that suit ey'd gotten on was ready fer th'rag-mon, an' 'is fancy shoes were wet through an' laubed up with clee.

"Th'lad's mother got on to us when 'er seyd 'im. 'Er said wey'd done it on purpose, but wey 'adna. Th'lad 'ad just tried fer do wot wey did, an' ey wonna very good at it.

"Ey were frittened death o' animals o' aw sorts. Thee couldstna get 'im anywheer near a steeble, or a pigstee, or a feyld o' cows. An' th'poer lad were a bit tickle-stomached ower smells.

"Ar remember wey tuk 'im in th'farmyard one dee fer show 'im rind. Th'farmer 'appened fer bey cartin' muck at th'tarme an' this lad started coughin' an' 'eavin' – ar thowght ey were goin' bey sick on th'spot.

"It gets a bit owerpowerin' when it's forked up, dunna it? Mind thee, ar reckon it's a good 'ealthy smell fer aw that.

“But ey fergot aw abite th’smell when th’owd gander put ‘is neck ite an’ come fer ‘im. Ey squeyled larke a stuck pig an’ ran off dine th’village ter ‘is mother.

“Some o’ th’lads thowght ey was a bit of a ducky-darlin’ an’ meede fun on ‘im. But ar nowticed as when theyse lads funt ite wot a lot o’ pocket-money ey’d gotten thee aw gethered rind fer ‘elp ‘im spend it!

“This lad ‘ad a funny road o’ talkin’ – wey couldna understand ‘im at fost. Mind thee, it wonna ‘is fawt – aw them London folk talk a bit funny, dunna thee?

“Ar remember tellin’ ‘im wey didna put ‘batter’ on us bread up this road – wey meede pon-cakes ite on it!

“After a few wiks, wey’d larned ‘im a thing or two an’ ey was beginnin’ fer luk a bit larke a village lad. Wot dust think ey said to us when it were tarme fer ‘im go back London?

“Ey said: ‘Ar’ll come an’ sey yer aggen as soon as ar con!’ So, thee seyst, wey’d larned ‘im fer talk reyght an’ aw. Mind thee, th’lad’s mother didna think so when ‘er ‘eerd ‘im! “

Th'owd skinflint

The installation of the first telephone in the village was a notable occasion. It provided a new and convenient method of transmitting information from one place to another.

However, it supplemented rather than replaced several other time-honoured ways of doing the same thing. Tradesmen who toured the villages in the district acted as unofficial postmen and gave same-day delivery.

Requests for a visit by the doctor were left at one of the houses he was known to be calling at that day. Messages for men in the pit were given to the lamp-house man, and so on.

Many messages, however, were delivered directly by hand. More precisely, this meant delivery by foot or, to put it in village parlance, by Shanks's Pony".

A lad could often look forward to a double payment for this service – one by the sender and one by the recipient. A penny or twopence was considered to be a satisfactory reward for a walk of several miles – sixpence was untold wealth.

"Ar remember takkin' a message fer a woman wot was a bit of a skin-flint," said Jabez. "'Er said 'er'd pee me when ar got back. Ar was ony a bit of a lad an' it was gettin' on fer threy miles theer an' back.

"On th'road wom ar was wonderin' if 'er'd give me a penny or twopence, an' ar was plannin' wot ar'd buy with it. In me mind's eye ar spent that money ower an' ower aggen.

"Anyroad, when ar got back 'er said: 'Ar'll give thee summat next tarme ar sey thee – ar anna got any cheenge.' For prove it 'er tuk a ten-bob note ite o' 'er poss an' 'eld it up. But ar'd 'eerd th'chink o' money when 'er oppened th'poss.

"Ar thowght: Jabez lad, 'er's coddin' thee. 'Er's fer doin' thee ite o' thee money.' So ar said: 'That's awreyght, ar'll get it cheenged fer yer,' an' ar snatched th'note ite o' 'er 'and an' went beltin' fer th'shop.

"Ar towd th'shop-woman ar didna want any coppers in th'cheenge – just silver. Ar thowght ter messel' 'er'll 'ave give me a tanner nar, an' it sarves 'er reyght fer tryin' diddle me.

"But bless mey, when ar tuk th'cheenge back 'er said: 'Wot dust think Jabez? Ar've funt a penny lyin' abite wot ar didna know ar'd gotten.' Ar reckon them folks wot cawed 'er a skin-flint wonna fer ite.

"Talkin' abite sendin' messages," Jabez went on, "thee wouldstna remember Pollymary wouldst? 'Er 'ad a sister wot lived in a little cottage in th'bottom o' th'valley. Gettin' on fer 'afe a mile awee it was.

"Pollymary used shyte messages ter 'er. It dunna seym possible does it? But 'er 'ad a reyght good pair o' lungs an' 'er voice travelled well dine that valley. 'Er used come ter th'top o' th'bonk an' cup 'er 'ands rind 'er mythe an' shyte 'Coo-ee. Coo-ee.'

"Just nar 'er sister 'ud come ter th'doer an' thee'd bey shytin' ter one another fer many a wheyle.

"But wey pleed a trick on 'er one dee. Ther were two on us pleein' in th'gorse-bushes 'afe-wee dine th'feylds when Pollymary come fer 'ave a shyte ter 'er sister.

"Th'sister's 'usband musta bin poerly, 'cos Pollymary shyted: 'Is Billy any better?' Wey got behind th'bushes an' imitated th'sister's voice an' shyted up: 'Billy's jed.'

"Wey didna think 'er'd bey takken in as easy as that, but 'er was. 'Er come runnin' dine th'feylds an' wey expected 'er go neck an' crop any minute. 'Er 'ad fer 'ave a bacca at th'second stile – th'owd lass was blowin' larke a brokken-winded 'oss.

"Wey didna stop fer find ite wot 'appened when 'er got ter 'er sister's. Pollymary was a big woman, – 'er coulda picked both on us up be th'scruff o' th'neck an' banged us yeds 'gether. Mind thee, ar think wey desarved it, dustna they?

'Er was a grand lass

I was strolling through the village one evening with the intention of calling on Jabez. As I approached the cottage, he emerged with a smartly dressed lady whom I judged to be about his own age.

They stood for a moment or two at the gate and then, with a laugh at some parting remark of his, she walked away towards the other end of the village. As he turned to go indoors he saw me and called out: "At comin' in?"

I hadn't recognised his visitor and I was more than a little intrigued to find out who she was. As we sat down he said: "Ee, that brought back some memories."

He sat gazing into the fire for a while and I waited for him to go on. He must have sensed my curiosity because presently he said: "'Er used live in th'village as a child but 'er lives off Leyk road nar.

"It's a good many yeers since ar seyd 'er. Wey were just talkin' abite some o' th'things wey did an' some o' th'owd folk wey could remember. Ar used plee with 'er a lot afoer wey were owd enough go schoo'. 'Er was as pretty as a picture an' 'er could twist mey rind 'er little finger.

"One o' me earliest memories was beyin' with 'er in a feyld at th'back o' their 'ice. Wey couldna 'ave bin moer than threy or foer yeer owd. 'Er beleyved in fairies an' 'er towd me as theyse fairies popped ite o' flowers when thee opened ther petals.

"Wey sat wetchin' some buttercups an' deesies for many a wheyle but ar never seyd any fairies – 'er said it was because ar didna beleyve in 'em! It's funny wot little things stick in thee mind, inna it?

"Ar reminded 'er abite th'tarme when 'er used send me inter th'middins. Them folks wot lived in th'terrace 'ises didna 'ave dust-bins in them dees – thee 'ad big brick middins fer put ther esses an' rubbish in.

"This lass used send me ferritin' abite in theyse middins fer find peyces o' brokken pleetes an' owd soce-pons an' things so's 'er could plee 'ises with 'em. Th'teeble 'ud bey an eringe-box with a peyce o' owd wo'-peeper on it fer a teeble-cloth.

"Th'dresser was another box, or a pile o' bricks, with a jamjar full o' weyld flowers on it, an' ther'd bey an owd bag on th'floer fer a carpet.

"Ar was supposed fer bey th'usband an' ar 'ad fer eat aw sorts o' stuff off theyse brokken pleetes – raw taters an' chonnucks, aw sorts o' berries, 'awthorn buds fer cheyse, vetch pods fer peys, an' them little red an' yeller flowers wot wey cawed eggs an' beecon.

"Ar 'ad fer wesh it dine with cowd weyter ite o' an owd cracked cup from th'middin. It's a wonder ar didna 'ave bally-ache or woss!

"Er was tellin' me it was mey wot larned 'er fer swing a canful o' milk withite spillin' any. Wey used fetch th'milk from th'farm in a can with a weyer 'andle an' a lid.

"When thee gotst th'knack on it thee couldst tak th'lid off an' swing th'can rind an' rind thee yed withite any comin' ite. Mind thee, it was best fer practice with weyter afoer thee triedst it with a quart o' milk!

"As this lass got owder 'er turned inter a reyght tum-boy. When th'other wenches were pleein' 'opscotch or pleein' with ther dolls, 'er'd bey pleein' bodger or rinkers with us lads, or climbin' treys or gettin' inter some mischief on 'er own somewheer.

"Ferluk at 'er nar thee wouldstna think as th'farmer once ad fer fish 'er ite o' th'pig-swill barrel. 'Er'd bin messin rind th'farm an' decided fer feyd th'pigs. Th'trouble was th'barrel was neyly empty an' when 'er leyned ower th'side fer ladle some ite er owerbalanced an' fell in! 'Er musta stunk summat terrible cos th'farmer 'ad fer pour buckets o' weyter ower 'er afoer ey dost let 'er go wom.

"Er mother used despair on 'er at tarmes. Ar remember takkin' 'er wom one dee when 'er'd gashed 'er leg open on some barbed weyer.

"Ar towd 'er mother 'er'd lost a lot o' blood but dust know wot 'er mother said? 'Er said: 'It'll do'er good! 'Er could do with some o' that mad blood lettin' ite on 'er.'

"But 'er was a grand lass fer aw that."

It wonna a rest dee

In times past, the village had an enviable reputation for producing Methodist local preachers.

Most of them were miners and, in addition to their preaching duties, they held office in church or Sunday School or both.

It was not uncommon for one of them to take a morning Sunday School Class in the village, an afternoon service in a chapel several miles away, an evening service in another chapel, and then to change into "delph-rags" for the night-shift at the colliery.

"Ar reckon that bloke wot wrote that hymn 'O day of rest an' gladness' 'adna 'eerd abite theyse local preychers trampin' up an' dine th'country," said Jabez. "It wonna exactly a rest-dee for *them.*

"Tak owd Daniel fer instance. Ey musta preyched fer nigh on 50 yeer. Ar con remember one Sundee mornin' when ey eksed me if ar'd larke go with 'im ter a little chapel off Crewe road.

"Ar'd bey in me early twenties at th'tarme. Wey'd just come ite o' Sundee Schoo' an' ey was goin' tak th'arvest Festival services at this chapel. It was a nice dee at th'back-end o' September so ar said: 'Awreyght, ar'll go with thee fer company. Wot tarme are we startin' off?'

"Ey' said wey were goin' nar – straight awee. Ey reckoned it'd tak us th'best part o' two 'ours fer get theer, an' ey'd bin invited ter a farm-'ice fer 'is dinner an' tey. So wey struck off.

"Ar soon funt ite as owd Daniel 'adna much use fer roads an' paths unless thee 'appened fer bey on th'crowline. If thee wonna, ey just cut straight across th'feylds.

"It 'ad bin a leete harvest an' there were a lot o' corn still weetin' fer bey carted. Owd Daniel lukked at it an' said: 'Ther's one hymn wey shanna bey 'avin' terdee. Wey conna sing 'All is safely gathered in' withite tellin' lies, con we?'

"Wey got ter this farm abite one o'clock. Ar've never seyn ser much stuff on a dinner-teeble eether afoer or since. Ther was enough fer feyd an army!

"Ar was that famished ar 'ad me kneyfe an' foke at th'ready afoer owd Daniel 'ad finished th'grace. Ar didna 'ear much o' 'is sermon in th'afternoon – ar was full ter bostin' an' ar think ar musta dozed off.

"Wey went back ter th'farm fer us tey but ar wonna aw that ungry. Th'farmer's weyfe thowght ther was summat up with me.

Owd Daniel did it justice though, an' ey give 'em a good threyquarters of an 'our sermon at neyght.

"Dust know, ar con still remember 'is text – it was ite o' the' Owd Testament: 'Thou shalt not wholly reap the corners of thy fields, neither shalt thou gather the gleanings of thy harvest – thou shalt leave them for the poor and the stranger.'

"Th'farmer would 'ave us goin' back ter th'farm fer some supper. Theyse farmers dunna 'afe get through some snappin'! Wey 'ad cheyse, pittled damsons an' wom-beeked bread. It was dark be this tarme an' wey'd got a couple o' 'ours walkin' fer do.

"Anyroad, th'farmer said ey'd get th'pony an' trap ite fer tak us dine th'leene as fer as th'meen road.

'Ar thowght th'farmer 'ud bey comin' with us, but ey said: 'When yer get ter th'meen road just turn th'pony rind an' start 'im back wom – ey'll bey awreyght.'

"Wey stood an' listened fer a bit ter th'pony trottin' back up th'leene an' then owd Daniel struck off across th'feylds aggen. Th'owd feller 'ad got bey up at 5 o'clock in th'mornin' fer go dine th'pit. Ar reckon somebody ought ter 'ave given 'im a medal.

Come fer think on it though, p'raps SOMEBODY did!

Th'coal harvest

Whatever else the villagers went short of in the 1926 coalstrike, it is true to say that very few of them went without coal.

Women and children and the old men went "chattin'. " This was the name given to the operation of collecting scraps of coal from the local colliery dirt-tips.

From a distance the tips began to resemble giant ant-hills whose defences were under attack by a host of marauders. Those lucky enough to possess bicycles balanced the bags of hard-won gleanings on the handlebars or across the pedals and pushed them home up the steep fields.

Others used wheel-barrows, or prams, or trucks made specially for the purpose from a box and a pair of mangle wheels. Most of the coal, however, came from a different source. The large area of woodland to the north of the village contained many shallow seams of coal. The miners were quick to take advantage of such a convenient harvest. Shafts were sunk amongst the trees, tunnels were driven into the slopes, and outcropping seams were worked on the open-cast system.

Trees were felled for pit-props, buckets and ropes and winches were "acquired", cabins were built, and the coal flowed out. There was much good humour to be found and, for the children, it was a happy, exciting time.

"Thee 'adst fer bey careful wheer thee wast walkin'," said Jabez. "Ther were little pits an' tunnels aw ower the'opper. Did ar ever tell thee abite them two brothers wot dug a tunnel inter th'side o' a bonk?

"Th'seym o' coal wonna much moer than a foot thick, but it was a bit o' good stuff. Theyse brothers 'ad a box on some runners with a peyce o' rope tied ter eych end. One on 'em 'ud crawl inter th'ole with a candle, draggin' th'box after 'im.

"When ey'd filled th'box with coal, ey'd give a couple o' tugs on th'rope. Th'other brother pulled th'box ite an' emptied it, an' then signalled fer it bey pulled back aggen.

"But one dee when ey pulled th'box ite ther wonna any coal in it – ther was a brid's neyst in it with foer eggs! Ey stood theer scrattin' 'is yed an' gawpin' at this neyst. Ey couldna understand it but ey shyted dine th'ole: 'Dust want 'em fried or poached?'

"Wot dust think 'ad 'appened, sirree? This tunnel 'ad gone straight through th'bonk an' come ite on th'other side under a bush!

"Ey towd 'er get off sleyp with 'er, but 'er wouldna rest. 'Er werritted that much ey 'ad fer get up. When ey oppened th'stairfoot doer, th'kitchen was full o' smoke!

"Ey shyted: 'Nell! Theyst better come dine – me trysers are on fire. "Er said: 'Oh my lors. Costna dite 'em?' Tum shyted back: 'Ar've dited 'em but ar shanna bey eeble go work in 'em – thers 'oles in th'legs big enough get thee yed through.'

"When 'er come dine 'er said ey 'adna got any moer fer go in. Ther was ony 'is best blue an' 'is flannels, an' 'er wonna lettin' 'im go in them. So 'er funt a peyce o' cloth ite 'o th'rag-bag an' petched 'em fer 'im.

"Then 'er said: 'Them'll 'ave do. Ar conna sey wot ar'm doin' withite me glasses an' ar'm blessed if ar con think wheer ar've put 'em. Theyt 'ave manage with 'em 'till ar con get thee a pair o' mowl-skins ite o' th'maxim.'

"So thee went back bed an' th'next thing 'er remembered was Tum shytin': 'Nell! Come dine quick. Ar'm in a reyght mess – ar've lost th'use o' me leg!' 'Er said: Theyst wot? Wotever's up with thee nar?' So ey shyted back. 'Well, eether ar'm paralysed from the weest dine or else theyst meede a reyght owd cobble o' theyse trysers. Ar conna move.'

"Dust know wot 'er'd done, sirree? Some road or other 'er'd stitched th'legs 'gether betweyn th'kneys.

" 'Ee!' ey said. 'They 'adst me worried fer a bit. Next tarme thee mendst me trysers in th'middle o' th'neyght meeke sure fer put thee specs on. Ar was beginnin' fer think theydst 'ave push me work in th'wheyl-barrer.' "

Every dog 'as its dee

It is a disturbing thought that each generation believes that the "old-days", the days of their youth, were best.

Our grandparents and parents were convinced of it, and we in turn experience this same feeling. A pessimist might reasonably conclude that things must therefore be getting steadily worse and worse. But are they?

Might it not be that each ageing generation dons its rosy tinted spectacles and recalls the pleasant things rather than the unpleasant ones? One remembers the long summer days of childhood, but not the longer wet ones. Or could it be that we are all striving constantly to escape from the present?

This train of thought was triggered off by something Jabez said as we watched one of the early combine-harvesters at work.

"Ar reckon every dog 'as its dee," he said. "At one tarme th'corn were awwees cut wi' a sickle or a scythe. Then th'reypin' macheynes come, an' then th'beynders, an' nar this greet lummockin' contraption.

"Thee cost 'ardly credit as when th'childer livin' nar get owd thee'll luk back an' tell their childer wot a grand seyght it was fer wetch this greet thing go through a feyld spewin' ite corn an' straw.

"Ar wonder wot some o' th'owd uns 'ud think abite it? In them dees, two acres o' wuts was a good dee's work fer a mon wi' a scythe. An' then it 'ad fer bey put up in sheyves an' stooked.

"Th'owd folks used reckon fer leyve th'stooks standin' on th'stubble 'till it 'ad 'eerd th'church bells ring on threy Sundees. Then it 'ad fer bey carted an' stacked fer weet fer th'thresher come rind.

"Ar'll tell thee wot though, ar used enjoy beyin' in th'arvest feyld in th'owd dees. Mind thee, it was 'ard work an' th'dees were lung an' th'pee were poer.

"But some-road or other folks seymed fer bey moer contented. Ar'm aw in favour o' takkin' th'ard work ite o' a job providin' a mon con get some satisfaction ite o' doin' wot's left.

"As ar luk at it, a mon's got fer bey comfortable with 'imsel', if thee gets me meynin'. An' if ey dunna get some satisfaction ite o' 'is job it's as sure as God meede little apple thers trouble brewin' fer somebody somewheer.

But no matter how the harvest is gathered – and the grain harvest is only part of it – there seems to be a deep-seated urge in most of us to express thankfulness for the joy and the wonder and the splendour of it.

Just a little while ago, the country chapels and churches were filled with the sweet aroma of ripe fruit and vegetables, flowers and grain, and within their walls was a feeling of warmth and security.

Even in this sceptical age, the Harvest is still the Church's most popular festival and it is surely more than mere tradition that fills the pews.

I asked Jabez about it. He said: "Theyt sey folks at th'arvest festival wot thee wutna sey at any other service bar a buryin' or a marryin'.

"It inna aw that lung ago since a good 'arvest meant th'difference betweyn a full bally an' a empty 'un in th'winter. Thers bin a two-threy cheenges since then but a mon still conna do withite 'is snappin.

"Wey con do some clever things but ar anna 'eerd tell abite a mon meekin' a bleede o' gress yet, let alone a grain o' corn. Ar reckon that's th'top an' bottom on it.

Tarmes were 'ard

In times of depression and unemployment, those households with large families of young children had a rough time.

The greater part of the heavy burden of work and worry fell onto the shoulders of the woman of the house.

In addition to her frequent child-bearing and her multifarious domestic duties, she often had to hide her own feelings and to forget her failing health in order to boost the morale of a depressed and frustrated husband unable to find a job or in danger of losing the one he had.

With a totally inadequate income, she had to pinch and scrape and scheme to provide even the bare necessities of life for her offspring.

Bread and potatoes in various guises formed the bulk of her family's diet. Lobby was a frequent item on the menu, and a slice of "spotted-dick" was a good filler.

A hungry child would be given a "peyce", or some pobs, or a sugar-butty made with "maggy-ann". A "peyce" was a thick slice of bread on which was spread some dripping or black-treacle or home-made jam.

"Ar used larke sey a lad tackle a good peyce," said Jabez. "Some o' them peyces were as thick as doer-steps.

"It was now use 'eksin' 'im fer seeve thee th'crusses though – ey'd eat them fost. An' th'sparrers didna get very fat on th'crumbs eether.

"Ar think ar towd thee as when ar was a bit of a lad ar used go rind with th'butcher-mon in 'is pony an' trap. Ther was one thing wot puzzled me fer a lung tarme – th'poerest family in th'village 'ad th'biggest parcel o' meyt.

"Dust know wot it was, sirree? A greet big lump o' udder, an' thee 'ad it neyly every wik-end. Ar didna fancy it mesel' but ar reckon it was eether that or nothin' fer th'poer souls.

"Another thing that family used 'ave a lot on was bread puddin'. Ther musta bin seven or eight childer at th'tarme ar'm speykin' abite. Ar could never keyp kynt o' them childer – ther awwees seymed fer bey another un since th'last kynt.

Anyroad, 'er used meeke this puddin' in a big jowl. Ar' ad many a lot on it. Ar used plee with some o' theyse childer an' when thee were 'avin' bread-puddin' fer ther dinners thee'd eks me fer 'ave some.

“Ther was nowbody could meeke bread-puddin’ larke that woman. Th’top on it ‘ud bey neyce an’ crisp with some bryn sugar on it.

“Er put aw sorts o’ things in it – a bit o’ rhubub or a two-threy goose-gogs, or some wind-blown apples, or black-berries, or owt wot was in seyson.

“When ‘er ‘adna got owt else, ‘er’d put some currans or reesons in, but when thee funst one thee ‘adst fer shyte ‘oo-ray ‘cos ther’d ony bey a ‘andful on ‘em in that big jowl.

“One o’ th’little lads used put me off a bit though. Ey awwees seymed fer ‘ave a couple o’ candles runnin’ dine ‘is nose on ter ‘is puddin’. Mind thee, th’little chap couldna ‘elp it, ey ‘ad one o’ them everlastin’ cowds in th’yed.

“Ey’d never ‘ad a proper ‘enkerchief an’ ‘is gansy-sleyve were a bit rough on ‘is little nose. But it was rattlin’ good breadpuddin’.”

Knockin' th'stuffin' ite

"That's a geeme wot's stood th'test o' tarme," said Jabez.

We were watching a couple of lads having a game of "conkers", and, as far as we could tell, the actions and the vocabulary they used were identical to those we both used as lads.

But what has happened to some of the other games we used to play? I still see boys in the village with their marble-bags but the games they play with them nowadays seem to be rather tame affairs.

In days gone by there were "taws" and "pugs", "alleys" and "stonies", "spotties" and "shotties", and "glassies" and "rinkers". With these different varieties and with the addition of such accessories as iron "bobbers" and stone "duckers" many different games were played.

The most boisterous and, at the same time, the most hazardous of these games was one involving the use of an iron disc some 6 or 7 inches in diameter and about 1/2 inch thick. "Wey used scrat a cirtle on th'grind abite foer foot across, an' us lads 'ud put a scoer' or moer taws in it apeyce," said Jabez. "Ther'd bey threy or foer 'undred awgether in this cirtle.

"Then wey'd draw a mark abite 30 yards awee, an' slat this iron pitcher at th'taws in us turn. Th'idea was fer drop it just in front o' th'cirtle so's it skidded inter theyse taws an' knocked 'em ite.

"They couldst 'ave aw them wot went iteside th'cirtle. Mind thee, a lot on 'em got brok, 'specially if thee 'appenst fer owerpitch it an' drop reyght on top on 'em.

"It peed thee fer stand well back when somebody else was pitchin' – some on 'em slat a bit weyld an' that theer iron pitcher coulda takken thee yed off thee showders."

Another energetic game was "peggy" or "tip-cat". This was best played in a field. A piece of wood about 3 inches long, cut from a mop or broom handle, was placed on the edge of a brick and given a sharp tap with a stout stick or a pick-shaft so that it went a few feet up into the air.

As it descended it was clouted good and hard. The striker then challenged the opposing side to cover the distance it had travelled in a certain number of running strides.

If any of them could stride it in that number they added it to their score. Otherwise, the striker added it to his score. It was a game requiring a considerable amount of skill, a steady eye and a sound judgement of distance.

"Ar've offen wondered." said Jabez, "if 'peggy' wonna th meekin' o' some o' th'good cricketers weyn 'ad in th'village. An ar'll tell thee another geeme wot thee dustna sey pleed nar-a-dees – bodger.

"Ee! ar've welly brok me back a tarme or two pleein' bodger. Foer lads on each seyd were abite th'best number, with th'fattest 'un fer th'bally-bunter.

"Th'bally-bunter stood with 'is back ter a wo' an' one o' th'lads bent dine with is yed in this bally-bunters bally. Then th'other two bent dine an' cushioned ther yeds in th'backside o' th'lad in front on 'em.

"When thee'd aw gotten dine th'other foer lads wot were goin' fogger 'ad fer leyp-frog on ter theyse threy lads' backs. Th'fost lad wot jumped 'ad fer try an' clear th'fost two backs an' land on th'third 'un.

"If ey didna it meant as ther was ony one back left fer aw th'other threy lads fer jump on to. It was now joke 'avin' threy 'efty lads on thee back, an' aw on 'em fangin' 'owd on thee somewheer so's thee wouldna fo' off. Thee 'ad fer stee theer withite touchin' th'grind 'till one on 'em 'ad kynted two, foer, six, eight, ten, bodger!

"Ar'll tell thee wot sirree, some o' th'lads weyn gotten nar-adees wouldna get inter ser much trouble if thee 'ad some o' th'stuffin' knocked ite on 'em with a two-threy geemes o' peggy or bodger. "

Th'magic -lantern mon

Some years ago I called on Jabez to tell him that I was going on holiday and to ask if he would keep an eye on my garden.

He had a poor opinion of my gardening abilities. Quite recently, for example he had pretended to mistake my beetroots for some new variety of radishes.

I was therefore expecting some further disparaging remark, and I was not disappointed. He said: "Ar'll 'ave a luk at it nar an' aggen but ar dunna reckon ar con do it much 'arm."

But I knew my Jabez. While I was away, the garden would be weeded and tidied, and there would be some new rows of plants from his own garden. As I was leaving his cottage he called out: "Bring us a stick o' rock back or a monkey up a stick."

I brought him a mammoth stick of rock but was unable to find a monkey up a stick. I gave him the rock and showed him some colour slides of the places I had visited.

"Ee!" he said. "Anna thee neyce? Dust know wot thee remind mey on, sirree? Them owd magic-l antern shows wot wey used 'ave. Ther was a mon wot used give theyse lantern-lectures on a wik-neyght in th'Sundee Schoo'. Ey 'ad a greet big lantern aw brass an' meeogony.

"It run off that theer 'cetylene gas – thee knowst, that stuff wot wey used 'ave in us bike lamps. Ony this mon 'ad a big gasometer thing wot stood on th'floer.

"Ar dunna reyghtly know wot sort o' contraption it was but ey used fill it with weyter an' put theyse big lumps o' carbide inseyd it. It didna 'afe stink!

"When ey'd lit th'burners in this lantern ey fastened a wheyte sheyt up on th'wo'. Ey 'ad some sleydes with hymns on 'em an' wey'd 'ave a good sing fer start off with. Then ey'd put two or threy funny sleydes on fer us childer.

"Ar con remember one on 'em – it was an owd mon in bed with 'is mythe weyd oppen. just nar ther come a mouse from under th'bed an' ran up th'bedclose an' across th'bed an' dine this owd mon's throat.

"Theyse meyce kept comin' from under th'bed – dozens on em – an' thee aw went inter 'is mythe. It was th'fost movin' picture a lot on us 'ad ever seyn an' wey thowght it was marvellous.

"After wey'd 'ad th'funny uns ey showed pitchers o' fereign parts an' talked abite 'em. Thee were mostly abite missionaries.

Sometarmes ey showed pitchers abite th'evils o' strong drink an' ey'd 'ave us singin':

"Dare to be a Daniel, dare to stand alone, dare to pass the public-house and take your money home.

"Some o' th'older lads wot sut at th'back pleed tricks on this mon. Ther was a rubber pipe wot went from this gasometer ter th'lantern an' theyse lads used put ther feyt on it an' squeze it.

"Th'leyghts 'ud start goin' ite an' th'mon 'ad keyp turning' th'gas up. Just when ey'd got it reyght theyse lads lifted ther feyt off th'pipe an' th'lamp shot up reyght through th'top o' th'owd lantern. It's a wonder ey didna set th'place afire.

"One neyght th'leyghts went ite awgether, an' then ther was an awmighty bang. Panic set in, an' th'folks started meekin' fer th'doer an' foin' ower one another.

"Th'pleece was as dark as a bag 'cos aw th'paraffin lamps 'ad bin turned ite. Anyroad up, somebody 'ad th'nowce fer kindle one o' theyse lamps an' thee funt this lantern-mon lukkin' larke a drynded rat.

"Aw th'weyter 'ad bin blown ite o' 'is gasworks an', be th'luk on 'im, most on it ad 'gone aw ower 'im. Ar dunna know whether them lads at th'back 'ad 'ad owt do with it but it was a long wheyle afoer ey come aggen. "

"Thee wouldstna remember me cousin Amos, wouldst?" asked Jabez.

"Ey lives at Congerton nar. Ey was ower this road a wheyle back an' wey 'ad a reyght good natter abite th'owd dees. Ey lived next doer when ey was a lad.

"Me granmother on me feyther's side lived with us at that tarme. 'Er was a bit of a strait-laced un was me granmother an' 'er an' Amos didna 'it it off aw that well.

"Er reckoned ey'd bin spoilt in th'rearin', but ar dunna think ey was that bad.

"But ey was one o' them lads wot couldna keyp 'is fingers ite o' things, 'specially things wot'd gotten 'oles in 'em. An' it wonna ony 'is fingers eether.

"If ey seyd a 'ole ey 'ad fer put 'is finger in it, or 'is arm, or 'is yed if it were a big 'ole. Got 'is finger fast in a knot-'ole in th'closet doer awmost afoer ey could walk, an' th'fost dee at schoo' ey got 'is 'and stuck dine a grid in th'plee-grind.

"It seymed as if ey couldna resist 'oles. Funny thing, wonna it? Ey used get fast in aw sorts o' things, an' ey 'ad many a good thrashin' fer it.

"Most tarmes thee were able fer get 'im unstuck, but tweyce thee 'ad fer tak 'im up th'Infirmry – once on accynt o' 'im 'avin' 'is finger stuck up a peyce o' iron-pipin', an' once with 'is 'and in an owd stone pittle jar.

"Is mother was fer takkin' 'im ter th'blacksmith fer 'ave this iron-pipin' sawed off 'is finger but Amos wonna 'avin' any. Ey could remember goin' theer once afoer fer 'ave a soce-pon tuk off 'is yed.

"Ey'd got this soce-pon fast when ey was pleein' sowjers in it dine th'feylds. Somebody 'appened 'it 'im top o' th'yed an' it stuck fast.

"When thee tuk 'im ter th'blacksmith fer get this soce-pon off ey picked up 'is big 'ommer an' said: 'Just put thee yed dine on th'anvil, lad.' Ey didna meyn it thee knowst, but it put Amos off blacksmiths.

"So 'is mother 'ad fer walk Silverdeele with 'im an' tak 'im on th'tram ter 'Artshill. Thee didna 'ave much trouble gettin' 'is finger ite 'o th'iron-pipin' but th'stone pittle jar caused a bit o' bother. "Ey 'adna towd 'is mother wot was in this pittle jar. When thee brok it oppen at th'Infirmary ite pops a snake. Th'nosses squeyled an' skidaddled but it was only a gress-snake an' Amos stuffed it in 'is pocket.

But 'is mother wouldna sit at th'side on 'im on th'tram n' back – 'er couldna abide snakes.

"But it wonna lung afoer it was Amos's turn fer do a bit o' squeylin'. At that tarme me granmother kept some leyches in a jar in th'pantry. 'Er used luk after bad folk in th'village an' 'er was a big beleyver in lettin' a bit o' blood ite.

Whenever ey spied 'is chance, Amos 'ud go an' wetch theyse leyches in th'pantry. Ar knew fer certin as sooner or leeter ey'd put 'is 'and in th'jar – an' ey did.

" Ey didna get 'is 'and fast this tarme but one o' th'leyches fastened on ter 'im. They shouldsta 'eerd 'im – ey squeyled blue murder. A bit touchy abite blood was Amos.

"Ey come runnin' inter th'kitchin screymin' at me granmother fer get it off 'im. But 'er wonna in aw that big a 'urry fer tak it off. 'Er said: 'Ee, that un's got a good 'owd on thee. Ar reckon theyt goin' tell me thee didstna put thee 'and in th'jar – it just jumped up an' bit thee.'

"Then 'er said. 'Dunna bey such a mard babby – it'll drop off thee when it's 'ad its fill.' But that meede 'im ten tarmes woss. In th'end 'er 'ad fer go an' cut a lump o' sawt off th'block fer get this leych off 'im.

"But it didna larn 'im – it wonna moer than a wik or two afoer thee funt 'im with 'is Yed stuck in th'razzervoy reelins. Poer owd Amos!

Thunder an' leyghtnin'

It was a warm summer evening and as I approached Jabez's cottage I could see that the front door was wide open.

He was sitting in his well-loved rocking chair and he appeared to be asleep. I was about to go quietly away and leave him to his slumbers when he called out:

"Ar anna asleyp if that's wot thee't thinkin'. Ar con tell thee footstep anywheer. They walkst just larke thee feyther used do – a bit 'eavy on th'keggy foot. Come in an' sit thee dine."

I sat on the old high-backed settle and made some suitable remark about the weather.

"It's bin a puthery sort o' dee, anna it?" he said. "Ar reckon wey shan 'ave some thunder afoer lung.

As we sat talking the thunder-heads were building-up in the western sky. A wind stirred the tops of the tall sycamores by the farm across the field, the bird-song was hushed and there was a rumble of thunder in the distance.

"Wey shan get it sooner than ar thowght," said Jabez. "Thee mitst as well stop wheer thee at 'till it's past ower.

"In th'owd dees me mother 'ud bey goin' rind th'ice coverin' up aw th'mirrors, puttin' aw th'kneyves an' fokes an' spoons awee, drawin' th'blinds dine, an' oppenin' th'doers. Folks used think as if th'leyghtnin' come dine th'chimney it'd go ite through th'doer withite doin' any mischief.

"When ar was a lad me mother used tell me if ever ar got caught in a thunder-storm th'best thing fer do was go ter th'middle o' a feyld an' lee dine on th'grind. Ar thowght abite 'er a two-threy yeer back when ar got owertakken be a storm dine in th'valley yonder.

"But theedst luk such a foo' lyin' dine on th'grind in th'pourin' reen, wutstna? So ar meede tracks fer wom. Ar 'adna gone moer than a cockstride afoer ther was a awmighty crack.

Th'leyghtnin' 'ad struck a oak trey just up th'road. It tuk a strip o' wood ite o' this trey from th'topmost twig ter th'grind. Kilt it stone jed, it did!

"Ar thowght ter mesel': Jabez lad, they shouldsta done wot thee mother towd thee. If theydst bin a bit aimer tote that trey theydsta bin split reyght dine th'middle! So it's dine on th'grind fer Jabez next tarme, choose wot folks think."

We sat and watched the awesome display of nature's fireworks on the grand scale, and then welcomed the cool rain that followed.

Jabez smiled and said: "Theedst 'ardly beleyve it but owd Charlie wot used live in th'wheyte-weshed cottage at th'bottom o' th'leene woulda slept through that thunder weyn just 'eerd.

"A terrible 'eavy sleyper was owd Charlie – ey seymed fer go jed. Dust know, sirree, 'is missus peepered th'bedroom one dee with owd Charlie asleyp in th'bed.

"Ey was on neyghts at th'pit at th'tarme, but 'er was determined fer get this new peeper on th'wo' wheylst th'childer were at schoo'. An' 'er did it an' aw. 'Er shunted th'furniture rind, an' th'bed an' aw, an' ey never 'eerd a thing.

"Ey wok up when 'er was puttin' th'last peyce on. When ey went sleyp th'wo's 'ad gotten autumn leyves on 'em, but when ey wok up thee were covered in roses. Ey rubbed 'is eyes an' lukked arind 'im an' said ter 'is missus: "Well, ar'll bey jiggered. Thers now wonder ar feyl 'ungry ar've gone an' slept reyght through th'flippin' winter.' "

Dolls an' clee-pipes

Jabez was doing his winter digging. I stood by the garden gate and watched him.

There was a certain rhythm in his unhurried movements that gave the impression that he could go on digging all day. He made it look so easy.

He must have caught sight of me out of the corner of his eye because, without looking up, he shouted: "Ar've gotten another spade in th'shed if thee't short o' a job. A bit o' diggin' 'ud do thee a world o' good. They't puttin' a fair bit o' fat on thee bones just leetly. "

Presently he stuck his spade in the ground and said: "Come on in, ar want show thee summat." He delved into one of the capacious pockets of the jacket that was draped over the garden hedge and put something into my hand.

"Wot dust meeke o' that then?" he asked. It was the head and shoulders of what must have been a small "china" doll.

"Ar musta dug a dozen or moer o' them up in me tarme" he said. "Belonged ter me sister them did. Yer could buy them little dolls fer a penny or twopence. Th'bodies were meede ite o' a peyce o' rag stuffed with sawdust.

"This rag was poer stuff an' it wonna lung afoer it bosted. Me sister used pretend theyse dolls were bad when th'saw-dust started comin' ite. 'Er'd keyp stitchin' 'em up but thee soon bosted ite aggen.

"When 'er couldna stitch 'em up anymoer 'er'd pretend thee were jed an' bury 'em in th'gardin. 'Er musta spent many a lot o' Satdee pennies on theyse dolls – ar keyp comin' across 'em aw ower th'opper."

A robin alighted on the handle of the spade and warbled his plaintive little song. He had picked up many a juicy morsel as Jabez turned over the soil. "Just 'ark at yon youth," he said. "Ey thinks ar do this diggin' fer 'is benefit – ey's bin follerin' me arind aw mornin'." The robin gave us an encore of his song and Jabez called out to him: "Owd thee whip a bit me owd friend – ar'm just 'avin' five."

We sat on the garden seat and Jabez lit his pipe. After a while he said: "Talkin' abite diggin' things up, 'ast ever noticed wot a lot o' owd clee-pipes ther is in th'feylds arind th'village?

"They 'ave a luk in any o' th'feylds just after theen bin ploughed. In spittin' distance thee cost pick up a 'andful o' peyces o' clee-pipe. A lot on 'em anna bin smoked eether – cleyn as a whistle thee are.

"Ar've offen wondered if somebody in th'village didna meeke clee-pipes at one tarme." He puffed away at his pipe and then said:

"Did ar ever tell thee abite th'fost smoke ar' ad in a cleepipe? Ar'd bey in me teyns at th'tarme an' ar come across Big Jim wot used work at th'bottom farm.

"Ey was ploughin' that feyld back o' th'Chapel an' ey'd got dine under th'edge fer a bite o' snappin'. When ey'd finished 'is bread an' cheyse ey cut a bit o' thick-twist an' put it on top o' th'dottle in 'is owd clee-pipe an' lit up.

"It smelt grand! This clee-pipe 'ad burnt ter th'colour o' meersham. Th'stem was ony abite a couple o' inches lung, an' th'bowl were just under 'is nose. Ar'd smoked many a lot o' dreyd leyves in a acorn pipe with a peyce o' straw stuck in it, but ar'd never smoked any reyl bacca.

"Ar eksed 'im if it teested as good as it smelt, an' ey said. "Thers nowt larke findin' things ite fer theesel', an' ey give me 'is pipe.

"Ar didna 'afe fancy mesel' with this clee-pipe but it wonna lung afoer ar began feyl a bit funny. Big Jim said: 'Wot's up me owd cock-sparrer? Theyt lukkin' a bit greyn arind th'gills.'

"Just nar owd Big Jim started goin' rind an' rind, an' then th'osses started goin' rind an' rind, an' then Big Jim an' th'osses aw started goin' rind th'Chapel.

"Ee! ar did feyl bad sirree. Ar managed fer get on me feyt an' stagger ter th'geete but th'geete wouldna stand still eether. Then aw of a sudden th'grind come up an' 'it me. Ar dunna remember much after that but ar've never fancied a clee-pipe since."

Th'collier barber

I found Jabez on his knees in the front garden planting bulbs in anticipation of a Spring display.

He glanced up at me, and then took a rather closer look and said: "Didst 'ave gas or cocaine?" It was many years since I had visited a dentist so I was at a loss to understand what he was getting at.

He laughed at my puzzled expression and said: "Ar meyn when thee 'adst thee 'air cut. Ar reckon it musta bin reyght peenful fer 'ave them two-threy 'airs o' thine cut as short as that.

'It's a wonder ter mey as that barber con give thee thee money's woth withite meekin' thee as bawd as an egg! Ey dunna charge thee full price, does he?"

Truth to tell, Jabez's own "thatch" was, if anything, a trifle thinner than mine, but he couldn't resist a dig at what he sometimes referred to as my "Bar-foot yed."

With a grunt or two he got up off his knees and said: "At one tarme ther used bey an owd collier in th'village wot did a bit o' 'air-cuttin' an' sheevin'. Ar dunna reyghtly remember if it was a penny or tuppence fer a 'aircut but it was one o' th'two.

"Us lads 'ad fer go on a Satdee mornin'. Ar tried fer get ite o' goin' if ar could, 'cos ther were a lot moer interestin' things fer a lad fer do on a Satdee mornin' than 'avin' 'is 'air cut.

"Ey did this 'air-cuttin' an' sheevin' in th'kitchin. Ey used put a cushin on one o' th'kitchin cheers fer us lads an' thee 'adst fer kneyl on this cushin an' lee owd o' th'back o' th'cheer.

"Ey awwees had a canary in a keege 'angin' up on th'wo', an' thee 'adst keyp lukkin' at this canary so's theedst keyp thee yed still. Ar dunna think ey'd larned any barberin' anywheer – ar reckon ey'd picked it up as ey went alung.

"Mind thee, considerin' ey were moer used ter 'andlin' a pick an' shovel than a comb an' scissors, ey didna do aw that bad a job. Thee lukst a bit larke a shorn lamb when ey'd finished with thee but it lasted thee a lung wheyle.

“Ey ‘ad this habit o’ suckin’ an’ blowin’ through ‘is mythe aw th’tarme ey were cuttin’ thee air’ – it synded larke a little steym-injin at th’back on thee. Ar remember ey ‘ad a finger missin’ off ‘is left ‘and. When ar fost went theer ar used think ey musta bin a bit careless an’ snipped this finger off with ‘is scissors.

“An’ ther used bey a little wooden box dine in one corner with cotton wool an’ peeper in it with blood on ‘em. “Ar didna larke th’luk o’ this box, an’ one dee ar eksed ‘im wot it was fer. Dust know wot ey said, sirree? Ey said it was fer puttin ears in wot ey’d cut off be mistake, an’ if ar didna keyp me yed still ther’d bey one o’ Jabez’s ears in th’box afoer ey’d finished.

“So ever after that ar kept me eyes fixed on th’owd canary, just in case.”

Weyter-cress an' bilberries

The long valley that almost circumscribes the village is still a popular and rewarding place in which to gather blackberries.

In former days, however, the blackberries were just one of many wild crops that could be harvested there.

Over the years Jabez showed me where to find wild raspberries and strawberries, gooseberries and bilberries, hazel nuts and chestnuts, crab apples and sloes, watercress and mushrooms, all within the confines of that fertile valley.

I remember the time we went to gather watercress. "Theen gotten a bun-feyght on at th'Chapel termerrer an' ar promised 'em a bit o' weyter-cress fer it. Ar'll show thee wheer it is but dunna let on, or else folks'll pluck it ter death in now tarme."

I must have walked past that bed of water-cress a hundred times or more without noticing it. At a certain point in its course, the almost insignificant stream was completely obscured from view by a dense screen of bushes and undergrowth.

Hidden away, and accessible only by crouching low and walking up the bed of the stream, was a shallow pool of clear water filled with luscious water-cress from which Jabez soon filled his basket.

As we strolled back to the village Jabez said: "Ar never walk up this road withite thinkin' abite th'tarme ar went bilberrin' with me Uncle Danny. Ey'd 'eerd tell as ther was a good crop o' bilberries in a wood t'other side o' Keyle.

"It was one 'olidee tarme just afoer ar left schoo', an' ey tuk me with 'im. It's a back-breekin' job bilberrin' is, inna it? A lot o' folks musta 'eerd abite theyse bilberries though, 'cos be th'tarme wey got theer th'bushes 'ad bin welly stripped.

"Wey were in that wood practically aw dee an' wey ony got abite a couple o' pynd apeyce. Anyroad, wey were just comin' back through Keyle when this bloke stops us an' says in a lah-di dah sort o' voice: 'Where did you get those bilberries from?'

"Uncle Danny lukked this bloke up an' dine, an' ey didna seym fer tak to 'im 'cos ey said: 'Wot's it got do with they wheer weyn 'ad 'em from? They mind thee own business.'

"Ar thowght Uncle Danny were beyin' a bit sharp with this bloke 'cos ey lukked a deycent enough 'soul. Thee couldst tell ey 'adna bin born in theyse parts though be th'funny road ey spok.

But ey musta cottoned-on as ey wonna goin' get very fer with Uncle Danny, so ey spok ter mey.

Ey wanted know if ar'd sell 'im me bilberries – ey said ey'd give me a shillin' fer 'em. Ar thowght abite aw th'things ar could do with a bob, an' wheylst ar was thinkin' abite it this mon said: 'Where did you say you got them from?'

"Ar were just goin' fer tell 'im when Uncle Danny tipped me th'wink fer keyp me trap shut. This bloke kept rattlin' th'money in 'is pocket an' eksin' me wheer weyd bin. Ar didna know wot fer do – ar coulda bought now end o' things with a bob in them dees.

"An' then ar thowght abite th'teeste o' that bilberry pie wot me mother 'ud meeke, an' then me mythe started weyterin' when ar thowght abite that bilberry an' apple dumplin' ar was goin' ave. In th'end me bally won th'dee – ar said ar wonna goin' sell em.

"When wey'd gotten ite o' ear-shot Uncle Danny said 'Ee! they 'adst me on tenterhooks fer a wheyle, lad. Dust know who that bloke was? Ey bought that bilberry-wood a two-threy yeer back wot weyn just trampled aw ower. If theydst towd 'im wheer theedst bin ey'd 'ad us in court next wik. An' thee dunna 'ave bilberry pie in gaol thee knowst – only bread an' weyter'."

Th'village dogs

"Ar could wreyte a book abite th'dogs weyn 'ad in this village," said Jabez.

"Ar reckon thers as much difference betweyn dogs as ther is betweyn folks. Thers good uns an' bad uns, an' thers clever uns an' mad uns.

"Thers them thee cost trust wi' thee leyfe an' thers them thee costna trust any further than thee cost spit.

"But th'queerest dog weyn ever 'ad in th'village was one neemed Turk. Funny neeme fer a dog, wonna it? Ey was wot ar caw a liquoreece dog. Ey was aw sorts – a bit o' this an' a bit o' that an' a bit o' everythin' else.

"Th'dog was 'armless enough but ey didna 'afe luk funny. An' th'funniest thing abite 'im was ey walked sideroads. 'Is back-end didna foller 'is front-end – if thee seyst wot ar meyn.

"Folks reckoned ey'd bin sut on when ey was a pup an' ey'd sort o' got twisted rind a bit. Ey lived ter a good age though, an' ey didna seym fer mind folks laughin' at 'im.

"An' then ther was one neemed Rex. Ey was a different kettle o' fish awgether. Ey was one o' th'best-lukkin' collies ar've ever seyn – ey was a beauty. Yer felt as though yer just 'ad fer stroke 'im an' pat 'im, an' tell 'im wot a grand-lukkin' dog ey was.

"But that's when folks funt ite wot a grand set o' teyth ey'd gotten. Ey couldna bear anybody touch 'is yed. Theydst ony got pat 'is yed an' ey'd 'ave thee 'and in 'is mythe up ter thee elber.

"Then ther was that big black un wot thee cawed Prince. 'Ast ever nowticed as some dogs seym fer 'ave a grudge aggenst certin folks? This dog belonged a widder-woman wot lived with a married doter.

"Th'doter's 'usband was a sowjer so thee didna sey much on 'im, an' th'dog were company fer 'em. Ey was a good dog but ther was one or two folks wot ey couldna stand th'seyght on.

"One o' th'folks ey 'ad a grudge aggenst was a relative o' theyse women – a mon neemed Frank. Ey lived dine th'other end o' th'village an' ey used 'elp 'em with th'gardin an' suchlarke.

"But whenever ey come ter th'ice theyse women 'ad fasten th'dog up somewheer. Ey'da etten Franky if ey'd gotten at 'im. Dust know, that dog could tell as soon as Franky lifted th'latch on th'geete. Uncanny it was.

"Franky 'adna got put 'is foot on th'path afoer th'dog 'ud bey barkin' an' growlin' behind th'doer.

"Anyroad, one mornin' when theyse women got up owd Prince seymed fer bey poerly. Ey was under th'big chest o' drawers in th'kitchin an' ey wouldna come ite. Thee tried ticin' 'im ite with aw sorts o' titbits but it was now good.

"Tote dinner-tarme thee began fer get worried abite 'im, an' when th'doter got dine on th'floer fer' ave a luk under this chest o' drawers, 'er started blartin'.

"Er said ey was as cowd as ice an' ey musta gone jed in th'neyght. So thee both started blartin' an' then th'doter said 'er'd better go an' get Franky fer 'elp 'em shift th'drawers an' bury poer owd Prince in th'gardin.

"Franky wonna in at th'tarme but 'is missus said 'er'd send 'im across as soon as ey come wom.

"So theyse two women sat comfortin' one another an' talkin' abite wot a good dog ey'd bin. Thee said thee'd get another pup as soon as thee could, fer tak ther minds off it.

"An' then aw of a suddin Prince shot ite from under th'chest o' drawers larke a rocket, an' was barkin' an' growlin' at th'doer. It could ony meyn one thing – ey'd 'eerd Franky comin' fer bury 'im.

"Theyse women couldna beleyve ther eyes, an' thee never did manage fer convince Franky as thee 'adna bin 'avin' 'im on."

Talkin' abite me sister

"Ar was tellin 'thee abite me sister a wheyle back, wonna ar?" said Jabez. "Ar was thinkin' abite 'er aggen th'other dee.

"Er was a funny mixture when thee comst think abite it. Ther were tarmes when 'er was that full o' beyns 'er'd bey up 'er neck in mischief.

"An' then ther were tarmes when 'er seymed fer go reyght inter 'er shell an' 'er'd bey as touchy as anythin'.

"Ar remember th'tarme when wey funt 'er scrykin' 'er eyes up in bed one neyght. It was a lung wheyle afoer wey could find ite wot was th'matter with 'er.

"Theydst never guess wot it was in a month o' Sundees. It was th'ice-martins wot 'ad upset 'er.

"In them dees, theyse 'ice-martins used neyst under th'eaves. Every yeer, thee built ower th'top o' th'winda o' th'bedroom wot me sister slept in, an' 'er used luk forward ter 'em comin'.

"'Er'd lie in bed at neyght listenin' ter 'em twitterin' 'specially when thee'd gotten young uns. 'Er said thee were company fer 'er an' it meede 'er feyl 'appy, 'cos theyse brids were aw neyce an' cosy in th'neyst, an' 'er was aw neyce an' cosy in bed.

"But when th'autumn come an' thee flew off 'er felt sad an' lonely. An' 'er didna 'afe get dine in th'dumps fer think as theyse little brids could fly from 'er bedroom winda aw th'wee ter Africa an' yet 'er 'ardly knew th'road ter 'Castle.

"An' that's wot 'er was blartin' abite! Me mother did 'er best fer comfort 'er an' towd 'er as p'raps 'er'd bey able go ter some o' theyse fereign pleeces one dee.

"But th'poer lass never managed it, an' even when 'er was grown up 'er used 'ave a little blart when th'ice-martins left us.

"Ar reckon 'er got some o' theyse funny notions from reydin' too many books. 'Er read anythin' 'er could lee 'er 'ands on. 'Er'd curl up in a cheer with a book an' thee wouldstna get a squeak ite on 'er – 'er seymed fer go miles awee.

"Dust know, sirree, 'er never went up th'yard withite takkin' summat fer reyd. 'Er'd bey up theer many a wheyle, an' it didna seym fer strike 'er as somebody else mit want go. It was as though 'er fergot wheer 'er was.

"But ar rowsted 'er ite one dee! At that tarme one o' th'blokes wot emptied th'closets 'ad one o' 'is 'ands missin'. Ey 'ad a big iron 'ook instead o' a 'and. It was a reyght 'andy thing fer carryin' th'buckets.

"Me sister was frittened death o' this mon – 'er'd run a mile if 'er saw 'im comin'. Anyroad, one dee 'er'd bin stuck up th'yard th'best part o' an hour an' ar was tired o' weetin'. Things were gettin' a bit desperate.

"Wot dost think ar did, sirree? Ar crept ite o' th'front-doer an' rind th'back, an' ar got a couple o' empty buckets an' rattled 'em 'gether behind th'closet.

"That did th'trick. 'Er thowght it was th'mon with th'ook comin'. 'Er shot ite o' th'closet an' dine th'yard with 'er bloomers danglin' rind 'er ankles. It was a lung wheyle afoer 'er spok ter me after that."

Th'owd cottage

Opposite the site of the old village green there stands an ancient cottage with its back to the road.

The reason it was built that way is not apparent until you walk round to the front of the cottage. To the South it looks out on a wide vista of undulating country with the tip of the Shropshire Wrekin just visible on the horizon.

To the West it overlooks the fertile Cheshire plain with the mountains of Wales as a backcloth.

A superb spot for a cottage and yet, strangely enough, it was originally a stable. just when the conversion took place is not known with any certainty.

In one corner of the living room some cunning carpenter built a staircase with such economy of space that it could be mistaken for a cupboard. The upper floor is supported on a massive oak beam that spans the room below.

No doubt successive occupants of the cottage learned to "duck" under the unyielding oak but many a visitor must have left with a very sore head.

Many and varied are the tales associated with this cottage and its former tenants. The one I like best concerns Charles and Jane who, just about 100 years ago, moved into the cottage from Wrinehill, their bits of furniture on a borrowed hay-waggon and a religious fervour aflame in their hearts.

The village chapel had yet to be built and their humble home became a temporary House of God, its walls echoing to the lusty singing of Methodist hymns. Twice-weekly services were held in the living room for several years.

After tea, the table with its lace-fringed cover was moved to the corner by the staircase, the great family bible with its brass corner-plates and clasps was placed upon it, and chairs were arranged for the congregation.

When all was ready Jane took off her apron, put on her best black bonnet, and sat in her accustomed place near the fire. Charles in his Sunday-best hovered near the door to receive the preacher and to welcome the worshippers.

“Me feyther used tell me abite it,” said Jabez. “Ey went theyse services reglar. Thee didna ‘ave a ‘armonium or owt thee knowst – somebody ‘ad fer start th’singin’. If th’preycher couldna start ‘em off, somebody in th’congregation ‘ad do it.

“Sometarmes th’tune didna fit th’words proper an ‘thee’d get ter th’end o’ a line an’ find thee’d eether gotten some words left ower or else thee’d gotten too much music. But thee managed fer pucker it in someroad or other.

“One owd feller was very fond o’ a tune with a ‘Glory, glory’ chorus to it. Ey started this tune up as offen as ey could with th’result that thee once funt thersels singin’ and devils fear and fly, singing glory, glory, glory!’

“One neyght, just afoer th’preycher started ‘is sermon, ther was a terrible smell o’ burnin’. It got woss an’ woss, an’ then aw of a suddin it struck Jane wot it was.

“Ther’d bin a two-threy taters left ower at dinner-tarme an’ er’d meede some tater-cakes an’ popped ‘em in th’oven. ‘Er’d fergotten aw abite ‘em. ‘Er sidled across ter th’oven-doer an’ tuk theyse tater-cakes ite. “Thee were as black as ‘er bonnet, so ‘er slat ‘em on th’fire an’ sut dine aggen. But th’owd preycher saw th’funny side on it an’ ey said p’raps ey shoulda preyched a sermon on th’sixth chapter o’ Jeremiah.

“Jane didna know wot ey were gettin’ at ‘till ‘er lukked it up after ey’d gone. It said: ‘Your burnt-offerings are not acceptable, nor your sacrifices sweet unto me.’ ‘Er ‘ad fer laugh when ‘er thowght abite them black tater-cakes.”

Th’owd Cottage

"In me younger dees," said Jabez, "some o' th'owd uns towd me a greet lot o' things abite th'village an' abite th'folks wot lived in it.

"It's still in me yed somewheer but it dunna 'afe tak a bit o' fetchin' ite theyse dees. Ar reckon me yed's a bit larke me gardin shed – thers that much rubbitch in it ar conna find owt ar want. If ony ar'd written it aw dine ar shouldna 'ave scrat me owd yed ser much.

"Me granfeyther used tell me as ey could remember th'tarme when th'village were 'afe-a-dozen cottages, two shoe-meeker's shops an' threy farms.

"When ar said as them folks in th'village musta weared a lot o' shoes ite fer keyp two shoe-meekers goin', me granfeyther said: Dunna bey daft lad – them two men meede shoes fer folks fer miles arind.

"In them dees thee 'adst a pair o' shoes meede fer fit thee feyt. If theedst gotten corns or bunnions, thee 'adst thee shoes meede fer go rind 'em. An' thee couldstna wear 'em ite in a 'urry either.

Jabez got up from his rocking-chair and said: "Nar ar come think on it ar've gotten a pair o' shoes upsteers wot one o' theyse owd shoe-meekers meede – ar'll fetch 'em dine fer thee.

They were a pair of child's shoes, beautifully made and still in remarkably good condition except for a small slit at the front of each shoe where the toe-nails of growing feet had finally pushed their way through.

The tiny hand-stitches were barely visible and there was never a nail to be seen. I asked Jabez how old they were. He said: "Ey meede 'em fer 'is doter, Sarah Ann, an' ar've figured it ite as them shoes musta bin meede abite eighteyn-foty, give or tak a yeer or two.

"Wot dust reckon theedst 'ave pee nar-a-dees fer a pair o' and-meede shoes larke them? Thee'd cost th'earth, wouldna thee?"

He put the shoes back carefully into the box in which they were kept, and then said with a laugh: "Ther was a teele me granfeyther used tell abite one o' theyse shoe-meekers.

“ It appears ther was a poacher wot was awwees braggin’ abite ‘is exploits. Ey wonna aw that good a poacher but ey kept tellin’ this shoe-meeker wot a clever bloke ey was. Ey said th’geeme-keypers were too slow fer ketch a cowd, an’ thee’d ‘ave larn some new tricks afoer thee could ketch ‘im.

“Th’owd shoe-meeker couldna abide braggin’ folks but ey didna see much ter ‘im. Ey just reminded ‘im as pride goeth afoer a fo’, an’ got on with ‘is shoe-meekin’.

“But it wonna lung afoer this poacher kept gettin’ ketched tarme after tarme. It was as though theyse geeme-keypers could reyd ‘is mind – thee seymed fer know every move ey meede.

“Th’poacher couldna understand it, but th’owd shoe-meeker coulda towd ‘im th’answer. Ey’d got that fed up with this poacher’s braggin’ ey decided fer teych ‘im a lesson.

“So when ey mended this poacher’s shoes ey meede a sort o’ pattern on th’soles with neels. But it wonna exactly a pattern - it was this poacher’s neeme written backerd’s! Whenever ey trud on a bit o’ muddy grind theyse keypers could reyd ‘is neeme as pleen as a pikestaff. “Thee were as pleysed as Punch with this shoe-meeker, an’ fer a lung wheyle ey funt a hare or a pheasant ‘angin’ on ‘is back-doer in a mornin’.

“Th’poacher never funt ite who was givin’ th’show awee ‘cos ey’d never bin schoo’ an’ ey couldna reyd ‘is own neeme!”

Sarah Anne’s shoes

"Ar come across an owd tooth-comb in one o' th'drowers th'other dee," said Jabez. "Ee! it tuk me reyght back ter me schoo'-dees.

"Ther used come a noss rind th'schoo' lukkin' at us yeds fer nits. Some mothers didna keyp ther childers 'air aw that cleyn an' it got full o' theyse nits. Aw th'wenches 'ad lung 'air in them dees an' it tuk a lot o' keypin' cleyn.

"Me mother was frittened death o' me sister gettin' any o' this livestock in 'er yed. 'Er used comb it with one o' theyse tooth-combs two or threy tarmes a wik. Me sister's 'air was welly dine ter 'er weest an' it didna 'afe tak some doin' with one o' theyse combs.

"Lung 'air larke that used get a lot o' lugs in it an' aw theyse lugs 'ad fer bey combed ite one at a tarme fear lest ther was owt livin' in 'em. Me sister awwees finished up scrykin' – it musta bin reyght peenful.

"Some folks used keyp dippin' th'comb in paraffin but me mother used oil o' sassafras – it didna 'afe meeke them little lodgers run, an' it didna smell queyte as bad as paraffin. At th'wik-ends, or if me sister was goin' anywheer special, 'er 'ad 'er 'air done up in curling-rags.

"It 'ad fer bey weshed fost, an' then 'er sut in front o' th'fire 'till it was dry. Theyse curlin' rags were lung strips o' owd cotton sheyt or summat larke that.

"Me sister 'eld th'end o' one o' theyse strips on top o' 'er yed wheylst me mother wun a bunch o' 'air rind it an' tied it at th'bottom. When it was aw done it lukked larke a lot o' sausages angin' dine. But th'next dee when theyse rags were tuk ite 'er air was aw neyce an' curly.

"But ther come a tarme when wenches started 'avin' ther air cut off – bobbed, thee cawed it. Th'owd folks threw up ther 'ands in disgust.

"Some reckoned it was a sin an' some reckoned it were sheemful fer a lass 'ave 'er 'air cut off. But it was th'fashion, an it wonna lung afoer most o' th'village wenches 'ad it cut off.

"Mind thee, it was a lot easier fer keyp cleyn, an' th'owd tooth-comb an' sassafras oil wonna used ser offen. Ar remember one lass whose feyther wouldna let 'er 'ave it cut off. 'Er'd gotten a grand yed o' auburn 'air.

“Er begged an’ pleyded with ‘im but ey wouldna ‘ear on it. Ey said if ‘er ‘ad it cut larke a lad’s ey’d meeke ‘er wear lad’s close an’ aw.

“But anyroad, when ey come wom from work one neyght this lass ‘ad ‘ad ‘er ‘air bobbed, an’ ‘er was wearin’ a pair o’ trysers just larke ey’d towd ‘er. Ey was just abite fer give ‘er a good thrashin’ when ‘is missus walked inter th’room.

“Yer coulda knocked ‘im dine with a fither. ‘Is missus ‘ad bin bobbed an’ aw, an’ ‘er’d gotten a pair o’ trysers on.

“Ey stood theer with ‘is mythe weyd oppen but it was a lung wheyle afoer ey could get any words ite.

“Then ey said: ‘Awreyght, yo win. Yer con both tak them trysers off. Ar think ar coulda got used ter me doter turnin’ inter a lad, but ar'm blessed if ar con stomach th'idea o' 'avin' a weyfe as luks lark a mon.”

Village sounds

In the period between the two wars, the village changed little in appearance. Indeed, in the 1930's the news that a new house was to be built became the major topic of conversation.

In due course, each stage of the operation, from the lifting of the first sod to the application of the last lick of paint, was minutely inspected and freely commented upon by a critical audience of villagers.

Many more houses have been built since the war, and some of the old ones demolished. There have been changes in other directions too. For generations, village ears had grown accustomed to the medley of sounds that emanated from the colliery in the valley below.

These mechanical noises, mercifully muffled by distance, provided a background against which all other village sounds were heard.

There was the accelerating "chuff" of the winding engines, the squeal of tortured metal from the screens, the repetitive clang of waggon buffers, the harsh clatter of coal-tub wheels on rail-joints, the ring of hammer on anvil from the blacksmith's shop, the apologetic whistle of the little fat-bellied shunting loco, and the bassoon-like buzzer that measured out the day and night in terms of working hours and eating minutes. But these and other familiar sounds have gone, abruptly silenced by the untimely closing of the colliery. Its demise marked the end of an era for the village.

"Dust know, sirree," said Jabez, "ar couldna sleyp of a neyght fer many a wheyle after thee closed th'pit. Ar couldna think wot was th'matter wi' me. Ar used drop off sleyp larke a babby ter th'synd o' th'pit goin' full blast.

"It's funny, but sometarmes yer dunna miss somethin' 'till it's gone – if thee seyst wot ar meyn.

"An' ar could lee in bed an' tell thee th'neeme o' practically every collier wot went passed. Thee aw meede different synds. Ther was little Tummy – ey was a grown mon but ey wonna moer than foer-foot nothin' in 'is stockin' feyt.

"Thee couldstna misteeke 'im – ey synded just larke a little lad in 'is fost pair o' clogs.

" An' there was Sampy. Ey awwees 'ad a wokin'-stick an' ey synded as though ey'd gotten threy legs – clogs on two on 'em an' a slipper on th'other.

“Some on ‘em went clatterin’ passed as though thee couldna weet fer get at th’coal, an’ some on ‘em synded as though thee could ‘ardly drag one foot in front o’ th’other.

“Then ther was owd Charlie – ‘im wot was a local preycher – ey was awwees singin’ or whistlin’ hymns. But ther was one youth wot was awwees leete – ey ran most o’ th’wee ter th’pit. Ey must bey one o’ th’few blokes wots fell ower a cow.

“It appears ey tuk a short cut across th’little medder one dark neyght an’ went neck an’ crop ower this cow. It was leed dine chewin’ its cud but ey was in that big a ‘urry ey never seyd it.

“It was a toss-up who was most takken aback – ‘im or th’cow.

Local Miners

Sonny

Jabez was showing me a letter that had come into his possession. It was written in 1923 by the Pastor of a large Presbyterian Church in North Dakota, U.S.A.

"It's too lung fer reyd nar," he said. "Tak it wom with thee, but tak good care on it 'cos ar wouldna larke owt 'appen to it.

It was indeed a lengthy letter – closely-typed foolscap pages that read like a fairy story. This eminent man of God was once a poor uneducated lad who had worked at the farm by the village chapel.

As a child he lived in "The Gothic" at Silverdale, and his earliest recollections were of cowering in the corner of the kitchen to escape from his drunken father, and of crying himself to sleep night after night with hunger.

He recalls going with his brothers to gather nettles for his mother to boil for them to eat.

At eight years of age, he was selling Sentinels and begging bread from his customers. When he was a little older the farmer in the village had taken pity on him and given him bed and board in return for such light work as the lad's undernourished body could attempt.

His letter spoke of many things, but over and over again he referred to the influence on his life of the little village chapel.

Of how, from the farmyard, he watched the children going into Sunday school and wished he had some respectable clothes so that he could join them,

And when the children sang such hymns as: "When He cometh to make up His jewels" and "Jesus loves me, this I know", the words seemed to touch some hidden chord within him and he would run down into the wood and break his young heart.

In the summer, the evening service was sometimes held on the village green near to the farm gate. The little congregation were unaware of the presence of the ignorant lad crouching behind the farmyard wall, but their singing and the words of the preacher made such a lasting impression upon him that 30 years afterwards in his book-lined study, 5,000 miles away, tears flooded his eyes at the memory of it.

He was now the Pastor of a city church, and a frequent lecturer at many American colleges. The day before he wrote the letter this one-time beggar-boy of Silverdale had conducted the funeral service of a United States senator in the presence of a congregation of over 1,000 people.

"Folks in th'village cawed 'im Sonny," said Jabez. "It's a wonderful letter, inna it? Didst reyd that bit abite wheer ey signed th'pledge? Ee! it musta tuk a bit o' courage fer th'lad tell them farm leebourers ey couldna drink any moer ale with 'em in th'ay feyld.

"Cost imagine wot thee'd see ter him? Thee'd pull 'is leg unmerciful, wouldna thee? Ar larke that bit wheer ey says as every tarme ey gets up fer preych in that big church ey gets a vision o' th'little village chapel.

"Them owd chapel-folks didna know as that young lad was wetchin' 'em an' listenin' ter 'em. If one on 'em 'ad done summat wrung, or said summat ey didna ought ter said, it coulda turned that lad alung a different path awgether. It meekes thee think, dunna it?"

The "Sonny" story is in fact the story of Dr Ernest E Parkes, the following are extracts from a long letter (11 typed foolscap pages) received in 1923 by Mr. Thomas Bloor, Wilfred Bloor's father . Dr. Parkes was born in the "Gothic" at Silverdale and for some time was employed as a labourer at Scott Hay on the farm adjoining the Chapel. He was known in the village as "Sonny". It is a truly remarkable story of the son of a drunken father who, from a background of extreme poverty, became an eminent man of God in the United States of America.

Minnewaukan, North Dakota,
United States of America.

March 6th 1923

My dear, dear friend,

How shall I manage to express my thoughts to you in a letter? I feel that in attempting to do so I am attempting one of the hardest tasks of my life. You will I am sure understand what I mean. It is now 10 o'clock at night, the family has gone to bed, and for the last hour I have been sitting before the fire in my study all alone thinking, thinking, thinking of the dear old days of yore. With the determination in my mind not to go to bed tonight without writing my long due letter to you. I have given myself up to an hour's meditation of those far away days when as a lad called Sonny I lived at Scott Hay.

I confess I have sat moved and melted into tears as I have lived again in memory those far off days and have followed the years down to today.It is all like a dream. How marvellous, how wonderful are the ways of God.

I have seen myself a poor half-starved lad, the son of a drunken father, at eight years of age selling the Staffordshire Sentinel, and remembering myself going round Keele and Madeley begging bread from door to door, and at one time going out and with my brothers gathering nettles for mother to boil for us to eat. And yet today I have been in a large city 50 miles away to conduct the funeral of a United States Senator, and 1,000 people listened to my funeral sermon.

For the past 10 years I have been in this country a Presbyterian Pastor preaching at least three sermons each week, and of an average two or three public civic addresses in addition to funerals etc. When I think of the beggar lad and the Pastor of today I am melted at the thought of the infinite love and guidance of God. And it is because in my attempting to write to you these two contrasts, the early and the later years of my life, are so vivid before me that I say I find it difficult to write to you. For, as you will understand, I cannot think of you and the old Chapel without thinking at the same time of my early days.

However, I am doing my best to express a little of myself, not only because you have been so kind to write such beautiful brotherly letters to me which I treasure so very much, but I also want to pay my little tribute to the influence of your work at Scott Hay, you and your Chapel. Nothing but the light of the Eternal world will ever reveal the full total influence which that little Chapel on the hill has had over the lives of mortal men and women.

In one of your letters to me you remark that we never know the hidden potentialities of a young life. That is perfectly true, and it is equally true that we never know the influence for good which a Christian man has in the world. Oftentimes, all unknown to him, he is influencing others for good, causing thoughts and feelings to arise within the heart. I know I was a poor lad without any early Christian training, ignorant of the simplest prayer, when I first went to your village but I used to see you crossing the bank there going to Chapel or Sunday School, or starting off to preach somewhere and it used to stir something up within me, some hidden longing to be good and useful. I well remember lying night after night in my bed thinking about you and what made you so different from most men I had known.

Then on some Sabbath mornings as I stood in the farmyard I would see you and the teachers and the scholars going into Sunday School, and presently there would come floating over the air the words of that beautiful hymn:

"Sing them over again to me Wonderful words of life". or

"When He cometh to make up His jewels".

Oh: what feelings used to come over me as I stood listening to those strains. They seemed to touch some hidden cord within me and I would go down into the wood and cry for hours. And sometimes you would hold your service on summer evenings by the farm gate and I would be listening behind the gate and the impressions I received behind that gate Heaven only will reveal. Oh yes, only a few of God's people holding a service on the village green and they couldn't see the poor ignorant lad behind the gate, but a merciful God was using that service for the making of impressions upon that young life, and tonight, thirty years afterwards, that one-time young life still feels the impressions made upon him by those services as he now sits in his study 5,000 miles away under the spire of his Church wherein he has preached three times a week for almost four years. The most ineradicable, the most permanent conviction of my heart tonight is the fact that my first impressions for good, my first longings for religious service, my first awakening to a higher, nobler, better life, all is the result of the influence of the little Primitive Methodist Chapel away there in old England on Scott Hay, and he whose name somehow I cannot dissociate from that Chapel - Thomas Bloor.

My earliest recollections are as a little ragged urchin living in the Gothic by the Church in Silverdale. I see my Dad coming home blind drunk, I hear to this day my mother calling out "murder", I see morning come and no food in the house, and I see my oldest sister (now dead, God bless her) going out and begging for bread from people across the street, and it was those people who again and again gave us bread. Two names are ever in my mind as I think of those dark, dark days, for they were the people who gave us bread. One I remember was named Ellams, Frank Ellams' parents. The other people were named Seabridge. At that time they kept a sweet shop and a joiners shop behind. Good, good people they were, and they will never know how, away out here in America, there is one who remembers them with grateful rememberance for what they did 35 years ago in giving bread for hungry children. The good Lord reward them.

And now after all these years I look back to those days of my youth I see there, in my stay in your village, the foundation which was laid for all which has followed in my life. For it is my conviction that I owe my earliest awakening to the influence of your Chapel in those far off days. It was in that Chapel where one night at a temperance meeting in the year 1894 I signed the pledge and by the grace of God from that day to this no intoxicating liquor has crossed my lips. I remember, as though it was last night, going from the Chapel and saying to George Mountford the farmer: "I signed the pledge tonight at the Chapel and I am not going to drink any more ale in the hayfield".

Well, I wish I could stay to mention by name all the friends at Scott Hay to whom I would like to be remembered, but it is now 7 o'clock in the morning and I have had a whole night in the writing of this letter except an hour spent in the Church. You will kindly give my Christian love to all my friends at Scott Hay. I delight to read from your letters of the splendid way in which first one and then another has risen to useful and honoured positions, and what a number of them must feel as I feel that they can trace back under Heaven all that is best in their life to the influence, the guidance, and the direction of that little Primitive Methodist Chapel there. Greater, vaster, more enduring is its work than many a cathedral in a large city. Here in this city on the prairies of the United State of America, 5,000 miles away from that little Chapel, is a Church with its large pipe-organ and its weekly crowded congregation. In its pulpit there stands a Minister preaching, and in that Minister's mind and memory there is ever the vision of a little Chapel away back there in old England. He thinks of it with reverence, he thinks of it with gratitude, and as he receives first one token and then another of being of some use to the Kingdom of his Master he thanks God that when a poor lad of a drunken father he was ever led to come under the influence of that little Chapel at Scott Hay. Between that Primitive Methodist Chapel in England and this First Presbyterian Church in Minnewaukan there is a link binding which time shall never break.

With fondest Christian love to you all, asking that sometime in the old Chapel a prayer will be offered for the one in a foreign land, far, far away, yet one of you in memory, love and service.

The one-time Sonny of the farm,

With affectionate love, Ernest E. Parkes

Th'scarlet feyver bug

"Ar wonder wot's 'appened ter th'scarlet-feyver bug," said Jabez. "Thee dustna 'ear much abite it theyse dees, dust?

"At one tarme folks thowght it was a terrible thing. It was mostly childer wot got it, an' thee 'ad fer go ter th'feyver 'ospital fer wiks an' wiks.

"Th'ambulance used come fer 'em an' thee'd bey carried ite on a stretcher covered in blankets. Ther'd bey a cryd o' folks rind th'ambulance wetchin' everythin' wot went on. Some o' th'women ud bey blartin', an' some on 'em 'ud bey comfortin' th'child's mother.

"When th'ambulance went back through th'village folks 'ud bey standin' at th'front doers talkin' abite it, an' tut-tuttin', 'an waggin' ther yeds. Th'other childer 'ud bey everser queyet an' everser sad fer many a wheyle. It was larke 'avin' a funeral in th'village.

"Ar was knockin' on fer 20 when ar 'ad it. It musta bin a good yeer fer it an' aw, 'cos aw th'feyver 'ospitals were full up. So, ther was nowt else fer it – ar 'ad stop at wom. Ee! theyst never seyn such a palaver. Th'ony folks wot could come inter th'bedroom were th'doctor an' me mother.

"That young doctor tuk 'is job too serious ter mar wee o' thinkin'. Ar did me best fer cheer 'im up but ey awwees 'ad a feece as lung as a bass-fiddle.

"Me mother 'ad fer soak an owd blanket in some sort o' disinfectant an' 'ang it ower th'doer, an' ther was a bowl o' stuff iteside wot 'er 'ad wesh 'er 'ands in everytarme 'er went ite o' th'room. It was larke 'avin' foot an' mythe, ony thee didna shoot me.

"Ar was as reyght as neynpence after a fote-neet but ar 'ad stee in that room fer nigh on seven wik. Talk abite solitary confinement! Ar just 'ad fer find summat fer keyp me from goin' rind th'bend.

"As it 'appened ther was a lass in th'village wot ar'd set me cap at. Ar got me mother fer bring me a lung peyce o' string an' some peeper. Ar dostna tell 'er wot ar wanted 'em fer. Dust know wot ar did, sirree?

"Ar writ a letter ter this lass an' fastened it on th'end o' this peyce o' string. Then when ar 'eerd me granfeyther potterin' up th'yard ar oppened th'bedroom winder an' dangled this letter dine.

"Ey was a good owd spoert an' ey soon cottoned-on ter wot ar was up to. Mind thee, ey shuk 'is fist at me, but ey put 'is jacket on an' toddled off up th'village with me letter. An' it wonna lung afoer ey was back aggen with th'answer.

"Ey 'ung abite a bit 'till me mother was ite o' th'road an' then ey signalled terme fer let th'string dine so's ey could fasten this lass's letter on it.

"Ey used trot back an' to with theyse letters threy or foer tarmes a wik. Dust know, sirree, ar'll swear th'owd rascal 'ad a twinkle in 'is eye every tarme ey set off fer sey this lass!"

Th'seventh-'and bike

It was not often that anyone in the village bought a brand new bicycle.

The few who did were usually the target for such caustic remarks as: "Ar didna know yer'd 'ad a fire at yoer 'ice," or "Ast come up on th'maxim then?" or " 'As thee rich uncle deyd aw of a suddin?"

Most people had to be content with second-hand ones, some of which had plainly been constructed by taking parts from several different machines. Others were so ancient as to come within the category of antiques or heirlooms.

The bicycles ridden by the lads of the village were often devoid of such refinements as brakes and mudguards, and there were those individuals who even considered that tyres were not absolutely essential.

When a village lad managed to acquire a road-worthy cycle, he soon discovered that he possessed a valuable asset. There was money to be had for the running of errands and the taking of messages. His less fortunate fellows were ever eager to hand over such desirable items as fag-cards, marbles, conkers and sweets in return for a ride round the village.

"Ar remember th'fost bike ar 'ad," said Jabez. 'It was supposed fer bey a second-'and un but ar reckon it was abite seventh-'and if th'truth were known.

"Th'wheyls 'ad bin puntured them many tarmes as th'innertubes lukked larke petch-work quilts – there was moer petches than tube. But me feyther fettled it up a bit an' give it a coat o' peent. Dust know, sirree, ar lived on that theer bike – ar went everywheer on it.

"Me mother said it was a wonder ar didna go up th'yard on it! Ar went th'shop on it, an' ar awwees fetched th'milk on it from th'farm. It wonna ser bad if th'milk were in a can but it was a bit tricky with a quart jug full.

"Th'farmer's weyfe said: 'Some o' yo young uns shoulda bin born with wheyls instead o' legs. When thee killst theesel' on that thing dunna come blartin' ter mey.'

"One dee when ar was 'sposed fer bey fetchin' th'milk ar funt mesel' in th'shop instead o' th'farm. Ar musta bin wool-getherin' or summat. Ee! ar did feyl a foo', an' ar could 'ear th'shop-woman comin' through from th'back. Ar thowght ter mesel' 'Jabez lad, 'er'll think theyt goin' soft in th'yed comin' ter th'shop fer milk.'

"So ar 'ad fer think pretty quick if ther was owt in th'shop wot ar could 'ave in a jug. Ar could ony think o' two things paraffin an' vinegar.

"So ar 'eld me jug ite an' said ar wanted a peynt o' vinegar. 'Er went rind ter th'vinegar barrel an' drew me a peynt off an' put it in th'jug.

"An' then ar remembered ar adna got any money fer pee fer it! Wey awwees peed fer th'milk at th'wik-end, but me mother never would 'ave tick at th'shop. So ar was flummoxed.

"Th'shop-woman lukked reyght through me an' 'er musta twigged wot 'ad 'appened. 'Er said: 'Jabez, they atna owd enough fer bey in love so it conna bey that. But theyt owd enough fer know th'difference betweyn a shop an' a farm. Th'ony conclusion ar con come ter is theyt losin' thee buttons.'

"Er tuk th'jug off me an' emptied th'vinegar back in th'barrel an' went an' weshed th'jug ite. Then 'er said: Nar, get thee off ter th'farm, if thee cost remember wheer it is. An' next tarme thee meekst a daft misteeke dunna bey frittened o' ownin' up – it'll seeve thee a lot o' trouble in th'lung run.'

"Ar coulda gone dine a mouse-'ole, but arve never fergotten th'owd woman's words.

Bikin' ter Rudgud

"Dust remember mey tellin' thee abite that bike ar 'ad?" asked Jabez. "Mey an' another youth went fer a ride rind Rudgud road one dee.

"Wey tuk a bit o' snappin' with us an' a bottle o' weyter, an' wey 'ad us dinner at th'side o' th'leeke. Wey 'adna got enough money for 'ave a go on th'boats but wey 'ad some fun wetchin' other folks. Ar dunna reckon some on 'em 'ad bin in a boat afoer, judgin' be th'road thee performed.

"It was a grand dee, an' tote th'middle o' th'af'noon ther come a lad dine ter th'weyter in a pair of beethin' drawers. Ey 'adna picked a very good spot fer it though – ther were a lot o' rough peyces o' rock at th'edge o' th'weyter.

"Ey 'adna gone inter th'weyter moer than a two-threy yards when ey let ite a yell an' started comin' ite aggen. So wey ran dine ter 'im an' 'elped 'im ite. Ey'd gashed 'is foot on one o' them lumps o' rock, an' ey was bleydin' larke a stuck pig.

"Wey carried 'im ter one o' th'ises an' begged some bandage an' iodine fer 'is foot. Ey didna 'afe squeyl when th'iodine went into this cut.

"It turned ite ey lived in Leyk an' ey'd come dine on 'is bike fer a swim. Wey didna larke th'idea o' 'im bikin' back ter Leyk with 'is foot – it wanted stitchin' up be reyghts. Wey towd 'im ey ought leyve 'is bike at th'steetion an' go back on th'treen.

"But ey said ey couldna 'cos ey adna got any money. Be th'tarme wey'd give 'im 'is treen-fare weyd got a penny left ower.

"Wey tuk 'im an' 'is bike dine ter th'steetion an' left 'im fer weet for th'treen. But dust know sirree, wey'd barely got rind th'corner when this lad come beltin' ite o' th'steetion on 'is bike! Th'young monkey 'ad pocketed th'treen-fare an' was going larke th'wind fer Leyk. Wey didna wish 'im any 'arm – wey just 'oped is rabbits deyd.

"But ther was moer trouble fer come. Wey decided fer go wom be a different road, but wey musta tuk a wrung turnin' somewheer 'cos wey finished up on Biddle Moer. Be th'tarme wey got dine inter Tunster it was goin' dark. Wey'd gotten carbide lamps on th'bikes but wey 'adna got any carbide. Wey wonna reknin' on beyin' ite after dark.

"Wey funt a shop in Tunster an' talked th'mon inter sellin' us a pennorth o' carbide. That's aw th'money wey'd got left after this lad 'ad done th'dirty on us.

"But that carbide musta bin a bit o' owd stock – it ony lasted ter Silverdeele. Wey were just comin' up be th'Stone-wo' when th'bobby stopped us. Ey said: 'Wot an yer got in them lamps – glow-worms?'

"So wey towd 'im th'sad story abite givin' this lad from Leyk us money, an' abite this Tunster mon wot 'ad sowd us a pennorth o' owd carbide.

"Th'bobby said: 'Dunna tell me any moer, ar conna stand it. Yer breekin' me heart.' But ey musta 'ad a soft spot somewheer 'cos ey put 'is little black book back 'in 'is pocket, an' towd us wey'd better push th'bikes through Silverdeele 'cos th'sergeant was up at th'top end be th'Bush.

"Fer tell thee th'truth ar was abite ready fer a spell o' walkin'. That theer bike-saddle was as 'ard as bell-metal. Every tarme ar went ower a bump ar felt as though me backbone was goin' come up through th'top o' me yed."

Some reyght ronk stuff

In recent years there has been a widespread revival of interest in some of the old-fashioned remedies.

It has been fostered no doubt by overcrowded doctors' waiting-rooms and by a growing awareness of some of the side effects of our modern drugs. Many village families in times of sickness resort to lotions and potions made from recipes handed down through several generations.

"In me young dees ar used get dosed reglar with aw sorts o' stuff," said Jabez. "Ar can sey me mother nar, standin' theer with summat or other in a cup an' a teyspoonful o' jam, or a lump o' sugar, fer 'tice it dine.

"It seymed as though th'woss it teested th'moer it did yer good, an' th'otter th'better. Ar've 'ad some reyght ronk stuff pushed dine me gullet in me tarme.

"An' when any on us got a bit chesty in th'winter, wey were rubbed back an' front with goose-greyse or camphorated oil, an' if wey got chilbleens wey 'ad 'em rubbed with a lump o' taller. Ar reckon if somebody 'ad struck a match wey shoulda aw gone up in fleemes

"Mind thee, ar've got a lot o' feeth in some o' th'owd remedies, an' ar con vouch fer a lot on 'em. Ar conna remember th'last tarme ar went sey a doctor.

"Ar reckon fresh air's th'best medicine but when ar've bin off side ar've awwees managed dose mesel' one road or another. But fer aw that ar larke fer think thers a doctor 'andy if th'wost comes ter th'wost.

"Ar 'ad a stiff showder a two-threy yeer back, so ar meede mesel' some embrocation. It's an owd recipe wots bin in th'family fer donkey's yeers. Me mother used meeke many a lot on it. Th'cricketers an' th'footboers used swear be it.

"When ar was rubbin' me showder ar couldna 'elp but think abite a woman from Augers Bonk wot come ter me mother fer some o' this embrocation.

"'Er'd kenched 'er kney an' 'er was 'obblin' abite larke a leeme duck. Me mother put 'er some in a bottle an' towd 'er fer rub 'er kney with it th'last thing at neyght an' th'fost thing in th'mornin'.

"But th'next tarme me mother seyd this woman 'er 'ad such a teele fer tell. It appeyers as this embrocation 'ad welly put peed ter 'er owd mon. Th'poer feller 'ad gotten a terrible 'ackin' cough an' ey kept a bottle o' glycereyne an' 'oney on th'wesh-stand.

"One neyght ey'd wokken up coughin' an' got ite o' bed an' groped 'is wee ter th'wesh-stand fer a swig o' this cough-stuff. 'Is missus wok up an' funt 'im on th'floer spittin' an' splotherin' an' feyghtin' fer 'is breath. 'Er couldna meeke ite wot was th'matter with 'im an' it was many a wheyle afoer ey could tell 'er.

"Wot dust think 'ad 'appened sirree? After 'is missus 'ad rubbed 'er gammy leg with this embrocation 'er'd put th'bottle on th'wesh-stand. Th'owd mon 'ad 'ad a swig ite o' th'wrung bottle. It's a wonder ey didna cock 'is toes up 'cos it's gotten turpentine in it an' vinegar an' ammonia!

"It's a funny thing, though, but after ey'd gotten ower this dose o' embrocation ey reckoned 'is cough was better than it 'ad bin fer yeers.

"Ar'll tell thee wot mey an' they could do with," said Jabez. "Wey could do with some o' that 'air-growin' ointment wot th'doctor meede up fer me brother.

"Ey was ony abite twelve or thirteyn at th'tarme but aw 'is air started foin' ite. Ey finished up as bawd as an egg – th'lad adna got a solitary 'air on 'is yed. It was some sort o' diseyse – ar dunna reyghtly remember th'neeme on it – but th'doctor said it was brought on be nerves or mebbe a shock o' some sort.

"Me mother was 'eart-brokken. 'Er couldna think o' any shock ey'd 'ad woth mentionin'. 'Er said 'er'd tanned 'is backside pretty reglar, an' 'er'd clipped 'is ear-'ole from tarme ter tarme. But th'doctor said that wonna exactly th'kind o' shock ey was thinkin' abite.

"Th'poer lad 'ad fer sit with 'is cap on in schoo' so's ey wouldna luk ser naked. Th'doctor meede some special ointment up fer put on 'is yed. It 'ad fer bey rubbed on tweyce a dee. Me mother used laub this ointment on neyght an' mornin', an' ther was a two-threy tears rubbed in with it an' aw.

"Th'doctor reckoned it'd grow 'air on a billiard-bo' but nowt much seymed fer bey 'appenin' ter th'lad's yed.

"Then one dee me mother said 'er thowght summat was growin'. 'Er shyted ter me feyther fer go an' get next-doer's magnifyin' glass. Th'pair on 'em went ower th'lad's yed with this glass. Me mother was certain 'er could sey somethin' but me feyther said ey was blessed if ey could.

"But me mother was reyght – in a dee or two wey could aw sey it. It was larke a bit o' that wheyte mowd wot sometarmes grows on owd cheyse. It was sproutin' up aw ower 'is yed!

"Me mother went an' 'ad a bit of a scryke – 'er was that pleysed fer think as th'lad was goin' 'ave a thatch on 'is knapper aggen.

"Every dee it grew a bit lunger, an' then th'next tarme th'doctor come ey said it'd aw got bey sheeved off. Me mother went reevin' mad. 'Er said if ey thowght 'er was goin' let anybody sheeve that 'air off ey'd got another think comin'.

"But th'doctor put 'is foot dine, an' me feyther got 'is reezor ite an' sheeved it off as cleyn as a whistle.

"When it started growin' aggen it come a lot thicker an' strunger. Th'owd doctor meede 'em sheeve it off threy tarmes awgether, an' in th'end th'lad 'ad as grand a yed o' 'air as yer could find in a dee's march.

"But me mother couldna rest 'till 'er'd funt ite abite this shock th'lad was supposed fer 'ave 'ad. 'Er got it ite on 'im. It turned ite ey'd neyly drynded in a poo'.

" Ey'd got fast amongst th'branches o' a trey wot 'ad fell in th'weyter. Th'young beggar 'ad never said a word abite it, but from wot wey could gether ey musta bin lucky fer get ite o' this poo' alive.

"Ar reckon it's a pity th'owd doctor's jed – mey an' they coulda done with a jar or two o' that ointment. Or dust think weyn left it a bit too leete?"

Goin' Yelly Castle

Years ago on Good Fridays the village often had a deserted look.

The traditional way of spending this holy day was to walk through the fields and along the country lanes to Heleigh Castle.

"Ar dunna remember th'fost tarme ar went," said Jabez. "Ar couldna bey very owd 'cos me feyther towd me ey carried me th'biggest part o' th'road.

"When ar was a bit owder, ar used go with that owd woman ar towd thee abite – thee knowst, 'er wot used tak us blackberryin'. 'Er'd collect abite ten or a dozen on us an' tak us aw Yelly Castle. "Wey tuk some butties an' 'ot-cross buns with us in a basket. Th'owd woman awwees carried a sweyt or two fer them as behaved thersel's, an' a stick ite o' th'edge fer them as didna. Mind thee, ar never seyd 'er use it – 'er'd ony got waggle it at thee.

"When wey got dine inter th'valley wey stopped fer put summat in that bruk wot used run under th'road. It was weyter wot thee pumped ite o' th'pit, an' everythin' yer put in it turned ter stone. Th'owd woman wouldna let us paddle in it though – 'er said wey'd finish up with stone feyt!

"Wey awwees cawed at Devil's Well fer a drink o' weyter an' a sit dine. Ar've offen wondered whey it's cawed a well – it's awwees bin a spring as lung as ar've known it.

"Th'weyter was as cleyer as crystal an' as cowd as oky. Ther was a greet big lump o' rock with a flat top wot yer could sit on.

"Folks said th'devil 'ad carried it theer but ey'd fergotten pick it up aggen after ey'd 'ad a drink o' weyter. Some o' us young uns were a bit frittened fear lest th'owd lad come back fer 'is lump o' rock!

"When wey got ter th'castle wey 'ad push an' pull th'owd girl up th'bonk. It's a stiffish climb but 'er reckoned it wouldna bey a proper Good Freydee if 'er 'adna bin reyght ter th'top. Mind thee, ther wonna much fer luk at when thee gotst theer just a couple o' owd wo's mostly.

"But betweyn theyse two wo's ther was a bit of a 'oller in th'grind an' yer could just sey th'arch o' a doer-wee with threy stone fithers at th'top on it.

“Ar promised mesel’ ar’d go an’ dig dine ter this doer when ar grew up ‘cos ther’d larkly bey some owd treasure dine theer. But ar never got rind ter it.

“Wey’d plee arind th’castle a bit an’ ‘ave us ‘ot-cross buns, an’ then th’owd woman ‘ud tell us it was tarme fer bey meekin’ tracks fer wom. ‘Er gethered us up larke an owd ‘en with ‘er chickens.

“If wey lagged behind ‘er used shyte: ‘Come on. Just keyp puttin’ one foot in front o’ th’other. Nowbody ever got anywheer with standin’ still.’ An’ when one on us fell dine ‘er said: ‘Up yer get. Them as never fo’ dine never larn fer get up.’

“Ther’s a lot o’ truth in wot ‘er said. Ar reckon th’owd lass knew a thing or two, dustna they sirree?”

Pleein' with fire

"Me mother used reckon as if moer than two lads got 'gether yer could luk ite fer trouble," said Jabez.

"Ther was an owd seein' wot 'er used tell us – ar conna remember th'exact words, but it was summat abite one lad beyin' a lad, two lads beyin' 'afe a lad, an' threy lads beyin' a devil.

"Ar reckon th'owd soul was abite reyght an' aw. It seyms as though threy lads'll do things wot none on 'em 'ud ever think o' doin' on ther own.

"When ar think abite th'mischief ar used get into, it was neyly awwees when ar was with two or threy other lads. Mind thee, wey didna go arind 'ittin' owd folks ower th'yed but wey did some nowghty things fer devilment.

"Wey used get inter a lot o' trouble pleein' with fire. Now matter wot wey were doin' dine th'feylds or in th'woods wey awwees seymed fer finish up with a fire o' some sort. It's a wonder wey wonna burnt death a tarme or two.

"Ar remember one Satdee – it'd bey tote th'back-end – wey'd built a cabin dine th'feylds. Ther used bey some owd cottages dine be th'razzervoy wot 'ad bin partly knocked dine.

"Folks cawed 'em th'top-outs. In one pleece, ther was some steps dine ter wot musta bin a cellar. Wey shifted aw th'owd bricks an' rubbitch ite o' this cellar – it was a grand spot fer a cabin. Aw it needed was a roof an' a fire-greet.

"Wey went rind th'back o' th'dirt-tip at th'pit an' funt a couple o' sheyts o' corrigeeted iron an' a lenth o' pipe wot nowbody seymed fer bey usin'.

"Theyse peyces o' corrigeeted iron were just reyght fer puttin' a roof on this cellar, an' wey put clods on top on 'em so's nowbody 'ud sey 'em. Then wey meede a fire-greete ite o' owd bricks an' a two-threy peyces o' scrap-iron. Th'ony thing showin' above grind was th'chimney-pipe. "Ar remember wey 'ad a lot o' trouble leyghtin' th'fire – everythin' was damp. So wey went dine ter th'pit aggen fer some lamp-oil.

"Wey knew owd Bassy in th'lamp-'ice wouldna give us any, so two on us went ter th'front o' th'lamp-'ice fer talk ter 'im wheylst th'other lad crept rind th'back an' filled an owd popbottle full o' oil.

"Th'fire soon got goin' with this lamp-oil an' wey decided meeke some chips. Wey'd bin teeter-pickin' in th'wik an' th'farmer 'ad peed us a tanner a dee an' two roasters.

"So ar went up th'village ter th'shop fer get some lard, an' th'other two went lukkin' in th'middins fer a chip-pon. Aw thee could find was a big tin-can wot 'ad 'ad soft-soap in, but wey wonna fussy.

"Wey sat rind this fire-greete weetin' fer theyse chips cook. Ee! thee didna 'afe smell good – wey could 'ardly weet fer 'em go bryn.

" But aw of a suddin, summat seymed fer go wrung with th'fire – it stopped drawin'. An' then fleemes shot ite an' th'chip-pon fell ower an' set aleyght,.

"Th'cabin was full o' smoke an' burnin' fat, an' wey were foin' ower one another tryin' get ite. Thee shouldsta seyn us tryin' get up them cellar steps threy abreast?

"Dust know wot 'ad 'appened sirree? Somebody 'ad sneyked up an' tuk one o' th'clods off th'roof an' stuck it dine th'chimney. Wey never funt ite who it was but ey neyly 'ad threy roasted lads on 'is 'ands.

"Mind thee, it wonna th'cabin wey were bothered abite, it was that tin-can full o' wom-meede chips. Wey couldna fergive 'im fer that."

Postin' a letter

"When me feyther or me mother writ any letters thee used send mey fer fetch some stamps from one o' them owd cottages at th'fer end o' th'village," said Jabez.

"Ar dunna know whey theyse folks sowd stamps – thee couldna meeke any money ite on it, could thee? Mind thee, when ar come think abite it, p'raps thee larked a bit o' company nar an' aggen.

Thee seymed fer bey lonely folk. Thee didna mix very much – kept thersels ter thersels, if thee knowst wot ar meyn.

"Th'mester was a stiffish little mon with a wheyte beard an' 'tash. Ey'ad a rind red shiny feece an' lukked a bit larke Santa Claus. 'Is missus was a taw thin woman, abite as fer through as a tram-ticket. 'Er awwees lukked sad, as though somebody 'ad just towd 'er some bad news.

"Ther was a growed-up son wot lived with'em an' ey was fer everlastin' carvin' wood up with a big kneyfe. Tell thee th'truth, ar was a bit frittened on 'im. Ey never said nowt but ey used stare at me with this big carvin'-kneyfe in 'is 'and.

"Ey meede bundles o' spills – some fer sellin' an' some fer 'is feyther leyght 'is pipe with. Th'kitchin' awwees smelt o' burnin' wood an' bacca smoke. Ar remember it meede me eyes weyter everytarme ar went in.

"Besides spills, this youth used meeke some things cawed totee-ponies. Thee were larke little spinnin'-tops. Ey carved 'em ite o' cotton-spoles, an'then stuck a peyce o' wood with a sharpened end dine th'ole in th'spole. Ey sowd 'em fer a a'penny apeyce.

"Sometarmes me mother let me buy one if ther was a a'penny cheenge ite o' th'stamp money. Ey seymed everser pleysed when ey sowd one, an' it was woth a a'penny fer stop 'im starin' at me. "Theyse stamps ar was tellin' thee abite were kept in a big bacca-tin in th'top drower o' th'dresser. Th'missus's eyes wonna aw that good an' 'er used 'ave tak th'stamps ter th'winda or ter th'lamp so's 'er could sey fer rip 'em off

"Nar an' aggen 'er run ite o' stamps an' then thee 'adst weet fer th'postman come empty th'letter-box. Ey come on a big red bike from Silverdeele an' ey mostly carried a two-threy stamps with 'im.

"Ey used come trudgin' up th'leene in aw sorts o' weather pushin' this big bike. Ar never knowed 'im fer bey leete. Moer offen than not ey was a bit early but ey wouldna empty that letter-box 'till th'big wetch in 'is westcot pocket said 6 o'clock.

"Ar remember this postman 'ad a funny road o' gettin' on 'is bike. It 'ad a little step stickin' ite at th'end o' th'back axle. Ey'd point th'bike dine th'bonk an' put one foot on this back-step, an' then 'urtle 'imsel' fer'erd onter th'saddle.

"Us lads awwees reckoned ey'd come a cropper one o' theyse dees -- an' ey did. One neyght ey missed th'saddle awgether an' dropped dine onter th'back mud-guard. It didna do th'poer mon any good at aw. Th'bike shot off dine th'bonk withite 'im, an' it ran up th'edge-bonk an' buckled th'front wheyl.

"Ey 'ad walk back Silverdeele 'owdin' this buckled wheyl off th'grind. But ey was back th'next neyght fer empty th'box dead on 6 o'clock.

"Wey never seyd 'im use that back-step aggen though."

Spring-cleynin' feyver

"As soon as Eyster was turned," said Jabez, "me mother used get th'spring-cleynin' feyver.

"Everywheer 'ad fer bey rimsoned ite from top ter bottom, an aw th'peentin' an' peeperin' 'ad fer bey finished afoer th'Charity. Me feyther couldna abide th'ice beyin' turned upside dine. Ey used get bad-tempered an' go arind chunterin' ter 'imsel'. But it was now use – ey'ad put up with it.

"Ey wonna any good at theyse decoreetin' jobs, an' ey kept ite o' th'road as much as ey could. But me mother awwees meede 'im do th'wesh-'ice an' th'closet. Aw ey did was slap some wheytewesh on th'top 'afe an' some gas-tar on th'bottom 'afe an' ey'd finished. Me mother did aw th'rest o' th'peentin' an' peeperin' 'ersel'

"One o' mar jobs as a lad was cuttin' th'edges off th'rowls o' peeper with a pair o' scissors. Some folks ony cut one o' th'edges off but me mother 'ad both on 'em cut off. It was woe betide thee if thee didstna cut 'em straight, an' ar'll swear some o' them rowls o' peeper were 'afe a mile lung.

"Ar remember one yeer when me feyther musta said summat abite it takkin' a lung tarme fer do th'front bedroom. Ey was tellin' me mother it'd bey a lot quicker fer cut up aw th'rolls o' peeper inter th'reyght length afoer 'er started.

"Me mother said: 'Awreyght then, they get 'em cut.' So ey did. But wot dust think ey did, sirree? Ey was in that big of a sweat fer get it done ey went wrung with 'is measurin'.

"Ey cut up five rowls o' peeper inter lengths an' thee were aw a foot short. Me mother 'ad a dicky fit. It tuk 'er tweyce as lung fer peeper th'room 'cos 'er 'ad go rind on 'er 'ands an' kneys puttin' little peyces o' peeper aw rind th'bottom o' th'wo's.

"Me mother used do aw th'ceylin's an' aw. 'Er was a dab 'and at it 'till one yeer 'er kenched 'er back an' 'ad give it up.

"Ther was a bloke dine 'Ommerend wot did ceylin's fer a bob apeyce if yer funt yer own stuff. 'Er was fer sendin' fer this 'Ommerend mon but me feyther said ey wonna peein' now shillin' fer 'ave a ceylin' done – it wonna woth it. Ey said ey'd rather do it 'imsel'.

"So me mother mixed 'im a bucket o' distemper an' towd 'im get crackin'. Ee! they shouldsta seyn 'im sirree. Ey distempered everythin' 'cept th'ceylin'.

"Ey' was flirtin' it aw ower th'opper, an' it was runnin' dine 'is arm an' droppin' off th'end o' 'is elber. Me mother was runnin' rind tryin' weyp th'splashes off th'wo's an' th'floer afoer thee dreyd. But 'er couldna keyp up with 'im – ey was geenin' on 'er.

"Just nar me mother said: 'Owd thee whip a bit sirree. Theyt supposed fer bey puttin' that stuff on th'ceylin'. It's reenin' distemper dine 'ere larke mad, an' ar'm gettin' soaked. Dust think it'd bey a good idea if ar fetched me umbrella?'

"Me feyther stopped an' lukked dine at 'er, an' then ey bost ite laughin'. Ey said: 'From wheer ar'm standin' theyt beginnin' fer luk a bit larke one o' them damnation dogs. Ar reckon wey'd best send fer that mon from 'Ommerend. If ey'll do a ceylin' fer a bob, ey's eether a lot better at it than mey or else ey's a devil fer punishment!' "

Weshin'-dee

"Weshin'-dee inna wot it was," said Jabez. "Them owd weshdees were donkey-work fer a woman – scrubbin' an' rubbin', dollyin' an' manglin'. Mind thee, a lot on 'em seymed fer thrive on it.

"Didst ever 'ave a go at twistin' one o' them owd dolly-pegs in a tub-full o' weshin'? It was a maulin' job, but th'road some o' them women went at it theedst think ther lives depended on it.

"An' dust remember them big owd mangles with wooden rowlers? Tuk a bit o' turnin' them did. Get a blanket in one o' them mangles an' thee 'adst fer 'ave muscles larke an ox fer shift them rowlers rind.

"Folks seym fer do ther weshin' any dee in th'wik nar, but Mondees awwees used bey weshin'-dee. Ther musta bin acres o' weshin' 'angin' ite in th'village on a fine Mondee.

"Them wesh-'ice chimneys 'ud bey belchin' smoke an' sut at th'crack o' dawn. Thee used burn a lot o' sleck an' owd rubbitch under them boilers – it didna 'afe meeke a puther. Ar awwees reckoned ther was moer smoke an' sut knockin' arind th'village on a wesh-dee than any other dee in th'wik.

"In th'summer, th'colliers' weyves got th'owd mon fer leyght th'boiler-fire afoer ey went on th'dee-shift at th'pit.

"Ar remember one owd collier tellin' me abite wot 'appened one Mondee when ey got wom.

"Ey'd lit th'boiler afoer ey went work but it didna luk as though 'is missus 'ad done any weshin'. Ther 'adna bin any reen, so it couldna bey that. Ey come ter th'conclusion 'er must bey bad. That was th'ony other thing wot 'ud stop 'er weshin' on a Mondee.

"When ey went in th'ice 'er was sittin' dine at th'teeble with er arms fowded. It was awwees a bad sign when 'er fowded 'er arms an' clamped 'er lips 'gether. 'Er didna luk bad but 'er lukked reyght narked abite summat.

"Ey said: Yer didna wesh then.' 'Er didna answer 'im an' ey could tell be th'luk in 'er eye as ey was in th'dog-'ice fer summat or other.

"Ey thowght ey'd better 'umour 'er a bit, so ey said: Didna yer feyl up ter it, duck?" Er got up an' went ter th'oven an' snatched 'is dinner ite. Then 'er slat it on th'teeble an' said: 'Ar conna wesh with 'ot air!'

“Ey thowght ter ‘imsel’: ‘Ot air? Wot on earth’s ‘er on abite? Th’woman’s losin’ ‘er buttons.

“So ey said ter ‘er: ‘Sit thee dine in that cheer me owd sparrer. Ar must bey goin’ deaf. Ar coulda sworn thee saidst summat abite weshin’ with ‘ot air.’

“Er said: ‘They ‘eerdst me reyght. They didstna put any weyter in th’boiler afoer thee litst th’fire. Be th’tarme ar got up th’bottom o’ th’boiler was red-’ot. An’ that wonna th’end on it eether. Ar tipped a bucket o’ weyter in it fer cool it dine an’ th’bottom dropped ite. So wot at goin’ do abite it?’

“Ey scrat is yed a bit an’ then bost ite laughin’. ‘Ee!’ ey said. ‘They adst me worried fer a bit. Ar begun fer think things were gettin’ on top on thee. Ar reckon ar’ll ‘ave go dine Silverdeele an’ get thee a new boiler. Ther’ll bey now living with thee’till theest done thee weshin’. If cleanliness is next ter godliness some o’ yo’ women should bey in th’runnin’ when it comes ter pickin’ a new Seent or two.’ “

Face beats edgercation

"Did ar ever tell thee abite owd Simpy an' them Wheyte Leghorns?" asked Jabez.

"It 'appened when th'manager at th'pit tuk it in 'is yed fer keyp some powltry. Ey 'ad a big 'en-cote built at th'back-side o' th'powder magazeyne. Th'joiner from th'pit meede it.

"Ey used best timber, an' ey put proper windas an' doers in it. It was a grand affair – good enough fer anybody live in. Ther was a greet big run fer th'ens with a seven-foot weyer-nettin' fence aw rind it.

"When it was aw finished, th'manager 'ad theyse Wheyte Leghorns sent be passenger-treen from Uttoxeter. Two dozen 'ens an' a cock ther was. One o' th'surface-men went with a 'oss an' cart ter th'steetion fer pick 'em up an' bring 'em dine ter this posh 'en-cote.

"Th'manager was weetin' fer 'em, an' ey wonna 'afe proud o' theyse brids. Ey said thee were th'very best yer could get an' ey'd peed th'earth fer 'em. Ey come dine aggen th'last thing at neyght fer put 'em bed – ey wouldna trust anybody else fer do it.

"But wot dust think, sirree? Ther wonna a sign o' them Wheyt Leghorns th'next mornin'! Thee'd aw gone. Every odd un 'ad vanished in th'neyght. Ee! th'manager wonna 'afe vexed.

"Ey sent fer th'bobby straight awee, an' th'pair on 'em picked up a treel o' wheyt fithers. Thee follered theyse fithers across feylds an' through woods an' ower'edges an' ditches. Thee were expectin' fer come across theyse Leghorns any minute.

"But just nar this treel o' fithers stopped jed – reyght in th'middle o' a big feyld just iteside Betley. Th'pair on 'em went aw rind th'feyld but ther wonna another fither fer bey seyn, let alone a Leghorn.

"Theydst never guess wheer thee were! Them two dozen 'ens wonna moer than 'afe a mile from th'encote. Thee were aw under owd Simpy's bed with ther necks wrung an' th'cock was in th'stew-pot in Simpy's mate's oven. Th'owd rascal 'ad got this mate fer 'elp 'im, an' peed 'im fer lee this treel o' cock-fithers fer put th'bobby off th'scent.

"It was awwees a bit of a mystery wot owd Simpy did with them two dozen Leghorns. It wouldna surprise me if ey didna get 'is missus tak some on 'em ter th'Potteries.

"Practically every Satdee 'er used come ite o' th'ice carryin' two owd tin 'at-boxes. Thee'd bey full o' summat or other – pheasants, partridge, rabbits – anythin' wot owd Simpy 'ad managed fer pick up.

"Sometarmes 'er walked aw th'wee ter th'Potteries, but if 'er'd got a copper or two 'er'd get on th'tram at Silverdeele.

"Er soon emptied th'boxes, an' Simpy 'ud bey sittin' at wom weetin' fer 'is money an' 'atchin' summat else up. "Th'manager 'ad this 'en-cote moved up inter 'is gardin wheer ey could keyp 'is eye on it.

"But owd Simpy couldna leyve well alone. Th'cheyky monkey went ter th'manager's 'ice an towd 'im ey'd 'eerd abite 'is bad luck with them Leghorns, an' then sowd 'im a broody 'en an' some eggs wot ey'd nicked from somewheer.

"Thee knowst, it's true wot folks see – face beats edgercation any dee."

Partridge an' rabbits

"Ar was talkin' ter a mon a wheyle back," said Jabez, "an' ey was tellin' me as when ey was a lad ey once 'elped owd Simpy ketch some partridge. This lad was flyin' a kite in th'feyld at th'back o' their 'ice.

"Just nar, ey spotted Simpy comin' alung th'edge-side with 'is gun. Ey come up ter this lad an' stood talkin' ter 'im fer a bit, an' then ey said: 'Thee seyst that theer gob o' rough gress tote th'middle o' th'feyld? Ar'll bet thee costna get thee kite fer fly reyght ower th'top on it.'

"Th'lad moved rind a bit 'till th'kite was flyin' in th'reyght derection an' then ey let a bit moer string ite. Owd Simpy patted 'im on th'yed an' said: 'Just 'owd it theer a minute or two.'

"Ey sneyked across th'feyld ter this rough gress with 'is gun cocked, an' ey wonna moer than a two-threy yards from it when a covey of partridge flew up from under 'is feyt. Ey let 'em 'av both barrels, an' two on 'em tumbled ter th'grind.

"Th'owd rascal musta known them partridge were theer, an' ey'd kidded 'em as th'lad's kite was an 'awk 'overin' ower 'em. Ey knew thee'd bey too frittened fer shift 'till ey was reyght on top on 'em.

"But ther come a tarme when owd Simpy got a bit too owd an' slow fer poachin', an' ey went workin' at th'Big-'ice dine Silverdeele. Thee tuk 'im on as odd job mon, an' ey did a bit o' geeme-keypin' fer 'em an 'aw.

"Ther was one tarme when ther was a visitor stoppin' at th'Big-'ice, an' one dee this bloke 'appened fer bey lukkin' through th'winda.

"Ey seyd owd Simpy runnin' rind th'feyld ketchin' rabbits with 'is 'ands an' poppin' 'em in a bag! Ey could 'ardly beleyve 'is eyes – ey'd never seyn a mon ketch rabbits larke that afoer.

"It turned ite as Simpy 'ad towd th'Mester as th'rabbits rind theer were in poer sheepe. Ey reckoned as ther'd bin too much in-breydin' an' thee neyded some fresh blood. Ey said ey knew wheer ther were some reyght good rabbits wot'd do th'trick, ony thee'd bey a bit expensive.

"So th'Mester 'ad give 'im some money fer go an' get 'em with. Simpy turned up with theyse rabbits in a bag, an' ey'd got a bill fer show ey'd peed fer 'em. Ey eksed th'Mester fer come an' wetch 'im let theyse rabbits loose.

"But wot dust think, sirree? Aw theyse rabbits were tame uns! Simpy knew thee wouldna go very fer, an' as soon as th'Mester 'ad gone ite ey went rind th'feyld an' gethered 'em aw up aggen. Ey was goin' sell 'em ter somebody else an' pocket th'money.

"If it 'adna bin fer that visitor, ey'da gotten awee with it an aw. Ey was as fawce as a cartload o' monkeys was owd Simpy

"Them as could affoerd it awwees 'ad new clothes fer th'Charity, – said Jabez.

"Th'Sundee Schoo' ran a clothing club fer 'elp folks ite. Yer peed a bob or two a wik aw th'yeer rind an' then yer drawed it ite just afoer th'Charity.

"Thee peed yer interest on yer money an' aw. Ar reckon a lot o' childer wouldna 'ad owt new if it 'adna bin fer th'Sundee Schoo'.

"A wik or two afoer th'Charity me mother used measure me up an' then fetch threy or foer suits from th'Co-op on appro.

"Er wouldna tak me ter th'shop 'cos 'er didna larke fer bey rushed inter buyin' things. 'Er could tak 'er tarme at wom an' 'ave a good feyl at th'stuff an' examine aw th'stitchin' an' sey if th'buttons 'ad bin sown on firm.

"It seymed fer tak 'ours fer try them suits on, an' in th'end er wouldna let me 'ave th'one wot just fitted me. Ar 'ad fer 'ave one wot was a bit big on me so's ar'd grow inter it.

"On Charity Sundee mornin' aw us young uns used walk rind in a procession fer show us new clothes off. Wey set off abite 'afe-past eight an wey walked miles.

"It's a funny thing but ar never remember it reenin' – it awwees seymed fer bey a roastin' 'ot dee. Ar used bey aw of a sweat in me new serge suit, an' me feyt 'ad blisters on 'em larke 'afe-cryns with me new shoes.

"Wey 'ad buns an' coffee 'afe wee through th'mornin', an' somebody awwees managed fer sheyd some coffee dine ther new clothes.

"After us dinner, wey 'ad fer bey in th'Sundee Schoo' just turned two o'clock ready fer go on th'steege. Th'wenches 'ad fer wear wheyte frocks on th'steege.

"Ar remember one yeer when ar was singin' a duet with one o' theyse wenches. Instead o' comin' in a wheyte frock 'er come in a breyght red un. Ee! it was a reyght bobby-dazzler. 'Er stood ite larke a soer thumb an' it fair put me off me singin'.

"Ther was a bloke neemed Ernie wot used sit on th'bottom row o' th'steege. 'Is job was fer sey we didna talk or fidget too much. But at th'service at neyght ey 'ad 'is 'ands full with them as fell asleyp.

"Wot with that big walk rind in th'mornin' an' aw th'excitement ther was awwees a little un or two wot fell asleyp on ther perches. Some on ‘em coulda dropped off th’steege onter th’floer if Ernie ‘adna bin theer fer ketch ‘em.

“Th’Chapel was awwees crammed full. Folks ‘ad fer come an’ ‘our or moer afoer service tarme if thee wanted bey sure o’ a seyt. Ar think ar towd thee abite that owd steward who was a dab-’and at packin’ folks in. It’s a wonder them Chapel wo’s didna start bulgin’ ite.

“Dust know, sirree, ar’ve seyn ‘im tak a fat un ite o’ a pew an’ put ‘im on a cheer an’ then put two thin uns in th’pew wheer ey’d ‘ad th’fat un from.

“Ar remember one yeer when th’minister’s weyfe turned up leete – wey were ‘afe-wee through th’fost hymn. Th’steward ‘adna got a seyt fer ‘er but ey didna larke th’idea o’ th’minister’s weyfe standin’ up. Ey tried pushin’ ‘er inter th’end o’ one o’ th’pews but ‘er said ther wouldna bey room fer everybody when thee sat dine.

“So ey said: ‘Ar’ll tell yer wot fer do missus – when yer get ter th’last line o’ th’hymn yo meeke sure fer sit dine fost, an’ them others’ll squeyze thersels in some road or other.’

“And thee did. But after th’service ‘er reckoned ‘er’d never bey th’reyght sheepe ever aggen.”

Larke two peys in a pod

"Ar've 'eerd tell as in th'owd dees th'feylds aw rind th'village were snived with little shaller pits," said Jabez.

"Them owd colliers 'ud sink a shaft an' bey drawin' coal in under a month. Thee used weynd th'coal up theyse shafts with wot thee cawd a gin-ring. It musta bin a bit larke a windlass but it was driven be a 'oss goin' rind an' rind in a cirtle.

"Across th'road from them two cottages at th'bottom o' th'leene ther were threy or foer little pits aw goin' at th'seeme tarme. Theyse pits were that shaller as when th'folks in them cottages were sittin' queyet thee could 'ear theyse colliers thumpin' an' knockin' underneyth 'em.

"At th'back o' th'cottages ther was a greet big sycamoer trey. It was said fer bey th'biggest trey fer miles arind. Th'owd folks reckoned it was ony th'roots o' this trey wot was owdin' th'cottages up! Ar dunna think ar'da bin eeble sleyp of a neyght wouldst they? Mind thee, th'trey's bin gone lung since but th'cottages 'anna fell dine yet.

"When theyse colliers 'ad gotten aw th'top-coals thee meede theyse shafts deyper an' drew coal an' weyter with a steym-injin' instead o' th'owd 'oss.

"Th'injin'-men at two o' theyse little pits were twin brothers neemed Dan an' Tum. Thee lived in one o' them two cottages, an' thee musta bin larke two peys in a pod.

"Ther own mother wonna awwees sure which was which, an' when thee were young 'er used buy 'em different coloured gansys.

"Ther was one tarme when one o' theyse twins 'ad brok a winda, an' th'mother didna know which on 'em 'ad done it.

"Neether on 'em 'ud own up so 'er decided fer scuft both on em. 'Er said 'er'd bey certain fer get th'culprit then.

"Th'fost un 'er threshed was Tum – 'er ketched 'im when ey come in fer 'is dinner. 'Er could tell it was Tum 'cos ey'd gotten 'is new blue gansy on. Th'one with a red gansy didna come wom'till bed-tarme but 'er was weetin' fer 'im with th'strap.

"Ey kept tryin' fer tell 'er ey'd 'ad th'strap at dinner-tarme, but 'er tuk now notice on 'im an' give 'im one or two extra fer tellin' lies.

"But th'lad was tellin' th'truth – 'er'd threshed th'seeme un tweyce!

“It turned ite as Dan ‘ad seyn Tum ‘avin’ th’strap at dinnertarme so ey’d kept ite o’ th’road fer th’rest o’ th’dee. Tote bedtarme th’pair on ‘em ‘ad bin pleein’ dine th’feylds an’ Tum ‘ad ripped is new blue gansy on some barbed weyer. Dan ‘ad spotted ‘is chance o’ workin’ a quick un on Tum. Ey towd Tum ey’d swop gansys with ‘im so’s ey wouldna get another threshin’ fir rippin’ ‘is new gansy.

“Tum didna twig nowt’till ey walked in th’ice with Dan’s red gansy on an’ got th’strap aggen.

“Tum used see ey wouldnera minded ser much but it wonna ‘im wot brok th’winda – it was Dan!’

Ar'll bet it was Betsy

"Ar reckon summat's 'appened ter eggs," said Jabez.

"When ar was a lad wey 'ad a little egg-tarmer with sand in it. It tuk just threy minutes fer th'sand run ite o' th'top inter th'bottom. If thee putst thee egg in boilin' weyter it was done just reyght when th'sand 'ad finished runnin' ite. But thee costna boil an egg in threy minutes nar – it taks moer larke five minutes afoer theer done.

"Mind thee, p'raps eggs are still th'seeme an' it's tarme wots altered. P'raps a minute's ony 'afe as lung as it used bey. It's a certin fact as ther dunna seyme fer bey as much tarme theyse dees.

"Me mother used send me ter th'farm fer fetch eggs in me cap. Everybody cawed th'farmer's weyfe Mam, but 'er never 'ad any childer o' 'er own. 'Er didna keyp a big lot o' 'ens, an' when thee wentst fer some eggs Mam neyly awwees 'ad fer go rind th'encotes fer find some.

" 'Er used tak an owd boiler-stick with 'er – one o' them sticks wot th'women got th'clothes ite o' th'weshin'-boiler with.

Mam 'ud firk under th'ens with this boiler-stick an' lift 'em up off th'neyst so's 'er could get at th'eggs. Ar used go rind with 'er an' 'owd me cap ite fer 'er put th'eggs in.

" 'Er 'ad neemes fer aw theyse 'ens, an' 'er used talk ter 'em. 'Er'd see: 'Nar then, Edith, yo'll 'ave do better than that. Ar've seyn bigger eggs in a pigeon-cote.'

"Ther was one or two wot tried peck Mam when 'er put 'er 'and underneyth 'em fer tak th'eggs. 'Er'd see: 'Yo peevish little bitch! Bite th'and wot feyds yer, would yer? Ar'll settle yoer ash one o' theyse dees me leedy.'

"Sometarmes one o' th'ens 'ud bey sittin' theer squawkin' its yed off an' er'd see ter it: 'It's now use sittin' theer aw dee squawkin' – them as shyte th'loudest dunna lee th'most eggs.'

"Then ther was one neemed Betsy. 'Er an' Mam, didna get on aw that well. Mam reckoned as Betsy ate tweyce as much corn as any o' th'others but ony leed an egg once in a blue moon. 'Er threatened Betsy with th'roastin' tin if 'er didna mend 'er wees.

"One dee when us lads were messin' arind th'farmyard wey come across a neyst full o' eggs under th'edge at th'back o' th'orchard. Ther musta bin two dozen eggs in this neyst. One o' Mam's 'ens musta bin leein' awee!

"Wey gathered theyse eggs up an' stuffed 'em in us pockets. Wey were fer goin' dine inter th'wood an' cookin' em. But one o' theyse lads 'appened fer squash one when ey was puttin' it in 'is pocket. It was a bad un, an 'it didna 'afe stink.

"Wey started laughin' at this lad an' ey didna larke it. Ey slat one o' theyse eggs at mey an' it ketched. me at th'side o' th'neck. That un smelt woss than th'fost un, an' th'laugh was on mey. "In th'end wey finished up peltin' one another with theyse eggs, an' every odd un was addled.

"Ar've offen wondered which o' Mam's 'ens was leein' awee – ar'll bet it was that owd Betsy."

Th'choir trip

"In th'owd dees, ther wonna many folk wot could affoerd fer go on ther 'olidees larke thee do nar," said Jabez.

"Some o' th'owd uns never saw th'sey, an' some on 'em 'ad never bin further than th'Potteries.

"At Stoke Weekes a two-threy families managed fer go on th'treen on one o' them dee excursions ter Blackpoo' or Rhyl. Thee didna 'afe tak some snappin' an' clobber with'em.

"Mind thee, thee wonna allowed fer tak any big luggage with em on theyse dee trips, so thee used split it up inter little bags an' parcels. Fer sey 'em set off theedst think thee were goin' fer a wik or a fortneet. Thee went ready fer anythin' from a snowstorm ter sunstroke.

"On Whit Mondee ther was awwees th'choir trip. Thee talked mey inter goin' Sytheport with 'em one yeer. It's a lung wee fer go, inna it? An' dust know sirree, ar never seyd th'sey aw th'wheyle ar was theer.

"Thee reckoned th'tide 'ad gone ite, but ar think somebody musta pulled th'plug ite. Th'sand was as dry as a desert. Ar coulda done a roarin' treede if ar'd 'ad a camel or two with me.

"Ther was a bloke theer givin' rides in an aeropleene. Ar dunna know wheer ey'd dug it up from – it wonna 'afe a ramshackle affair. Th'wings seymed fer bey fastened on with bits o' owd weyer, an' it'd gotten moer patches on it than me owd gardnin' jacket.

"It seemed fer tak it a terrible lung tarme fer get up off th'grind. Ar towd th'choir it put me in mind o' that owd Khaki Campbell duck wot thee 'ad at th'farm. This duck was awwees tryin' fly.

"It used go beltin' across th'farm-poo' many a tarme a dee, flappin' its wings larke mad. But it never managed fer get up off th'weyter an' in th'end it brok its neck be-runnin' full tilt inter th'bonk at th'fer end o' th'poo'.

"Anyroad, threy or foer o' th'choir were fer 'avin' a go on his aeropleene. Five bob it was fer go rind in a cirtle ower Sytheport. Judder was fost fer go – 'im wot was awwees pullin' other folks's legs. But this tarme it was Judder wot 'ad 'is leg pulled.

"Somebody give 'im all umbrella all' towd 'im if th'wost come ter th'wost ey could awwees come floatin' dine with this umbrella ower 'is yed. An' then one o' 'is mates went up an' shuk 'ands with 'im an' said: 'Thee didst tell me ar could 'ave thee gowd wetch when anythin' 'appened ter thee didstna?'

"Somebody else offered give th'mon an extra 'afe-dollar if ey'd loop th'loop when Judder was in. But Judder said: Dunna they do nowt o' th'sort. Ar get giddy spells when ar just bend dine fer leece me shoes up.'

"Wey aw weeved ter Judder as ey went cirtlin' rind, but th'owd soul lukked frittened death. Thee managed fer land awreyght but when Judder climbed ite ey was aw of a cowd sweat.

"Ey said: 'Dust know, Jabez, aw th'wheyle ar was up theer ar kept thinkin' abite wot 'appened ter that Khaki Campbell duck. Ar wished thee 'adstna towd me abite it.' "

Th'Sundee Schoo' treyt

"A wik or two after th'Charity wey used 'ave th'Sundee Schoo' treyt," said Jabez.

"Th'fost thing wey 'ad was a reyght good blow-ite in th'schoo'-room. Th'teebles were full o' snappin'. Ther were pleetes piled up with aw sorts o' butties an' cakes, an' greet big bowls o' jelly an' fruit, an' gallons o' tey in mugs.

"Wey used stand up an' sing th'Grace but wey 'ardly got th'Amen ite afoer th'battle commenced. Dust know, sirree, that snappin' vanished off them teebles larke snow in summer. Theedst think some o' them lads 'ad bin clemmed death.

"When everybody 'ad 'ad ther fill wey aw went dine th'cricket feyld fer plee geemes an' run reeces. But some o' us lads were that full o' snappin' wey could 'ardly walk, let alone run.

"Wey 'ad a lot o' singing geemes larke: 'Eringes an' lemons, an' poer Mary sits a-weepin', an' threy jolly fishermen, an' Lucy Lockett.'

"Th'wenches used tuck ther frocks inter ther bloomers fer th'reeces. Ther were sack-reeces, an' threy-legged reeces, an' egg-an -spoon reeces.

"One yeer a lad got inter trouble fer cheytin' in th'egg-an'spoon reyce. Ey was yards in front o' everybody else but just as ey got ter th'finishin' line ey fell dine ower a gob o' gress.

"Th'egg-an'-spoon went flyin' ite o' 'is 'and, but somebody nowticed a funny thing. Th'egg didna fo' ite o' th'spoon. Dust know wot ey'd done? Ey'd stuck th'egg dine with a lump o' chewed toffee: It tuk a long tarme fer 'im live that dine.

"An' then one yeer ther was neyly a tragedy. One o' th'wenches started chokin' an' goin' blue in th'face. Th'poer lass couldna tell em wot was th'matter with 'er, an' nowbody seymed fer know wot fer do fer th'best.

" 'Er'da bin a gonna if it 'adna bin fer Big Harry. Ey was a greet big mon – ey lukked larke a giant ter us lads.

“Big Harry tuk one luk at ‘er an’ then fanged ‘owd on ‘er be th’feyt an’ ‘eld ‘er upside dine. Then ey give ‘er such a clout on th’back with th’flat o’ ‘is ‘and.

Summat shot ite o’ ‘er mythe larke a bullet ite o’ a gun. Wot dust think it was sirree? It was one o’ them ther aniseyd bo’s.

“But mostly thee were ‘appy tarmes, an’ at th’end o’ th’dee wey were dished ite with an eringe an’ a bag o’ sweyts apeyce.

“Aw th’children were served alarke whether thee went Sundee Schoo’ or not. Wey didna think this was reyght, an’ one yeer wey grumbled abite it.

“Th’owd teycher wot was givin’ theyse eringes an’ sweyts ite lukked us up an’ dine an’ said: ‘Yo lads wot go Sundee Schoo’ anna learnt much, ‘an yer? Dunna yer reyd yer Bibles or summat? Th’good Book says as them wot sneaps a little child ‘ad better go an’ drynd thersels.’

“Wey ‘adna got any answer ter that.

Th'burnin' 'ay-stack

"Dunna that mown gress smell grand?" said Jabez. "It taks me back ter th'owd 'ay-meekin' dees.

"Us childer used 'ave some grand tarmes in th'ay-feyld. Th'wenches built 'ises an' shops with it, an' th'lads meede ships an' forts an' pleed sowjers.

"Wey were awwees a bit sad when it was dry enough fer bey carried, but wey used foller every load ter th'farm, an' then ride back on th'empty waggins. Th'men 'ad ther bread an' cheyse an' ale under th'edge. an' wey fetched bottles o' weyter an' jambutties an' sat with'em.

"When it'd aw bin carted th'farmer's weyfe – Mam wey cawed 'er – used put on 'er mob-cap an' go aw ower th'feyld getherin' up bits o' 'ay with a big wooden rake. Nowt was weested on Mam's farm.

"One yeer, thee built a 'ay stack betweyn th'end o' th'big barn an' th'farm-poo. Slap-bang up aggenst th'poo' this stack was. Ther'd bin a good crop o' gress an' it was a middlin' big stack.

"But one Satdee af'noon word went rind as this stack was on fire. 'Ast ever noticed as synd travels faster than leyght in a village?

"Thee'st ony got whisper summat at one end o' th'village an' in next ter now tarme them at th'fer end know wot thee'st said. Sometarmes thee dustna even 'ave whisper it – thee'st ony got think it! Them savages with ther drums anna a patch on us when it comes ter passin' th'word on.

"Anyroad, it wonna many cracks afoer th'farmyard was full o' folks gawpin' at this stack-fire. Th'ony weyter fer put it ite was th'farmyard pump an' th'poo'. Th'fire was on th'poo'-side o' th'stack so th'men waded inter th'poo' with buckets an' anythin' else wot'd 'owd weyter.

"Mam got inter a panic – 'er went in th'ice an' come rushin' ite with two chambers in one 'and an' a wesh-stand jug in th'other.

"But th'men in th'poo' were soon in trouble. Th'wind was blowin' th'smoke reyght across th'poo' an' thee couldna sey wot thee were doin'. Them as wonna chokin' death were slattin' weyter in aw derections – mostly ower one another.

"Then th'farmer 'ad a breen-weeve. Ey said if thee couldna put th'poo' on th'stack whey not put th'stack in th'poo'? This stack was built on baulks o' timber with gaps beween 'em.

"Ther was some lung planks in th'barn, so th'farmer got th'men fer push theyse planks under th'stack betweyn th'baulks. After a lot o' gruntin' an' groanin' thee managed fer tip this stack ower inter th'poo'.

"Ther was one thing thee 'adna allowed fer though. When th'stack went inter th'poo' th'weyter come ite! Aw them folks standin' gawpin' rind th'poo' got drenched.

"An' it wonna cleyn weyter eether. Wot with pond-weyd an' jack-sharps an' frogs an' farm-yard mud ther wonna 'afe some squeylin' an' bad language.

"But theest got fer admit it was a good road o' puttin' th'fire ite, wonna it?"

Rinkers an' a feyght

In days gone by the children of the village were not the only ones to play games in the street.

On warm summer evenings, the menfolk brought out their dartboards and ringboards, and hung them on the walls of the farm-buildings which backed onto the village green.

And across the road from the Chapel there was a flat patch of hard-packed dirt where they played the game of "rinkers". The "rinkers" were the size of billiard balls. Four of them were placed on the circumference of a yard-wide circle scratched on the ground and the fifth was put in the centre.

Spectators sat on the nearby field-gate or squatted under the hawthorn hedge. The object of the game was to knock the rinkers out of the circle by flirting a "shotty" at them. But the "shotty" must never come to rest inside the circle.

To the uninitiated it looked a simple enough game, but for the expert it was full of subtle moves and cunning tactics. The rules had a vocabulary of their own which included such terms as "slips" and "fudging", "brushes" and "crogging-on".

The exponents of the game developed such a delicacy of touch and such a sound judgement of rebound angles and velocities that they could position their "shotty" to the inch. The games went on for hours and there was much good-natured banter from spectators and players alike.

"Mind thee," said Jabez. "ar once seyd one geeme finish up with a feyght. Ther was two brothers pleein' at th'tarme an' thee'd bin rubbin' one another up th'wrung road fer a lung wheyle.

"Ar dunna think th'row was anythin' do with th'geeme o' rinkers. Ther was summat else behind it, but ar dunna think anybody knew wot it was. Thee were both grown men – thee'd bey in ther thirties an' thee oughtera known better.

"Anyroad, just nar th'eldest let fly at 'is brother, an' then thee both started slammin' inter one another. Some o' th'men were fer separatin' 'em but th'others said thee'd best let 'em feyght it ite. "So thee stood in a ring rind 'em fer sey fair plee.

"Th'mother an' th'feyther o' theyse brothers lived just across th'road, an' when thee 'eerd th'commotion thee both come ite an' shyted at 'em fer stop it. But it was now good – thee were goin' at it 'ommer an' tungs, an' th'blood was beginnin' fly.

"Th'mother got that upset 'er lukked as if 'er was goin' pass ite, so somebody fetched 'er a glass o' weyter an' a cheer fer sit on so's 'er wouldna miss nowt. 'Er sat theer dabbin' 'er eyes on er apron an' shytin': 'Oh! th'shame on it, an' reyght in front o' th'Chapel an' aw!'

"But after a bit 'er got up off th'cheer an' went in th'ice an' come ite with th'owd strap. 'Er pushed 'er road through th'crowd an' said: 'If yer goin' behave larke little lads ar'll give yer both th'buckle-end o' th'strap, as owd as yer are!'

"Er leed abite 'er with this strap'till theyse brothers 'ad fer defend thersels. And that was th'end o' th'feyght. 'Er meede 'em sheeke 'ands an' then thee went back an' finished th'geeme o' rinkers. "But nowbody let 'em ferget th'dee thee 'ad th'strap in front o' th'Chapel."

A greet big brid

"Ar've never 'ad any trouble at gettin' up in a mornin'," said Jabez. "An' once ar've wok up ar conna lay in bed. Mind thee, when ar'm asleyp ar tak a bit o' rousin'. Ar go sort o' jed if thee knowst wot ar meyn.

"But ar remember one mornin' when ar got wokken up with a start – somebody was knockin' me doer dine! It was still dark iteside an' it synded as though somebody was doin' ther best fer breek in.

"It put me in mind o' th'tarme owd Whacker wok up in th'neyght an' thowght ey 'eerd somebody rummagin' abite in 'is parlour.

"Ey went ter th'top o' th'steers an' shyted dine: 'If it's money they't lukkin fer ar'll come dine an' 'elp thee – ar've never bin eeble find any in this 'ice.'

"Anyroad, this bangin' on me doer started up aggen. An' then ar 'eerd somebody shytin' me neeme. Ar thowght ter mesel': 'Jabez lad, it synds as though they't wanted pretty bad. Theydst better get theesel' up sharpish.'

"So ar jumped ite o' bed, an' th'fost thing ar did was stub me toe on th'leg o' a cheer. Then ar couldna find me trysers anywheer. When thee't a 'eavy sleyper it taks thee a bit fer get thee bearin's, dunna it?

"In th'end, ar 'ad fer leyght th'candle so's ar could sey wot ar was doin'. An' aw this tarme me doer was 'avin' th'stuffin' knocked ite on it. Ar was comin' ter th'conclusion as nothin' less than murder 'ad bin done somewheer or other.

"When ar opened th'doer ar seyd it was owd Johnty's widder wot lived at th'top o' th'leene. Ee! 'er was in a state. 'Er was ony 'afe-dressed an' 'er started rattlin' that fast ar couldna tell wot 'er was on abite. It turned ite as 'er was tryin' tell me ther was a greet big brid in 'er kitchin'.

"So ar said: 'An yo got me ite o' bed in th'middle o' th'neyght fer tell me that?'

"An' then ar remembered – 'er was frittened death o' brids o' aw sorts. 'Er didna mind 'em at a distance but 'er just couldna abide 'em flutterin' rind 'er. Aw th'use used go ite on 'er. Thers a lot o' women larke that, thee knowst.

" 'Er said 'er'd gone dine in th'dark fer get a drink o' weyter an' this greet big brid 'ad come at 'er. 'Er 'adna seyn it but 'er reckoned it must bey a yard across or moer.

"Ar couldna think wot sort o' brid it'd bey. Th'most larkly thing 'ud bey an owl wot 'ad come dine th'chimney.

"Anyroad, ar tuk me blackthorn stick with me fer bey on th'safe side – them owls con bey a bit nowghty at tarmes. When wey got ter th'ice it was breekin' dee-leyght.

"Ar went inter th'kitchin a bit careful larke with me stick at th'ready. Ar tuk a quick luk rind but ar couldna sey a brid anywheer.

"An' then ar spotted wot it was – just comin' ite from behind th'sofa. Ar put me stick dine an' bost ite laughin'. Dust know wot it was sirree? That greet big brid was threy young throstles. Thee musta got in th'ice th'neyght afoer an' 'er 'adna seyn 'em.

"Ar picked 'em up an' tuk 'em ite ter 'er. Ar said: 'Thee dunna luk a yard across ter mey. Ar reckon they't goin' tell me thee flew at thee threy abreast!'

"But th'woman wonna in a fit state fer 'avin' 'er leg pulled, an' 'er'd gotten a mornin's cleynin'-up fer do. Them throstles 'ad bin terrible loose in th'neyght."

"Afoer thee put tarmac on th'leene ther was open ditches dine eether side." said Jabez.

"Th'road-mon used come an' cleyn 'em ite when th'fancy tuk 'im. Th'owd feller ony 'ad two speyds – dead-slow an' stop.

"It tuk 'im a terrible lung wheyle fer do it, but credit wheer credit's due – ey meede a rattlin' good job on 'em.

"Ey used put th'muck ite o' theyse ditches in little piles at th'side o' th'road, an' then ey'd bring a 'oss an' cart fer tak it awee.

"When me sister was little 'er couldna resist theyse piles o' muck ite o' th'ditches. 'Er used go trippin dine th'leene jumpin' on 'em an' squashin' 'em flat. Be th'tarme 'er'd finished 'er shoes an' stockin's wonna fit fer bey seyn.

"Er 'ad many a good tankin' fer it. Th'owd road-mon used go reevin' mad 'cos aw 'is nice little piles o' dirt were as flat as poncakes.

"Ar remember th'tarme me mother was goin' tak me sister inter 'Castle fer do a bit o' shoppin'. 'Er'd gotten 'er Charity clothes on, an' a pair o' them leather gaiters.

"'Er'd pestered me mother death fer 'ave theyse gaiters on. It wonna 'afe a performance puttin' 'em on, sirree. Thee'd gotten a dozen or moer buttons up th'side wot 'ad fer bey fastened with a button-'ook.

"Nar an' aggen me mother 'ud get a bit o' flesh caught up in th'ook an' me sister wouldna 'afe yell. Me mother used see: 'Pride must abide – yer would 'ave 'em on.'

"Anyroad, wheylst me mother was gettin' 'ersel' ready 'er sent me sister dine th'leene fer ask them folks at th'bottom-end if thee wanted owt bringin' back from 'Castle.

"But th'road-mon 'ad bin cleynin' th'ditches ite an' ther were aw theyse little piles o' dirt on th'road! 'Er managed fer resist th'temptation fer a bit but it couldna last – 'er just 'ad fer squash some on 'em flat.

"Er got theyse gaiters laubed up with muck, so on th'road back 'er decided 'er'd sneyk inter th'closet an' weype it off afoer me mother seyd it.

"But 'er didna get th'chance 'cos owd Dr. Maloney come trottin' up behind 'er in 'is pony an' trap. Ey was comin' fer 'ave a luk at me granfeyther, so ey give 'er a ride wom.

"Theydst never guess wot was up with me granfeyther. Ey'd 'ad hiccups fer a fortneet! Dee an' neyght ey kept it up.

"Nowbody in th'ice was gettin' ther proper sleyp, an' it was that lide as folks could 'ear 'im in th'streyt. Meede 'im as weyk as a kitten it did.

"Thee'd tried aw roads fer stop it. Ey'd drunk gallons o' weyter, an' ey'd 'eld 'is breath 'till ey went purple. But th'doctor 'ad gotten a new idea.

"As soon as ey'd gone upsteers ter me granfeyther me mother said ter me sister: 'Ar'll settle yoer ash young lady when th'doctor's gone.'

"But aw of a suddin everythin' went queyet – th'owd feller 'ad stopped hiccupin'!

"Me mother ran up an' funt th'doctor on th'bed. Ey was reyght on top o' me granfeyther! Ey was kneylin' on 'is stomach with aw 'is weight. Judgin' be th'road me granfeyther was groanin' it wonna doin' 'is stomach any good but it cured 'is hiccups.

"Th'owd feller slept th'clock rind tweyce, an' me mother was that chuffed 'er fergot aw abite me sister's leather gaiters.

Stuck in th'pantry

"Did ar ever tell thee abite th'tarme ar got stuck in th'pantry?" asked Jabez. "Th'pantry's under th'steers thee knowst, at th'top of th'cellar steps.

"One dee ar'd meede mesel' a bit o' custard fer go with some stewed rhubub ite o' th'gardin. Ar put this custard on th'pantry floer fer go cowd. Ar larke me custard thick, dustna they? Ar conna stand it when it's larke yeller weyter.

"Ar put a good dollop o' this cowd custard on me rhubub, but ther was summat matter with it. It was larke eatin' custard an' cinders. Dust know wot it was sirree? It was peyces o' owd plaster wot'd fell inter it! Th'plaster under th'steers was perishin', an' lumps on it kept foin' dine inter th'pantry.

"Ar kept tellin' mesel' ar'd 'ave do summat abite it. But thee knowst wot 'appens – yer keyp puttin' theyse jobs off, dunna yer? Anyroad, ar thowght ter mesel': Jabez lad, theydst better do summat abite that pantry. If thee getst much moer plaster dine thee theyt get bunged up solid!

"Ar decided th'best thing fer do was knock aw th'owd plaster ite an' put a proper ceylin' in lower dine. Then ar could put a doer at th'top o' th'cellar-steps an' shut th'pantry off from th'cellar.

"So ar shifted aw th'snappin' ite o' th'pantry an' set abite it. Ar'd gotten a bit o' timber wot'd do fer th'joises fer this ceylin'.

"Everythin' went grand 'till ar got ter th'fer end. Ther was one moer joist fer put in, but th'ony road ar could get at it was be standin' on top o' a pair o' steps balanced on th'cellar-steps.

"Ar shoulda 'ad moer nowce. Ar was just puttin' this joist in when th'pair o' steps went from under me an' went clatterin' dine th'cellar. Ar managed fer fang 'owd o' th'joist an' stop mesel' from follerin' th'steps.

"But after ar'd gotten me breath back it began fer dawn on me as ar was stuck! Ther wonna room fer pull mesel' up on ter th'joises an' ar dostna drop dine on ter th'cellar steps – ar shoulda brokken me leg, or woss.

"So theer ar was, danglin' dine in th'pantry. Ar felt such a foo'.

"Ar shyted a tarme or two but ther was nowbody abite. It musta bin 'afe an 'our or moer afoer ar 'eerd footsteps comin' up th'leen.

"Ar shyted at th'top o' me voice, an' it turned ite fer bey two colliers from Augers Bonk in ther pit-dirt. One on 'em was neemed

Ephraim, but ar ferget t'other uns neeme – ey was a fereigner wot 'ad come from Biddle road.

"Th'pair on 'em come ter th'pantry doer an' stood lukkin' at me danglin' dine. Eph said: 'Well ar'll bey jiggered. Owd Jabez's gone an' 'ung 'imsel' in th'pantry"

"Ar towd 'em fer stop messin' abite an' get me dine. But this Biddle mon said: 'Ey anna meede a very good job on it – ey's still talkin'!' Eph laughed an' said: 'Ee sirree, it'd tak moer than that fer stop owd Jabez talkin'!'

"Thee got me dine in ther own good tarme an' ar finished th'job off. But it's a funny thing – ar've gone reyght off rhubub an' custard."

In th'dentist's cheer

" Thers a lot o' talk theyse dees abite childer's teyth rottin'-off soon after theen growed 'em," said Jabez.

"Thee seym fer 'ave moer sweyts naradees than wey 'ad – p'raps that's got summat do with it. Mind thee, ar've 'ad me fair share o' tooth-ache.

"Me mother used put pepper on us teyth when thee ached. Ar dunna know whether it cured it or not, but it tuk yer mind off it. Yer forgot abite th'tooth-ache when th'pepper got on yer tungue.

"Ar wish me teyth 'ad bin as good as me feyther's. Ey was in 'is eighties when ey deyd but ey'adna got many missin'.

"Dust know, sirree, ey wouldna use a tooth-brush. Ey reckoned as th'bristles meede little 'oles in yer gums an' them little bugs burrered dine theyse 'oles an' rotted yer teyth. Ey awwees cleyned 'is teyth with 'is finger dipped in sawt.

"Ar remember 'avin' me fost tooth ite dine Silverdeele. th'dentist was a greet big mon – ey 'ad th'reyght sort o' build fer a blacksmith.

"When ey was ready fer tak thee tooth ite ey used send fer 'is missus. Er'd come up behind thee with 'er 'ands clasped 'gether an' pull thee yed back onter th'cheer.

"It was larke 'avin' thee yed in a vice – thee couldstna shift it. Then this greet big mon 'ud come at thee with 'is pliers an' ther was nowt on earth wot'd stop thee tooth comin' ite. Ar reckon them pair coulda yanked th'tusk ite o' an elephant.

"Th'fost tarme ar 'ad gas was at a dentists dine 'Castle. When ar come rind ar felt aw ower me mythe with me tungue an' ar said: 'They 'astna takken any ite!'

"Ey said ey 'adna bin eeble get anywheer near me. Ey reckoned ar'd gone reevin' mad under this gas, an' if ar 'adna bin fastened dine in th'cheer ar shoulda kilt somebody.

"Ar couldna understand it – ar'd bin as 'appy as anythin'. Ar'd 'ad such a grand dreym. Ar dreamt as everythin' wot 'appened ter us was awwees fer th'best.

"Ther was now neyd fer folks worry thersels abite owt, 'cos everythin' fitted 'gether larke one o' them jig-soer puzzles. An' then reyght at th'end o' this dreym ar was goin' bey shown God!

"Ar thowt ter mesel: Jabez lad, thee tarme's come – this's th'end o' th'road. Th'good Book says as nowbody's seyn God an' lived.'

"But dust know, sirree, ar wonna a bit frittened. Somebody drew a sort o' veil back, an' wot dust think ar seyd? Ar seyd a face wot kept cheengin'. As soon as ar recognised who it was it cheenged ter somebody else.

"It kept cheengin' an' cheengin' 'till ar musta seyn practically aw th'folks ar've ever known. But ar never seyd God.

"An' then ar remember thinkin' ter mesel': 'P'raps that's th'answer – God's everybody an' everybody's a bit o' God.'

"It was a funny dreym, wonna it?"

It meekes thee wonder

I found Jabez sitting at his cottage door cleaning an old gun. I had never known him to use a gun, so it was something of a surprise to see him handling one.

As I greeted him he said: "They needstna bey frittened ar anna goin' shoot thee with it. Not just yet anyroad. It's bin in th'family fer donkey's yeers, but ar've never bin eeble lee me 'ands on it 'till nar. A nice lukkin' gun, inna it? But it once kilt a mon thee knowst."

He went on with his cleaning for a while, and then he said: "It 'appened one Stoke Weekes Sundee. Dust know that valley wot runs from 'Ommerend ter Cradduck's Moss? Well, ther was a geeme-keyper lived in a cottage on top o' th'bonk at th'fer side o' th'valley. It appears ey'd gotten 'imsel' in th'bad books o' a gang o' poachers. Thee'd gotten a grudge aggen 'im ower summat or other.

"Anyroad, this perticler Weekes Sundee neyght some on 'em were weetin' fer 'im come wom. It was just gettin' dark when thee spotted a mon comin' across th'feyld ter th'cottage. Thee wetched 'im go past th'leyghted cottage winda, an' then just as ey'd gotten 'is 'and on th'latch one on 'em let fly with this gun.

"But wot dust think, sirree? It wonna th'geeme-keyper – it was 'is son. It turned ite ey'd bin ter th'evenin' service at Aidley Church an' ey'd walked back across th'feylds. Ey was kilt stone jed, an' ther was ructions up.

"Th'bobbies arrested a youth ite o' th'village fer this murder. Thee'd funt this gun 'idden in th'granfeyther clock. It's an owd muzzle-loader thee knowst, an' theyse bobbies 'ad funt a peyce o' wad near th'geeme-keypers cottage wot matched up with some wads in a drawer in this youth's ice. So that was that.

"Th'nextmornin' was Stoke Weekes Mondee an' me granfeyther 'appened fer bey standin' at th'top o' th'feylds when another youth ite o' th'village come up ter 'im an' towd 'im ey was goin' dine Aidley police steetion.

"Ey said ey was goin' tell 'em this youth thee'd arrested adna done it. Ey reckoned as th'pair on 'em 'ad bin 'gether on th'Sundee neyght. But when ey got dine Aidley th'bobbies arrested 'im an' aw.

"After th'trial theyse two youths were 'anged at Stafford gaol. One on 'em was only 19 yeers owd, an' th'other was just turned 20. Mind thee, ther was a lot o' folks rind this road wot didna think thee'd done it.

"A good many yeers after it 'appened ther was an owd mon in th'village wot seymed fer know summat abite it. When ey was in 'is cups, ey used 'owd 'is fost finger up an' tell folks: 'This's th'finger wot pulled th'trigger.' "An 'there was another mon dine Leycitt wot sent fer an owd local preycher when ey was on 'is death-bed. Just afoer ey pegged ite ey confessed ter takkin' part in a shootin'. It meekes thee wonder, dunna it?

"Dust know, sirree, when ar come think abite aw th'bother this gun meede in th'village ar dunna know if ar want owt do with it nar ar've got it."

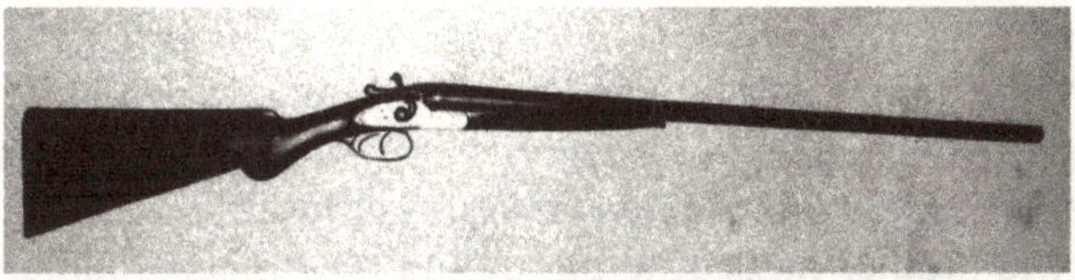

The gun which Wilfred inherited and was said to be the gun which 'kilt a mon'

Th'village doctors

"Folks seym fer go ter th'doctor a lot moer than thee used do," said Jabez.

"Ar dunna know whether it's 'cos folks get bad oftener or if it's 'cos thee dunna 'ave fork ite every tarme thee go. In th'owd dees yer 'ad fer bey at death's doer afoer yer 'ad th'doctor.

"Mind thee, at one tarme ther were threy doctors wot used come inter th'village. Some folks 'ad th'Aidley doctor, some 'ad th'Meedley doctor, an' some on 'em swore be th'Silverdeele mon.

"Th'Aidley doctor used bey in 'is element if ey could do a bit o' operatin'. If thee wentst dine ter th'surgery ey'd lance thee a boil, ar tak thee a couple o' teyth ite, or set thee a bone on th'spot.

"Ar remember one tarme when ey come sey me feyther. Ey'd gotten pleurisy an' ey was in a bad wee. As it 'appened me brother was off work at th'seeme tarme with a abscess under 'is arm.

"Me mother 'ad bin powlticin' it with red-'ot linseyd meyl. When th'doctor seyd it ey said it wanted openin' up, ony ey 'adna got 'is tranklements with 'im. But ey didna intend missin' th'chance o' doin' a bit o' carvin' up.

"Dust know wot ey did, sirree? Ey tuk 'is pen-knife ite an' sharpened it on me feyther's razor-strop. Then ey dipped it in boilin' weyter an' firked this abscess ite larke gettin' th'worm-'ole ite o' a tater. Me brother passed ite but ey 'ad now moer trouble with 'is abscess.

"Th'Meedley doctor awwees meede 'is own medicines up. Ey ad some black stuff wot was reckoned fer bey grand fer bad stomachs.

"Owd Martha in th'village used swear be this black medicine. 'Er'd 'ad a bad stomach fer yeers but one dee er'd run ite on it.

"So 'er got a couple o' lads fer walk ter th'surgery at Meedley fer 'ave 'er bottle filled up. 'Er give 'em th'money fer th'medicine an' a penny fer themsel's.

"When thee got dine Leycitt thee stopped fer 'ave a luk at th'sweyts in th'Post Office winda. Reyght in front o' th'winda ther was some lumps o' Spanish juice, so thee bought a pennorth betweyn 'em.

"Thee were just abite fer set off aggen fer Meedley when one o' theyse lads lukked at 'is mate an' 'ad a bright idea.

"Ey'd noticed as this other lad's chops an' tungue were as black as club ten with suckin' this Spanish juice. Ey said if thee put some on it in th'bottle with some weyter it'd luk just larke th'doctor's black medicine. It'd seeve 'em walkin' ter Meedley an' back, an' thee could pocket th'medicine money.

"So th'young monkeys put some o' this Spanish juice in th'bottle an' shuk it up with some weyter ite o' one o' them taps at th'back o' th'Leycitt 'ises. When thee give Martha th'bottle 'er said. 'Ee, yo are good lads, an' it anna tuk yer lung go Meedley an' back 'as it? Yer musta run most o' th'wee.'

"Thee kept ite o' Martha's road fer a dee or two but 'er never said nowt abite th'black medicine. Ar've awwees said as a lot o' theyse medicines are nine parts weyter an' one part o' faith. Ar reckon some on 'em do yer good if yer think thee wull."

Th'tin bath

"A lot o' folks used 'ang ther tin-baths up on th'wo' in th'backyard," said Jabez. "But one o' th'ises in th'village 'ad a posh un. It wonna one o' them oval uns – it was a lung narrer un, an' thee used 'ang it up on th'wo' at th'backside o' th'closet.

"It musta bin abite six foot lung with 'andles at th'ends.

"Mey an' this other lad decided it'd meeke a good boat if ony wey could get it dine th'feylds ter one o' th'poo's. Wey knew theyse folks wouldna want it 'till th'Freydee neyght – that was when thee aw 'ad ther baths.

"So wey spied us chance when theyse folks wonna in. Wey unhooked it off th'wo' an' balanced it on th'top o' th'gardin 'edge. Then wey went rind inter th'feyld an' pulled it ower.

"Wey dostna tak it through th'village 'cos everybody knew whose bath it was. So wey' ad carry it reyght rind th'village. Wey crept alung th'edge-bonks as much as wey could fear lest ther was anybody knockin' abite.

"Wey thowght wey'd try it ite on that little poo' wheer th'Independent pit used bey. It floated awreyght, an' wey could ardly weet fer 'ave a go in it.

"But wot dust think, sirree? As soon as wey got inter this bath it settled dine on th'bottom – th'poo' was too shaller.

"But wey wonna goin' bey done ite o' us fun. Wey decided tak it ter 'Ommerend razzervoy – wey knew ther'd bey plenty o' depth theer.

"So wey mauled it through th'wood an' ower th'stiles an' put it in th'weyter. Ee! thee shouldsta seyn us tryin' get inter it. It was larke tryin' get on a 'oss wot 'adna bin brokken in. It kept bobbin' up an' dine, an' tippin' ower.

"When wey did manage fer get in it wey 'ardly dost move th'flippin' thing kept tryin' tip us ite. Wey paddled it arind a bit with us 'ands but it was th'ockerdist boat ar've ever bin in.

"But ther was woss fer come. Wey got a bit too venturesome, an' th'next thing wey knew wey were both in th'weyter. When wey were comin' up fer air th'owd tin-bath went past us on its road dine ter th'bottom o' th'razzervoy. It sunk larke a stone.

“Wey swum ter th’side o’ th’razzer an’ got us breath back. Wey couldna sey this bath anywheer. Mind thee, it wonna surprisin’ ‘cos th’weyter was larke bryne soup – folks used drynd ther dogs an’ cats in it thee knowst.

“But some road or other wey’d got get this bath ite an’ put it back on th’closet wo’ afoer bath-neyght on th’Freydee.

“So th’next mornin’ wey went dine with a peyce o’ clothesline an’ a pot-’ook. Wey were reckonin’ on gettin’ this pot-’ook under one o’ th’andles. Wey spent aw dee fishin’ fer that bath. Thee wutstna credit some o’ th’things wey pulled ite o’ that razzervoy. But wey never funt th’bath, an’ fer aw ar know it’s still theer. Ar beleyve ther was ructions up when theyse folks come fer ‘ave ther baths on th’Freydee neyght.”

'Arvest tarme

"In me young dees," said Jabez, 'ar used think spring was th'best part o' th'yeer. Aw th'growin stuff in th'feylds an' woods was young an' fresh. Some road or other ar felt as though ar was part on it – it was good fer bey alive.

Ar still larke th'Spring but ar dunna feyl th'seeme abite it anymoer. Naradees Autumn's me feevourite 'cos ar'm gettin' reype an' meller mesel'.

Ar luk forrerd ter th'arvest tarme but it inna wot it used bey. Mind thee, th'owd kind o' harvest was 'ard sloggin' work an' ther was nowt much in thee pocket at th'end on it. Things 'ave cheenged a lot since then – some on 'em fer th'best an' some on 'em fer th'wost.

But when thee comst reckon it up things anna altered aw that much reyght dine at th'bottom. It's ony th'methods o' farmin' wots cheenged. It dunna matter wot sort o' fancy macheynery yern gotten, yern still got put th'seyd in th'good earth an weet fer th'sun an' th'wind an' th'reen fer do its work.

With aw us cleverness wey conna manage withite neeture. Ar've never 'eerd tell of a mon meekin' a little bleede o' gress yet, let alone a ear o' corn.

Thee knowst, thers summat abite th'arvest Festival as still attracts folks ter th'Church. It's a pity thee dunna get th'urge a bit offner – it'd meeke aw th'difference ter theyse little village Chapels.

Th'owd Chapel folks used caw it th'arvest Thanksgivin', an' some on 'em used give things thee couldna affoerd.

Ar've known a lot o' poer folks who oughta etten th'stuff themsels instead o' givin' it ter th'Chapel. On th'other 'and, some folks get th'wrung idea abite th'arvest.

Ar remember one woman who'd got a greet big marrer – ar adna better tell thee 'er neeme. Anyroad, 'er was goin' meeke some marrer an' ginger jam with it, but when 'er cut it across th'middle it was 'oller as a drum. Ther was 'ardly a bit o' flesh inseyde it.

Dust know wot 'er said sirree? 'Er said: 'Ee, inna it a sheeme, an' it's such a nice-lukkin' marrer. If ar'da known it was 'oller ar wouldnera cut it – ar'da sent it ter th'arvest.'

Ar dunna think er'd got th'reyght idea, dust they?"

Th'butcher-mon

"Dust remember me tellin' thee abite that butcher-mon ar used go rind with when ar was a lad?" asked Jabez.

"Ar used think ar was th'cock o' th'middin when ey let me drive that pony an' trap. Mind thee, ey didna tak much drivin' ey knew th'road better than mey.

At one tarme, ar used think that butcher-mon must bey one o' them theer millionaires. Ey was th'ony mon ar'd ever come across wot bought sweyts be th'afe-pynd.

Every Freydee ey cawed at th'village shop an' come ite with threy or foer big bags o' sweyts in 'is basket.

Wey delivered th'meyt on th'Freydee an' then ey went rind on th'Satdee fer collect 'is money. After wey'd gone aw rind th'village, wey used go ter some new 'ises up Keyle.

Dust know, sirree, ey reckoned yer could deliver ter them new 'ises at any tarme o' th'dee 'cos if ther was nowbody in yer could awwees get th'wik-end jynt through th'letter-box!

Ther was a trick ey used plee on me. Ey'd send me ter one o' th'ises with th'meyt an' then just as ar was comin' back ey'd start th'pony off dine th'road so's ar'd 'ave run after 'im.

But as soon as ar got a two-threy yards off th'back o' th'trap ey'd tickle th'pony up an' go a bit faster. An' th'faster ar run, th'faster ey'd meek th'pony go.

Ey sut theer in th'trap laughin' 'is yed off, an' ar think th'pony enjoyed it an' aw.

But ar put a stop ter 'is little trick one dee. Th'woman at th'ice 'ad peed me fer th'meyt cos 'er wonna goin' bey at wom on th'Satdee. So when th'butcher started th'pony off dine th'road withite me, ar just sut me dine at th'side o' th'road an' started pleein' jack-stuns with 'is money. When ey spotted wot ar was doin' ey wonna many cracks afoer ey turned th'pony rind an' come back fer me. Ey was frittened death lest some o' th'money rowled dine inter th'ditch.

That pony knew every 'ice wheer ey'd got stop. Ar remember ther was an owd woman lived in a little cottage just across from Keyle Church. 'Er could ony affoerd a bit o' scrag-end or summat larke that, but 'er awwees come ite fer give th'pony some lumps o' sugar. Ar con sey 'er nar in 'er lung black frock an' a peyce o' black velvet ribbin rind 'er throat. Ar think 'er musta seyn better dees 'cos er lukked a proper leedy.

Anyroad, one dee th'poer owd soul popped off pretty suddin an' thee tuk 'er across th'road ter th'Church yard. But nowbody 'ad towd th'pony as ther wouldna bey anymoer lumps o' sugar fer 'im.

Th'next Freydee when wey were up Keyle wey couldna get 'im passed that cottage. Th'butcher-mon got dine off th'trap an' wrostled with 'im but ey wouldna budge.

Ey showed 'im th'whip but it didna meek a scrap o' difference. It lukked as though wey were goin' bey stuck theer aw af'noon.

But just nar th'butcher got an idea. Ey got some sweyts ite o' one o' them big bags in th'basket an' gave th'pony one on 'em.

Theedst 'ardly beleyve it sirree, but ey wouldna shift 'til ey'd 'ad threy sweyts. That pony could kynt – that was th'number o' lumps o' sugar th'owd woman used give 'im.

An' then folks tell yer as 'osses anna 'uman."

"Ar'll tell thee wot ar've nowticed sirree," said Jabez. "Yer dunna sey as many drunks knockin' abite as yer used do. P'raps it's 'cos th'ale inna as strung as it used bey, an' theyse big drinkers come nigh ter bostin' afoer thee get drunk.

At one tarme yer could sey threy or foer drunks come totterin' back inter th'village at wik-ends. That last little bonk up th'leene used bey a bit too much fer some on 'em. Ar've seyn 'em get dine on ther 'ands an' kneys fer stop thersel's goin' backerds.

Th'wost un ar con remember was a big mon thee cawed Mad Alec. Ee! ey used get 'imsel' inter a reyght state. Thee shouldsta seyn 'im comin' up th'leene on a Satdee or Sundee neyght.

Ey was aw ower th'opper. It's a good job ther wonna any traffic abite in them dees – ey'da bin kilt a dozen tarmes ower.

Every Mondee when ey'd sobered up ey vowed an' declared ey wouldna touch another drop, but come th'wik-end yer'd find 'im lommerin' up th'leene aggen.

Ey come urtlin' inter th'Chapel one Sundee neyght just as thee were 'avin' a prayer-meytin'. Ey kept shytin' ey wanted bey seeved from th'deymon drink.

So thee seeved 'im. At anyrate thee got 'im sign th'pledge aggen. Ar reckon that mon musta 'ad a full set o' them pledges somewheer 'cos ey'd signed plenty on 'em. Mind thee, ey was that fer gone ey wouldna know whether it was a pledge-card or a pawn-ticket thee were givin' 'im.

One Satdee neyght, two blokes funt 'im at th'side o' that path wot runs across th'feylds from Augers Bonk. Ey was sittin' up th'edge-bonk with 'is yed in 'is 'ands blartin' an' goin' on abite summat or other.

Thee couldna get any sense ite on 'im fer a bit, but it turned ite ey was tellin' 'em fer go an' fetch th'bobby 'cos ey'd kilt a mon.

Thee yanked 'im on 'is feyt but ey wouldna go wom with 'em. Ey said ey was goin' weet theer'till th'bobby come so's ey could tell 'im abite this mon wot'd set on 'im.

Ey reckoned this mon 'ad come at 'im with a big stick, so ey'd 'ad a feyght with 'im, an' kilt 'im. Theyse two blokes come ter th'conclusion ey'd got a touch o' th'D.T.'s so thee moer or less carried 'im wom.

Anyroad, on th'Sundee mornin' one o' theyse blokes was goin' across th'feylds aggen fer a jar o' medicine afoer 'is dinner.

Ey 'adna gone very fer afoer ey come across a bowler-end, an' then a jacket.

A bit further inter th'feylds ey funt a pair o' trysers, an' then a big stick just larke owd Mad Alec 'ad said.

Ey stood theer scrattin' 'is yed fer a bit, an' then it dawned on 'im wot 'ad 'appened. Mad Alec musta wandered off th'path an' gone full tilt inter th'farmer's scarecrow!

Ey'd kilt it awreyght – ey'd tore it limb from limb! Ther were peyces on it scattered aw ower th'feyld. It's a good job it *wonna* a mon, wonna it sirree?"

Th'goose-gogs an' th'vicar

"Me granfeyther on me mother's side was mad on gardnin'," said Jabez.

"In th'summer ey'd do a couple o' 'ours in th'gardin afoer ey went work. Dust know, sirree, ar've known 'im bey trundlin' a barrer rind at foer o'clock in th'mornin'. Me granmother used see ter 'im: 'Ar wonder thee dustna bring that barrer bed with thee'.

Ey used put a lot o' stuff inter th'different shows, an' in th'Spring ey 'ad fer meeke 'is mind up if ther was goin' bey a frost in th'neyght. Ey'd go iteside an' study th'sky, an' 'ave a sniff or two o' th'air. Then ey'd come in th'ice an' tak a luk at th'fire fer sey if it was burnin' blue.

If ey decided it was going' bey frosty, everybody 'ad fer turn ite fer 'elp cover things up. Some o' th'plants 'ad fer bey covered with pots, some on 'em with straw, an' some on 'em with peyces o' muslin.

It wonna 'afe a palaver, an' woe betide yer if yer didna do it proper. Th'next mornin' everybody 'ad fer bey up with th'larke fer tak it aw off aggen.

Th'owd mon won a lot o' prizes with 'is goose-gogs. That part o' th'gardin wheer ey grew 'is goose-gogs was holy grind.

Nowbody dost set foot on it. Ar'll tell thee wot, sirree, none o' me granfeyther's family was born under a goose-gog bush – it wouldnera bin allowed.

Mind thee, them bushes were nowt fer luk at. Ther was ony abite 'afe-a-dozen little branches on 'em, an' ony abite threy or foer goose-gogs ter th'branch. But thee shouldsta seyn 'em – thee were as big as greyn-geeges.

Ey used feyd 'em with brandy! Ey'd put a drop or two o' brandy in th'palm o' 'is 'and an' kneyl dine at th'side o' th'bush.

Then ey'd 'owd 'is 'and up under every goose-gog so's th'end on it just dipped inter th'brandy. Ey said it swelled 'em up. Ar reckon thee'd a teested awreyght an' aw, but them goose-gogs wonna fer eatin'.

It's a pity th'owd Vicar from Augers Bonk didna know thee wonna fer eatin'.

Ey'd come sey me granfeyther abite summat or other, but ey wonna in. So ey said ey'd weet fer 'im come back. Me granmother meede 'im a cup o' tey, an' then ey said it was such a nice dee ey'd go an' 'ave a luk rind th'gardin.

Me granmother shoulda warned th'poer mon abite them goose-gogs, 'cos when me granfeyther was comin' up th'leene ey spotted this mon in th'gardin 'elpin' 'imsel' off th'show bushes!

Ee, ther was th'devil ter pee. Me granfeyther went berserk ey was fer gettin' th'double-barrel gun dine but me granmother begged 'im not fer do owt rash.

Ey was a good mon was me granfeyther, but ar reckon ey ruined 'is chances o' goin' heaven after th'things ey said ter that Vicar. "

Whey owd Isaac left 'is missus

"Ar larke things fer bey neyce an' teydy," said Jabez. "But ar conna stand theyse folks wot meeke a religion ite o' cleynin' an' polishin'.

Thee wouldstna remember owd Isaac, wouldst? Ey upped an' left 'is missus one dee, an' 'er never clapped eyes on 'im aggen. An 'it was aw on accynt o' 'er 'avin' this mania abite dust an' dirt.

Thee'd never bin eeble 'ave any childer o' ther own, an' ar think it musta affected 'er. 'Er was fer everlastin' rubbin' an scrubbin' an' cleynin' an' polishin'. 'Er was at it from mornin' 'til neyght. An' it wonna as though there was any neyd fer it – th'ice was awwees as cleyn as a new pin.

Dust know, sirree, 'er wouldna let owd Isaac set foot in th'ice with 'is pit-clothes on. 'Er used put some owd newspeepers dine on th'entry floer an' ey 'ad strip off in th'draughty entry. It's a wonder ey didna ketch 'is death o' cowd in th'winter.

An' then 'er tried stoppin' 'im comin' in th'ice with 'is best shoes on. 'Er wanted 'im leyve 'em in th'entry an' walk abite in 'is stockin' feyt. That put th'tin-'at on it – ey just up an' left 'er.

It appeyers 'er used bey just as bad when 'er went inter anybody else's 'ice. When 'er thowght nowbody was lukkin' 'er'd bin known fer turn back th'corner o' somebody's hearth-rug with 'er foot fer sey if ther'd bin any dirt pushed under it, an' 'er'd run er finger across th'top edge o' folks's doers fer sey if thee'd bin dusted.

There was another thing 'er used do an' aw. If 'er seyd a bit o' fluff, or owt larke that, on anybody's clothes 'er couldna resist pickin' it off. It didna matter who it was. Mind thee, one o' 'er brothers moer or less cured 'er o' that. Every tarme ey went sey 'er in 'is best blue suit 'er used go rind an' rind 'im takkin' bits off 'im larke a brid peckin' crumbs.

But one dee when 'er tried tak a bit o' cotton off 'is jacket sleyve 'er got moer than 'er bargained fer. th'moer 'er pulled at this cotton th'moer it come ite. 'Er finished up with yards an' yards on it in 'er 'and. Ey said: 'Wot on earth at doin', woman? Theyt 'ave me clothes droppin' peyces.'

Dust know wot ey'd done sirree? Ey'd put a spole o' cotton in 'is pocket an' threaded it up th'inside o' 'is jacket an' dine th'arm-'ole. Then ey'd left abite 'afe an inch pokin' ite through 'is sleyve. It larnt 'er a lesson that did.

But wot worried 'er moer than owt was speyders' webs – 'er couldna abide 'em. 'Er used go rind th'ice every dee, inside an' ite, ferritin' in ever nook an' cranny fer 'em. An' 'er was just th'seeme in other folks's 'ises. 'Er'd bey pokin' 'er nose everywheer lukkin' fer speyders' webs.

Th'owder 'er got, th'woss 'er got. A wik or two afoer 'er deyd folks reckon thee'd seyn 'er goin' rind th'gardin' 'edge with a feather duster rowstin' th'speyders ite.

But 'er brother towd me abite a funny thing wot 'appened when thee buried 'er. Just as thee were lowerin' th'coffin inter th'greeve th'sun shone across th'brass neeme-pleete. Fer a second or two it leyghted up one o' th'corners o' th'greeve.

Stretched across this corner was one o' th'neycest speyder's webs ey'd ever seyn! Wot dust reckon ter that, sirree?"

Owd Jim's wheyte shirt

"Ar tak after me mother when it comes ter wind," said Jabez.

"Ar dunna mind a nice breyze but ar conna abide them strung winds. Ar get that restless ar dunna know wot do with mesel'.

Ar've often wondered if it was owt do with that big ash trey wey used 'ave in front o' th'ice. On windy neyghts it moaned an' groaned larke a soul in torment.

When ar was a lad it used fritten me, so ar'd put me yed under th'bed-clothes an' stuff me fingers in me ear-'oles so's are couldna 'ear it.

But th'wost wind ar con remember musta bin abite 30 yeer ago. It lasted fer two dees an' neyghts, an' it did a terrible lot a damage.

Ther were treys an' chimney pots dine aw ower th'pleece. Ar've never known owt larke it. Dust know, sirree, it was that rough aw th'brids were walkin'!

Ar remember wetchin' owd Betsy tryin' get dine th'leene. 'Er wonna 'afe 'avin' a 'ommerin'. Any minute ar expected sey 'er go flyin' up in th'air larke one o' them witches thee reydst abite.

Ar thowght ar'd better go an' sey if 'er was awreyght. Mind thee, ar mostly kept ite o' Betsy's road 'cos yer couldna stop 'er from natterin'. Ar've awwees said as 'er tungue was hinged in th'middle an' 'er wagged it both ends.

Ar shyted at 'er: 'Wheer yo going' on a dee larke this? Yone get blowed awee.' Th'wind was full in 'er face an' 'er could 'ardly get 'er breath, let alone talk.

But after a bit 'er said: 'Ee, inna it rough. Ar've got go dine Silverdeele but ar do 'ope th'wind cheenges rind afoer ar come back!'

Ar'ad fer laugh at 'er but th'owd soul didna know 'er'd said owt funny.

It was on th'fost dee o' this wind when owd Jim's best wheyte shirt went missin'. Ey worked in th'pit an' lived in one o' them little cottages at th'top o' th'feylds. Ey was a big union mon was Jim, an' ey went ter a lot o' meytin's in th'Potteries.

Anyroad, just after loose-it, when th'colliers were comin' off th'dee-shift, owd Jim's missus was standin' at th'top o' th'feylds.

'Er kept going' up ter theyse colliers an shytin' in ther ear'oles: 'An yer seyn owt o' Jim's best wheyte shirt dine theer?'

But thee didna know wot 'er was on abite. It turned ite as Jim 'ad gotten a union meytin' that neyght so 'er'd weshed 'is best shirt ite an' 'ung it up in th'gardin fer dry. But 'er'd fergotten abite it, an' when this big wind got up owd Jim's shirt flew off

Ther wonna a sign on it anywheer, an' ey 'adna got another un. Ey'd 'ave put 'is owd flannel shirt on an' keyp 'is jacket buttoned up. So 'er went back in th'ice fer get 'is bath weyter ready. It wonna lung afoer ey come, an' afoer 'er could get a word ite ey said: 'Luk thee wot ar've funt up a trey dine th'feylds. Somebody's lost a rattlin' good shirt.

It inna aw that dirty dine th'front an' it's just abite mar size. Just run th'iron ower it an' ar'll wear it fer go ite in terneyght. Ar fancy mesel' in that shirt – it's a better un than marn.'

So ey went off th'Potteries in it. Owd Jim was that pleysed with 'imsel' 'is missus dostna tell 'im it was 'is own shirt ey'd funt.

Bobby Charlie

"Ar've towd thee abite some o' th'tricks Simpy got up to when ey was poachin', anna ar?" said Jabez.

"Ar was talkin' ter owd Ben th'other dee – 'im wot used bey a good cricketer. Ey was tellin' me a thing or two abite Simpy ar 'adna 'eerd afoer.

It appeyers Simpy turned up in th'village one dee wearin' one o' them theer flunky's suits. Thee knowst wot ar meyn, dustna? It was one o' them ite-fits th'mon-servants used wear at theyse big 'ises.

Ey musta met owd Charlie in th'village, an' Charlie said: 'Eh up, sirree, wot sort o' get-up dust caw that? They lukst a bit larke a dog's dinner in that lot. Dunna tell me theest started workin' fer thee livin'.'

But Simpy said that suit was woth its weight in gowd when ey was doin' a bit o' poachin' on th'big estates. If ey run inter any o' th'geeme-keypers ey could awwees cod 'em ey'd just started work at th'big 'ice.

Then ey towd Charlie ey'd got a better un than that at wom – ey'd got a bobby's uniform! Ey reckoned this uniform 'ad seeved 'is bacon many a tarme when ey'd bin poachin' at neyght.

Anyroad, one dee Charlie spotted some o' 'is mates doin' a bit o' gamblin' with cards behind one o' th'edges in that feyld across from th'Chapel. So ey went across ter Simpy's an' got 'im fer lend 'im this bobby's uniform.

As soon as ey'd put it on ey crept dine th'edge-side an' just showed 'imsel' through a gap in th'edge. Ey stood side-roads so's thee wouldna sey 'is face proper.

Theyse gamblin' blokes 'ad gotten a crippled youth keypin' a luk-ite, an' when ey seyd this bobby's uniform ey shyted:

It's th'Ommerend bobby!' Theyse blokes didna 'afe skiddadle. Thee didna stop fer gether th'cards up. Some went this road an' some went that. One or two on 'em meede off dine th'leene, so owd Charlie give 'em a bit of a start an' then went after 'em.

When ey'd got abite 'afe-wee dine th'leene, ey seys two women comin' towards 'im. It was two owd meeds wot lived in a little cottage set back from th'road.

One on 'em was shytin': 'Officer! Officer! come quick. A mon's just run inter th'ice an' ey's hidin' under th'sofa.'

Course, Charlie didna want ‘em get too close ter ‘im fear lest thee recognised ‘im. So ey shyted back ter ‘em: ‘Go back an’ lock th’doer on th’ite-side so’s ey conna get ite. Ar’ll come an’ get ‘im when ar’ve ketched th’others.’

Then ey turned rind an’ went back up th’leene aggen. But be this tarme aw th’village ‘ad turned ite fer wetch th’fun.

Owd Simpy ‘ad towd everybody wot ‘ad ‘appened, an’ folks wonna ‘afe ‘avin’ a good laugh abite owd Charlie’s trick.

Theyse gamblers musta crept back one be one during th’neyght but ther wonna ‘afe some red feeces th’next mornin’ when thee funt ite who th’bobby was.”

Th'black ointment

"When ar was in me early twenties," said Jabez, "ar started comin' ite in red blotches aw ower me body.

Ar didna tell anybody abite it fer a wik or so. Tell thee th'truth, ar'd worked mesel' up inter such a steete ar was convinced it was summat terrible, larke leprosy.

But when it spread ter me feece, me mother spotted it an' said: 'Wots up with thee feece, lad – it luks as though thee't sickenin' fer summat or other.'

So ar 'ad fer tell 'er aw abite it. When 'er seyd me body 'er said: 'Oh, my lors! Whatever 'ast got, lad? Ar've never seyn owt larke that afoer. Dust think it's summat theest etten?'

Theyse red blotches didna 'afe itch, an' thee started growin' sceeles on 'em larke a fish's. When me feyther seyed theyse sceeles ey said: 'Yer dunna think it's owt do with that peyce o' cod wey 'ad th'other wik, dun yer? Ar towd yer at th'tarme it was goin' off. Ar remember me Uncle Ralph used come ite in red spots if ey eat out ite o' th'sey.

Anyroad, me mother started laubin' me with elder-flower ointment, but it didna seym fer bey doin' any good. So 'er talked me into goin' th'doctors.

Ar sut theer in th'weetin'-room 'til it was me turn fer go in, but aw th'wheyle ar 'ad fer keyp scrattin' mesel'. Folks musta thowt ar'd gotten fleys.

When th'doctor seyd it, ey seymed fer know wot it was 'cos ey put a neeme ter it, but ar didna ketch wot ey said.

Ey give me a peeper fer tak th'chemists – it was fer a greet big box o' black ointment. Ey said ar'd got put this ointment aw ower me an' then wesh it off after a dee or two, an' put some fresh on.

It lukked an' smelt just larke gas-tar ony it was a lot thicker. Ar thowght ter mesel' : 'Jabez, theyt goin' luk a rum lad when theyst daubed this stuff on thee. Folks'll think thee 'astna 'ad a wesh fer months.'

Ee! ar did 'ave a tarme with that ointment. It was that thick yer couldna spread it proper – it just stuck ter me skin in gobs. Thee cost imagine wot it was larke tryin' spread it on me 'airy legs – it was agony.

But that was nowt compared with th'trouble ar 'ad gettin' it off. Ar got some good 'ot weyter in th'tin-bath an' put a 'andful o' weshin' soda in it, but th'soap wouldna touch this ointment.

Ar tried some o' me mother's soft-soap wot 'er scrubbed th'kitchin floer with, but that was now use eether. In th'end, ar weyped most on it off on th'towel an'then went dine th'chemists aggen. Ey give me some stuff cawed rape-oil, ey reckoned that'd get it off.

It fetched it off awreyght but thee shouldsta smelt it, sirree – it'd fetch ducks off th'weyter. Ar 'ad stee in th'ice 'cos everywheer ar went folks kept sniffin', an' lukkin' at me everser funny.

It tuk many a wheyle for theyse blotches clear up. Ar dunna think it was owt do with that peyce o' owd cod though, dust they?"

Danny's damsons

"Wey awwees 'ad us damsons from owd Danny Barker's, rind th'bottom o' Wilmer Hills," said Jabez. "It was a lung wee fer go an' fetch 'em, but me mother reckoned thee were th'very best damsons yer could lee yer 'ands on.

Ar remember one yeer when th'word come as Danny's damsons were reype, an' ey'd gotten moer than ey knowed wot do with. Ey was lettin' 'is reglar customers 'ave 'em fer nowt if thee come an' picked ther own.

Me feyther said wey'd best tak th'little clothes-basket if thee were goin' as cheyp as that. So wey set off on th'Satdee af'noon. Ar was ony a bit of a lad at th'tarme, an' goin' ter Wilmer Hills was larke goin' ter fereign parts.

Owd Danny wonna coddin' when ey said ey'd got a lot o' damsons. Th'treys were loaded dine. Ar reckon ther musta bin a lung winter an' th'blossom 'ad bin that slow in comin' ite it'd missed aw th'leete frosts.

Me feyther went up th'treys an' did most o' th'getherin'. Ey passed 'em dine fer us put in th'basket. Mind thee, ar think ar musta etten moer than ar put in th'basket 'cos ar didna feyl very well on th'road wom.

Me mother wouldna dreym o' meekin' jam or owt larke that on a Sundee, so theyse damsons 'ad fer bey dealt with on th'Satdee neyght.

Th'kitchen fire was stoked up an' th'big brass jam-kettle was fetched ite an' put on th'ob. Th'sugar was put in it fer get warm wheylst me mother sorted th'damsons ite.

Some on 'em were fer jammin', some on 'em were fer meekin' damson-cheyse an' some on 'em were fer picklin'. Me feyther was very partial ter a pittled damson.

Ther was a bowlful put on one side fer me granmother, an' then wot was left in th'basket were divided up betweyn th'neeghbours.

Me granmother awwees meede damson ale with 'ers. 'Er used put th'damsons in a big stone jar with some sugar an' the fill th'jar up with owd ale. Th'top o' th'jar was covered ower with a peyce o' bryn peeper rubbed with mutton fat, an' tied dine with string.

Then 'er put it at th'fer end o' th'pantry 'til Christmas.

Ar used larke go rind me granmother's on Christmas eve an' wetch 'er pourin' this ale off th'damsons.

It wonna 'afe a drop o' good. Mind thee, ar wonna supposed fer 'ave any o' this ale. But 'er awwees give me a drop in a cup if ar promised not fer tell me feyther an' mother.

Th'owd lass said it'd do me a world o' good, an' it'd grow hairs on me chest. Come fer think on it, though, it tuk a lot o' Christmases fer meeke it work."

Tater pickin'

"Wey 'used 'ave a wik's 'olidee from schoo' in October fer th'tater-pickin'," said Jabez. "It wonna aw that bad if th'weather was good, but if ther'd bin a wet spell wey got rowelled up.

In them dees th'farmer used pee us lads a tanner a dee an' two roasters.

It was now use thinkin' thee couldst tak moer than two roasters 'cos at th'end o' th'dee th'farmer stood at th'gate dishin' theyse tanners ite. Thee 'adst fer go up ter 'im fer get thee money an' ey could spot streeght awee if theedst gotten an extra roaster 'idden up thee gansy.

Us lads awwees knew wheer find th'biggest roastin' taters. Th'big uns never seymed fer grow wheer th'soil was fine an' close. Th'best pleece fer roasters was in th'roughest part o' th'feyld wheer ther was plenty o' clee an' th'grind was aw lumpy.

Me mother used buy a bag or two o' taters off this farmer, but fost of aw 'er got 'im bring a two-threy pynd as a sample.

If 'er was satisfied with'em er'd order a bag, but woe betide th'farmer if them in th'bag wonna as good as th'sample – er'd meeke 'im cart 'em aw back aggen. Folks 'ad fer wetch th'pennies in them dees.

Talkin' abite taters reminds me o' th'teele me feyther used tell abite a farmer dine Meedley. This farmer 'ad noticed ther was summat up with 'is feyld o' taters. Some o' th'tops 'ad deyd off a lot quicker than th'others.

So ey pulled a root or two up fer 'ave a luk at th'taters, but apart from a two-threy little uns ther was nowt on 'em. Ey couldna reckon it up.

In th'end ey put it dine ter some sort o' new diseyse, but whatever it was it seymed fer bey spreadin'.

Practically every dee ther was one or two moer tops wot 'ad deyd off.

An' then ey spotted summat up th'edge-bonk. It was an owd gardin fork partly 'idden in th'gress. Somebody was 'elpin' 'imsel' ter taters an' keypin' th'fork neyce an' 'andy an' aw!

Wot with this new diseyse an' somebody pinchin' 'em ey reckoned ey'd better 'arvest theyse taters afoer ey lost 'em aw. But th'next dee ey ketched this thief red-'anded an' cured th'diseyse an' aw.

It was a young lad ite' o' Meedley. Ther was a big family on em, an' ey'd bin keypin' em goin in taters. But wot dust think ey'd bin doin', sirree? After ey'd dug th'taters up ey'd bin plantin' th'tops back aggen ever ser careful so's nowbody 'ud notice!

Th'farmer scufted 'is ear-'ole reyght well, but ey couldna 'elp smilin' ter 'imsel' at this lad plantin' th'tops back.

An' if th'farmer 'adna spotted th'fork ey wouldnera twigged wot was goin' on in a month o' Sundees. "

Th'little bangers

"Abite this tarme o' th'yeer wey used bey 'angin' rind th'shop weetin' fer th'fireworks come in," said Jabez.

"Th'owd shop-woman used get a bit fed up with us. Every tarme that danglin' doer-bell rang 'er come bustlin' through from th'back o' th'shop expectin' sey a customer, but mostly it was just one o' us lads askin' abite th'fire-works fer th'umpteynth tarme.

Ar think 'er was glad when er'd sowd 'em aw – 'er seymed fer bey frittened death on 'em. Us lads only wanted th'bangers – wey wonna interested in them pretty uns.

It's a wonder wey didna 'ave some nasty accidents with them little bangers.

Yer dunna sey deenger when yer young though, dun yer? Wey funt ite yer could put lamps ite with them bangers.

If yer popped one through th'key-'ole inter somebody's back-kitchin it neyley awwees blew th'owd oil-lamp ite in th'kitchin. It musta bin a bit of a shock ter th'poer souls fer bey deafened an' plunged into darkness at th'seeme tarme.

An' yer couldna leyght them owd lamps straight awee eether. Yer'd got weet'till th'lamp-glass cooled dine or else 'unt arind fer a duster or summat fer fang 'owd on it with. As soon as thee'd got it lit aggen, wey used pop another un through th'doer.

Ther was another thing wey used do with theyse bangers. At that tarme ther was a lot o' owd pit-shafts dotted rind th'feylds, an' wey used throw leyghted bangers dine 'em. It was just larke a greet big cannon going' off – it didna 'afe meek a din.

Ar've offen wondered wot woulda 'appened if one o 'them pit-shafts 'ad bin full o' gas. Wey coulda bin blown ter smithereyns.

It's a funny thing, but th'nearest ar ever come ter beyin' blown up with a firework was after ar'd growed up. Ar'm godfeyther ter one o' young Tum's lads thee knowst, an' ar'd give 'im a bob or two fer get some fireworks.

Thee awwees 'ad a bit of a do at their 'ice on Guy Fawkes' neyght. Thee 'ad a big bonfire, an' Tum's missus meed toffee-apples an' parkin an' brandy-snap.

Anyroad, this neyght ar'm tellin' thee abite ar went across fer 'ave a luk wot thee were up to. Thee'd finished letting' fireworks off an' th'bonfire 'ad deyd dine. Thee were aw sittin' rind th'kitchin fire feydin' ther feeces with theyse toffee-apples an' stuff. At that tarme young Tum 'ad a terrier bitch an' two part-grown pups. Th'kitchin seymed fer bey full o' kids an' dogs.

Ar'd just sut me dine in a corner with a peyce o' parkin in me fist when ther was an awmighty bang. Th'kids screymed an' th'dogs yelped an' everybody meed fer th'doer at once. Mind thee, Jabez wonna th'last ite eether. There was another couple o' bangs afoer wey dost venture back inter th'kitchin. Wey couldna sey owt for smoke fer a bit.

Dust know wot it was, sirree? It was one o' them theer jumpin' jacks. It'd jumped inter a puddle in th'yard so thee'd brought it in an' put it on th'ob fer dry ite! Th'flippin thing musta bin smowlderin' aw th'tarme. Ar never bought that lad anymoer fireworks.

Deengerous things, anna thee?"

A terrible thing

Th'owd folks used tell me as th'biggest bang this village ever 'eerd was on th'dee after bonfire neyght in eighteyn ninety-threy," said Jabez. "It 'appened in a little cottage dine th'leene.

This cottage was just at th'bottom side o' wheer th'owd reelwee cuttin' is. It stood end-on ter th'road with a nice peyce o' gardin front an' back.

It'd bin empty fer nigh on a couple o' yeer, an' then a collier an' 'is weyfe neemed Charles an' Sarah went live theer. Charlie's brother, Horace, 'ad just come ite o' th'army an' ey moved in with 'em.

On this perticler neyght, just afoer it went dark, a widder-woman was walkin' dine th'leene. 'Er neeme was Alethea --nice neeme, wonna it?

Anyroad, er'd 'afe-a-mind fer caw at this cottage, but just as 'er got level with th'gate ther was this greet explosion.

Everythin' went queyet fer a bit an' then Horace staggered ite o' th'cottage shytin' fer 'elp. Ey didna seym fer bey 'urt bad, but ey was gropin' abite larke a blind mon. Th'widder-wornan ekst 'im wot 'ad 'appened, but ey was that dazed ey didna know wheer ey was. So 'er tuk 'im ter one o' th'cottages up thleene.

Be this tarme two or threy colliers an' some folks ite o' th'village who'd 'eerd th'bang 'ad got ter th'cottage. Thee couldna sey owt at fost fer smoke an' dust, but when it cleyerd thee could 'ardly beleyve ther eyes. Th'place was a shambles.

Thee funt Charlie on th'floer be th'doer. Ey was still alive, but ey was 'urt terrible bad. Ey deyd on th'road ter th'infirmary. Sarah was on a cheer be th'chest o' drawers opposite th'fire-pleece. Er'd bin blown reyght across th'kitchin an' some road or other 'er close 'ad got caught up in th'drawers. Th'poer woman was stone jed. Ther was 'ardly a bit o' th'fire-pleece left, an' most o' th'furniture was in splinters. Th'winda 'ad bin blown cleyn ite an' th'blast 'ad lifted th'ceylin' reyght up.

It turned ite as thee didna use th'boiler in th'owd range cos it'd gotten a crack in it. On th'Satdee neyght Charlie 'ad put a tin in this boiler. Wot dust think was in th'tin sirree? A pynd o' gelignite!

Ey used this gelignite in th'pit an' ey said ey wanted warm it ter th'reyght temperature.

A woman neemed Lizzie was in th'cottage on th'Satdee neyght an' seyd 'im put this tin in. 'Er remembered Sarah eksin' Charlie if it was deengerous, but ey said it wonna. Then ey went an' fergot aw abite it!

On th'Mondee neyght Charlie put a soce-pon o' weyter on th'fire fer wesh 'imsel' with. Horace was on th'sofa an' Charlie an' Sarah were sittin in front o' th'fire-pleece. Just nar, Charlie got up an' give th'fire a poke. That was when th'gelignite went off

It was a sad tarme fer th'village, but th'saddest part abite it was young Charlie an' Sarah 'ad ony bin married a wik.

Terrible thing, wonna it?"

LETTERS

ANNIVERSARY OF TRAGEDY A local village tragedy of 53 years ago this week is recalled in a letter from Mr. T. Bloor, of Scott Hay, who writes: On Monday, November 6, 1893, the village of Scott Hay was the scene of a terrible explosion in a cottage where a newly married couple resided—Mr. and Mrs. Charles Poulson. In those days miners were allowed to take home the explosives they used in the mines. Charles Poulson had taken a can of gelignite home some days previous to the day of the tragedy, and placed it in a disused grate boiler to keep it from freezing. He arrived home from the colliery, had partaken of his dinner, and was seated in an arm chair on the boiler side of the grate. His brother Horace was sitting on the other side, and Mrs. Poulson was sitting near the door, repairing the working trousers of her husband, when the gelignite, from the intense heat of the fire in the grate, exploded, destroying the grate, a peice of which struck Mrs. Poulson in the chest, killing her. The explosion blew the forearm off Mr. Poulson beside inflicting other injuries. The brother Horace escaped with severe injuries. Charles Poulson died on the way to the North Staffs. Infirmary. Horace remained in the infirmary for some time and fully recovered.

The walls of the cottage were rent, and it remained empty for a considerable time. Two workmen on their way to the Leycett Colliery were the first to arrive on the scene. As Gunpowder Plot was being celebrated on that day, many people got the impression that the explosion was the noise of a celebration somewhere. The couple had been married about a fortnight. The cottage was visited by many people from the surrounding district after the tragedy became known. The funeral was a most pathetic scene. They were buried in Silverdale Cemetery.

From the Newcastle Times 1946

Owd Jim an' th'bobbies

"Dust remember me tellin' thee abite owd Jim th'Union mon?" asked Jabez. "Thee knowst who ar meyn, dustna? It was that mon ar towd thee abite wot lost 'is best wheyte shirt in that big wind.

Ey was 'owdin' a meytin' one mornin' at th'back o' th'Swan dine Meedley. Ther was a strike on at th'pit an' ther musta bin close on 200 colliers at this meytin'. Owd Jim was 'owdin' forth – ey was a good speyker was Jim. Anyroad, when ey'd finished talkin' somebody pushed through th'cryd an' whispered summat in Jim's ear-'ole. It turned ite as this bloke 'ad brought word as th'road up ter th'pit was swarmin' with bobbies. Somebody musta started a rumour as theyse colliers were goin' march ter th'pit after this meytin' an smash it up.

Jim towd 'em wot ey'd just 'eerd, an' then ey said: 'Ar reckon somebody's tryin' meeke mischief. Ar dunna want any trouble with bobbies but ar dunna mind 'avin' a bit o' fun with 'em. Just do as ar tell yer an' wey shanna get in any bother.'

So ey towd 'em fer foller 'im up th'leene towards th'pit but thee munna block th'road, an' thee munna shyte or sing or owt. Ey'd got 'is yed screwed on 'ad Jim.

As soon as theyse bobbies seyd 'em comin' thee aw set off fer th'pit fer bey ready fer guard it. But just afoer th'colliers got ter th'pit Jim shyted ite: 'Reyght abite turn!' an' thee aw went back towards Meedley aggen. Th'brass-'at in charge o' theyse bobbies didna know wot fer meeke on it, but ey'd bin towd ey mustna let theyse colliers ite o' 'is seyght. So ey ordered th'bobbies fer foller 'em.

When thee got back inter Meedley owd Jim turned 'is men rind, an' back thee aw come ter th'pit aggen. Thee kept it up aw af'noon – backerds an' fererds betweyn th'pit an' Meedley.

It was a boilin'-'ot summer's dee an' it wonna lung afoer theyse bobbies were aw of a muck-sweat with them thick uniforms on an' them 'elmets on ther yeds. An' thee 'adna 'ad a bite fer eat since mornin'.

Th'colliers were awreyght 'cos thee'd bin eeble pop inter ther 'ises a two-threy at a tarme fer tak ther jackets off 'an 'ave a bite o' snappin'. Thee coulda kept it up aw neyght.

But th'bobbies 'ad 'ad abite enough. This brass-'at come up ter Jim 'an eksed 'im wot ey was pleein' at. Jim said ey wonna pleein' at owt. Ey towd ‘im th’men ‘adna worked fer wiks an’ there jynts were goin’ stiff, so ey was givin’ ‘em a bit o’ exercise.

In th’end ey begged Jim fer send ‘is men wom but Jim said: Now fear – yo started it, yo mun finish it’.

It was gettin’ on fer tey-tarme when th’bobbies cawed it a dee. Thee formed up an’ went off back ter ‘Castle. Jim’s colliers give ‘em threy rousin’ cheers as thee went marchin’ past.

Ey larked a bit o’ fun did owd Jim.”

Winter warmers

With me feyther beyin' a collier, wey were awwees pretty well stocked-up wi' coal," said Jabez. "Summer an' winter ther was awwees a good big fire in th'kitchin, but th'front-room fire was ony lit on Sundees, an' th'bedroom fire-greets were 'ardly ever used. If thee 'adst a fire in thee bedroom thee couldst bet thee bottom dollar thee wast terrible bad.

Me mother was one o' them folks wot 'ad everlastin' cowd feyt. As soon as th'leyves started turnin' on th'treys er'd get th'owd stone 'ot-weyter bottle ite an' fill it every neyght 'til th'cuckoo come. Us childer 'ad bey satisfied with a 'ot-brick or th'oven-shelf lapped in a peyce o' blanket. Ar never larked th'oven-shelf 'cos th'ony road thee couldst get thee feyt flat dine on it was be lyin' on thee back with thee kneys drawn up.

On cowd winter neyghts when us lads were pleein' in th'road wey used meeke a thing cawed a winter warmer. In them dees some o' th'feylds rind th'village were fenced off with weyer rope. Th'iteside on it was weyer but th'inside was meede ite o' rope wot'd bin soaked in creyosote, or summat larke that, fer stop it rottin'.

Anyroad up, wey used get a length on it ite o' th'fence an' tak th'weyer off th'iteside 'til ther was ony th'rope left. Then yer got a tin – a black-treycle tin was best – an' yer punched a lot o' 'oles in it rind th'bottom, an' then two moer 'oles up at th'top. Theyse two 'oles at th'top were fer puttin' a peyce o' weyer through fer meeke a 'andle fer carry it with.

Then yer lit this lenth o' rope an' stuffed it in th'tin an' jammed th'lid dine. When yer swung it rind an' rind be th'andle this rope glowed red-'ot an' meede th'treycle tin everser warm. It was a grand thing fer carryin' rind with thee fer warm thee 'ands on of a winter's neyght. Mind thee, it stunk a bit, but wey didna mind that.

One neyght ther was threy or foer on us with theyse winter-warmers, an' wey were pleein' in front o' that row o' cottages at th'fer end o' th'village. One youth was swingin' 'is tin rind an' rind in front on 'im when aw of a suddin th'andle brok. This tin went flyin' up in th'air an' ower th'top o' theyse cottages.

Wey listened ter it clatterin' dine inter one o' th'back-yards, an' then wey 'eerd somebody shytin'. Wey didna 'ang abite fear lest it'd done some damage. But wey 'eerd aw abite it th'next dee.

It turned ite as one o' th'women ite o' theyse cottages 'ad bin up th'gardin. 'Er was just comin' back with 'er candle in 'er 'and when 'er seyd this thing come ower th'roof an' drop in th'yard.

Ther was smoke an' fleemes comin' ite on it an' 'er dostna go passed it. So 'er shyted fer 'er 'usband come ite. 'Er said ter 'im: 'Luk thee dine theer. That thing's just dropped ite o' th'sky. Dust think it's one o' them theer shootin' stars or summatt?'

'Course ey knew wot it was as soon as ey seyd it, but ey didna let on. Ey picked it up on th'coal shovel an' doused it in th'reen-weyter butt. Then ey said. 'Inna it marvellous – yer larn summat new every dee, dunna yer? Ar'd never 'ave beleyved them shootin' stars were flyin' black –treycle tins if ar 'adna seyd one with me own eyes'."

" 'As it ever struck thee wot a lot o' good musicians weyn 'ad in th'villages rind this road?" asked Jabez. "Thers bin some top-notchers thee knowst, an' a good many on 'em were colliers. Thers bin composers, an' conductors, an' singers, an' folks wot could plee any sort o' instrument.

A lot o' th'talent seymed fer run in families but, on th'other 'and, ther were good musicians whose childer sung larke crows an' couldna plee a tin-whistle.

Two or threy ite o' th'village 'ad music lessons off an owd collier dine th'bottom o' Silverdeele. That mon could plee owt. Some folks reckoned thee'd 'eerd 'im plee th'national anthem on 'is clee pipe!

Ar knew one youth wot 'ad orgin lessons off 'im. On th'Satdee mornin' when ey went fer 'is fost lesson this owd collier said ter 'im: 'Just give us a 'and fer shift this orgin awee from th'wo'.'

When thee'd got it tote th'middle o' th'room th'collier fetched a screwdriver an' started takkin it peyces.

Th'lad was a bit mystified, but ey stood an' wetched 'im fer a bit. Then ey said: 'Is ther summat wrung with it, mister?' Th'owd collier shuk 'is yed an' said: 'Now – thers nowt matter with it, lad. Ar'm just goin' show thee its innerds. Theyt never meek a good orginist if thee dustna understand wot goes on inseyde it!' That was th'lads fost music lesson, an' ey never fergot it.

Some o' th'villages 'ad enough musicians fer meeke up a little orchestra.

Thee used go rind ter th'different chapels pleein' fer special services larke th'arvest an' th'Charity. One o' theyse little orchestras 'ad a rattlin' good piccolo pleer neemed Billy. Thee were pleein' off Cheshire road one Sundee, an' Billy 'ad burrered a monkey-suit off somebody. Ey didna 'afe fancy 'imsel' in it.

Anyroad, after th'af'noon service thee aw went ter different 'ises fer ther teas. Billy went ter a widder-womans, an' 'er give 'im a reyght good feyd. Er'd put a fire in th'front-room fer 'im, an' after thee'd 'ad ther teas 'er give 'im a tumblerful o' elderberry weyne an' towd 'im fer go and 'ave a rest afoer th'service at neyght.

At th'neyght service th'conductor got th'feylin as Billy was a bit off form. Ey couldna just put 'is finger on it but ther was summat wrung with Billy's piccolo pleein'. So after th'service ey 'ad a word with 'im. Billy said: 'Ee! ar wonna 'afe meythered. It musta bin that elderberry weyne. Ar could sey a lot too many notes on th'music, an' it was th'devil's own job sortin' th'reyght uns from th'wrung uns. Dust know, sirree, if ar'da pleed aw on 'em thee wouldstnera neyded th'rest o' th'orchestra. Thee coulda aw gone wom!"

Dine amongst th'gorse-bushes

"Theyse cowd winter neyghts ar larke fer think back ter them lung 'ot summers wey awwees seymed fer 'ave when ar was a lad," said Jabez. "Folks reckon as th'weather anna cheenged aw that much but it taks a bit o' beleyvin'. Th'trouble is yer dunna seym fer remember th'cowd wet dees wot yer 'ad when yer were young.

When it was too 'ot fer pleein' geemes or owt ar used larke get off dine th'feylds amongst them gorse-bushes. Thee'n practically aw gone nar but theyse bushes used bey in big clumps with neyce petches o' gress betweyn 'em. Yer could sit on this gress with th'gorse-bushes aw rind yer an' bey in a world o' yer own.

It was sort o' queyet but, on th'other 'and, it was surprisin' wot yer could 'ear if yer lee flat on yer back an' kept still. Besides listenin' ter th'brids an' th'beys an' th'flies yer could 'ear th'seyd-pods on th'gorse-bushes bostin', an' th'gress-'oppers chirpin', an' th'little gusts o' wind blowin' through th'lung gress an' meekin' th'hare-bells rattle.

Ar think ar musta 'ad a good imagination when ar was a lad 'cos ar used lie theer pretendin' ar was a giant in a land o' little tiny folks. Th'lung stalks o' gress were big forest treys, an' th'explodin' seyd-pods were theyse little folks's guns wot thee were tryin' fritten me off with. Th'chirpin' o' th'gress-'oppers was th'chatterin' o' th'crowds o' little folk wot'd gethered fer sey this big giant lyin' theer. Th'gnats bitin' me legs were theyse little folks's sowdjers stabbin' me with ther swords. Daft idea wonna it?

Ar still went dine among th'gorse-bushes nar an' aggen when ar was a young mon, but ar didna seym fer 'ear 'afe as much as when ar was a lad. Mind thee, ar 'eerd moer than ar was supposed fer do one dee.

Ar 'eerd somebody comin' dine th'feylds but ar didna tak much notice 'cos ther was a footpath not fer off. Just nar theyse footsteps stopped an' ar could 'ear two women talkin'. Thee'd sut themsels dine on wot wey cawed th'deesy-bonk, just th'top-side o' theyse gorse-bushes. Th'pair on 'em were a bit too owd in th'tooth fer meekin' deesy-cheens, so thee'd brought ther knittin' with 'em. It wonna lung afoer ther tungues were clackin' faster than ther knittin' neydles. Ar couldna ketch aw thee said, but ar gathered thee were doin' a bit o' muck-reekin'. Ar'll bet ther was a lot o' folks with smokin' ears in th'village that dee.

But ar did manage fer ketch summat thee said abite one woman in th'village, an' ar didna neyd fer guess tweyce who it was. Thee were takkin' this poer woman ter peyces bit be bit, but then one on 'em said:

'Mind yer, credit wheer credit's due, 'er keyps that 'ice spotless – yer could eat yer dinner off th'floer'.

But wot dust think th'other woman said? 'Er said: 'From wot ar've seyn o' 'er cookin', th'floer 'ud bey th'best pleece fer eat it off – it inna fit fer put on a pleete'.

Some o' theyse women can bey reyght catty, conna thee?"

Th'owd bull

"Some o' theyse owd farm leebourers knowed a thing or two abite animals," said Jabez. "When ar was a lad ar spent a lot o' tarme at one or th'other o' th'farms, an' ar larnt a lot abite th'different roads o' deylin' with animals. Mind thee, at fost ar used bey frittened death o' owt bigger than a chicken.

Th'best mon with animals worked at th'bottom farm. Ey was a rum owd stick but ey seymed fer understand 'em better than anybody. Ey reckoned as animals could smell fear, an' thee knew if yer were frittened on 'em afoer yer went anywheer near 'em. Yer couldna do owt with things larke 'osses an' cows an' pigs an' dogs if yer were frittened on 'em.

But ey reckoned bulls were a different kettle o' fish awgether. Bulls wonna fer bey trusted 'cos every bull 'ad a devil inside 'im wot was tryin' get ite.

Ey said: 'If anybody ever tells thee thee'n gotten a queyet bull, meek sure fer keyp ite o' 'is road or else one o' theyse dees ey'll meeke mince-meyt on thee'.

One o' th'bulls thee 'ad at this farm was an owd devil. This farm leebourer was th'ony one as could do any good with 'im. Th'farmer 'ad picked 'im up cheyp at th'Smithfeyld dine 'Castle. Ey wonna aw that bad at fost, but th'owder ey got th'moer cantankerous ey got. In th'end thee dostna let 'im ite in th'feylds at aw – ey'd 'ave a go at owt wot moved.

But this farm leebourer didna larke th'idea o' th'owd bull beyin' fastened up in th'shed aw th'wheyle, so most dees ey let 'im ite inter th'farmyard fer stretch 'is legs. Ar used get up on th'pig-sty wo' ite o' th'road – ar didna larke th'road ey lukked at me.

Ey seymed fer bey as queyet as an owd tup when this leebourer was with 'im. Th'ony tarme ey got a bit nowghty was when ey got th'smell o' th'cows on th'wind.

Anyroad, one Mondee af'noon th'farmer was dine 'Castle market an' th'bull was 'avin 'is exercise in th'yard. Th'farmer's missus was meekin' th'beds at th'tarme an' 'er 'appened fer open th'back-bedroom winda fer tell this leebourer summat or other – ar didna ketch wot 'er said.

Ey ony turned 'is back on that bull fer a two-threy seconds fer luk up at th'winda, but that was enough fer th'bull. Ey spied 'is chance an' come fer 'im!

Ar shyted ter ‘im an’ th’farmer’s weyfe screymed. Dust know, sirree, ar’ve never seyn an owd mon move as quick in aw me leyfe, but ey ony just meed it ter th’back doer.

Next tarme thee’t dine at th’farm ‘ave a luk at that doer. Yer can still sey wheer it was patched up. That owd bull didna ‘afe lambaste it.

Wey ‘ad fer weet’till th’farmer come wom afoer th’bull could bey put back in ‘is shed. Th’owd leebourer was reyght shook up, but ar’ve awwees remembered wot ey said terme. Ey said: ‘Thers summat ar fergot tell thee abite bulls. Never turn thee backside ter a bull – ey’ll get thee in th’end.’ “

Owd Percy's Christmas duck

"In a village ther awwees seyms fer bey somebody yer can go ter if yer run short o' summat, or if yer want owt done," said Jabez. "Me mother was one o' them folks wot never throwed owt ite, an' aw th'village seymed fer know it.

Folks were fer everlastin' comin' ter th'ice fer sey if wey'd gotten such-an'-such a thing. Thee'd walk straight in through th'back-doer shytin': 'Ar'm comin' in!' an' then thee'd see: 'Yer dunna 'appen fer 'ave a so-an'-so by yer, dun yer? or thee'd see: 'Ar've come abeggin' – ar wouldna bother yer but ar knew if anybody 'ad got so-an'-so it'd be yo'.

Ther were tarmes when it was just larke livin' on Crewe steetion with folks comin' an' goin.' Me feyther used see: 'Thee awwees know wheer come when thee want owt, dunna thee?' But me mother 'ad an answer fer that. Er'd see: 'They knowst as well as ar do, if ever wey were in want wey could go ter any 'ice in th'village an' thee'd give us 'afe o' wot thee'd gotten.'

An' then ther were them folks yer went ter if yer wanted owt done. Some on 'em seymed fer 'ave a knack fer doin' things better than anybody else. One o' th'busiest folks in th'village at this tarme o' th'yeer was a woman neemed Fanny. 'Er was a dab-'and at pluckin' fithers off owt. Meede a rattlin' good job o' dressin' powltry did Fanny. Er'd pluck thee a chicken fer a tanner or a goose fer a bob. An' 'er didna weeste th'fithers eether.

Ther was fither cushins aw ower th'ice, an' folks reckoned er'd got a fither-bed in th'front bedroom wot was nigh on two-foot thick when it was shuck up.

But them fithers 'er got off owd Percy's duck wonna much use ter 'er. Perce 'ad won this duck in a raffle. Ey decided fer feyd it up 'til just afoer Christmas, an' then kill it an' tak it ter Fanny fer pluckin'. Th'ony pleece ey'd got fer keyp it in was th'coal-'us.

This duck started off as a Khaki Campbell but be th'tarme it'd bin in th'coal-'us fer a wik it was as black as an owd crow.

Perce meede up 'is mind fer kill it on th'mornin' o' Christmas Eve. Ey'd never kilt a duck afoer, an' ey wonna sure which was th'best road fer do it. In th'end ey decided fer chop its yed off with th'axe! When ey went ter th'coal-'us doer with 'is axe in 'is 'and this black Khaki Campbell was sittin' on top o' th'coal.

Ey reckoned as when ey went fer fang 'owd on it it lukked at 'im everser pathetic an' started quackin'. Ter this dee ey swears it said ter 'im: Dunna do it mister – dunna do it!'

Mind thee, ar reckon ey was exaggeratin' a bit, but ey couldna bring 'imsel' fer kill it. Ey dusted it dine a bit an' tuk it up th'farm fer 'ave its neck wrung.

When ey tuk it ter Fanny fer pluckin' 'er said: 'Ey's a funny colour fer a duck. Ey luks as though ey's bin dine th'pit fer a wik.'

Perce reckoned ey didna enjoy 'is Christmas dinner a bit. Ey couldna 'elp thinkin' abite th'road that duck lukked at 'im when ey went fer it with th'axe."

Th'tin drum

'Dust know, sirree," said Jabez, "ar musta bin in me teyns afoer ar stopped 'engin' me stockin' up at Christmas. When ar was a young lad ther was awwees an apple an' an eringe an' some nuts in th'stockin' foot.

Somewheer amongst th'nuts ther'd bey a brand new tanner or a couple o' joeys. Them little silver joeys tuk a bit o' findin', an' it didna pee thee fer 'ave a 'ole in thee stockin.'

Then ther'd bey some sweyts or liquoreece leeces, an' a sugar mice, an' p'raps a chocolate wetch. Come fer think on it ar anna seyn any sugar meyce fer a lung tarme, 'ast they? Stickin' ite o' th'top o' th'stockin' ther'd bey a box o' peents an' a peentin' book, or summat larke that. Ther was wonder an' magic in Christmas when yer were young, wonna ther? Ar con still remember th'excitement o' weekin' up afoer it was dee-leyght an' tip-toein' ter th'bottom o' th'bed fer 'ave a feyl at th'stockin' fer meeke sure Santa 'ad bin.

Then sneykin' back inter bed fer weet'till it got leyght, an' thinkin' abite which o' them things in me stockin' ar was goin' eat fost, an' wot ar was goin' spend me tanner on.

Th'childer naradees seym fer do a lot better fer Christmas presents than wey did, an' good luck ter 'em. But ar dite whether thee get any moer fun ite on 'em. Ar'll tell thee wot ar've noticed sirree – young childer still seym fer get moer fun ite o' a two-threy odds an' ends than thee get ite o' some o' theyse expensive toys.

Ar've known a lad bey as 'appy as th'dee is lung with 'afe a dozen owd shoe-boxes an' a lenth o' string. When th'boxes were fastened 'gether one behind th'other it was a treen, an' as fer as th'lad was concerned it was as good as any treen wot ever went ite o' Stoke steetion.

It puts me in mind o' that teele owd Tum was fond o' tellin'. Ey 'appened fer bey dine 'Castle just afoer Christmas tarme an' ey popped inter a toy shop fer get a bit o' summat fer 'is lad.

Wheylst ey was 'avin' a luk rind ther come a woman an' a little lad inter this shop. 'Er was a well-ter-do woman be th'luk on 'er – 'er was dressed ter th'nines.

Anyroad, 'er let this lad loose in th'shop so's ey could pick wot ey wanted fer Christmas.

Tum reckoned as money was now object, an' this lad coulda 'ad owt ey wanted. Ey went aw rind th'shop lukkin' at this an' that, an' then ey spotted a little tin drum dine in one corner. It was ony abite eighteyn-pence but it was peented in breyght colours an' it'd gotten a red silk cord fer 'ang rind thee neck.

This lad sut 'imsel' dine on th'shop floer an' ey didna 'afe leather inter that drum! 'Is mother tried 'tice 'im inter 'avin' a little bike or a steym-injin' or some sowdjers an' guns, but it wonna any use. Th'lad 'adna got eyes fer owt else, an' ey wouldna 'ave it lapped up eether.

Th'last owd Tum seyd on 'im ey was marchin' dine th'Ironmarket in front o' is mother knockin' th'stuffin' ite o' this drum.

Just goes fer show, dunna it?"

Locked ite

"Folks go bed a lot leeter than thee used do," said Jabez.

"Barrin' Christmas an' New Yeer 'afe th'village used shut up shop an' bey in bed be ten o'clock of a neyght. Th'owd uns reckoned as th'neyght air was bad fer yer. Mind thee, ther wonna much fer stee up fer, an' most folks 'ad got bey up pretty sharpish in a mornin'.

Dust know, sirree, up'till ar was 21 ar 'ad bey in th'ice be 'afe-past ten or else ar got a good tickin' off. But ar never got locked ite larke that lass did wot used live at th'fer end o' th'village.

'Er was mashin' a youth from Augers Bonk, an' 'er'd bin towd tarme an' tarme aggen abite comin' wom leete. 'Er feyther 'ad threatened fer lock th'doer on 'er if 'er didna mend 'er wees.

Anyroad, this perticler neyght it'd gone eleven an' this lass was supposed fer bey in be ten. Th'owd mon kept lukkin' at th'clock an' gettin' up ite o' 'is cheer an' patherin' rind an' rind th'kitchin. But just nar ey knocked 'is pipe ite on th'ob, an' wun th'clock up, an' said ter 'is missus: Nowbody con see ar anna given 'er fair warnin'. Get thee ready fer bed, ar'm goin' lock th'doer.'

Th'lass's mother pleyded with 'im not fer lock 'er ite. 'Er said: 'Give 'er a bit lunger – ar'm certin' 'er's bin 'eld up somewheer.' But th'owd mon said: " ' Eld up, me foot. If anybody's 'owdin' 'er up it's that rapscallion from Augers Bonk. Ar never did reckon owt ter 'im – ey's a bit shifty in theen.'

So ey locked an' bowted th'doer an' blew th'lamp ite, an' off thee both went bed. But th'lass's mother couldna go sleyp. 'Er lee theer listenin' an' werritin'. It musta bin tote midneyght when 'er 'eered somebody try th'doer an' then start knockin'. 'Er was fer gettin' up but th'owd mon pushed 'er dine in bed an' said: 'Stop wheer thee at – ar'll show 'er who's boss in this 'ice.'

Th'knockin' got woss an' woss, an' then th'lass started shytin' fer bey let in. But th'owd mon wouldna budge. It wonna lung afoer aw this knockin' an' shytin' 'ad wok th'neebours up. Just nar thee 'eerd a mon's voice. It was th'bloke from next doer. Ey was up at th'bedroom winda an' ey was shytin' ter this lass, but ey was ony meekin' matters woss.

Ey said: 'It inna any use knockin'- thee wunna let yer in. You could come rind ter us but wey anna got a spare bed. Ar'll tell yer what yer can do though – yer con spend th'neyght in th'kennel. Go rind th'back an' rowst th'dog ite. Ey wunna bite yer if yer weeke 'im up gentle. Ar put cleyn straw in th'kennel th'other dee, an yer'll bey as snug as a bug in a rug. Ar'll give yer a shyte in th'mornin'.'

That put th'tin-'at on it! Th'lass started blartin' an' 'ommerin' on th'doer. In th'end th'owd mon come dine an' let 'er in. But ey said never a word ter 'er – 'er'd larnt 'er lesson.

'Er chucked th'bloke from Augers Bonk an' married a butcher from 'Castle. But ar bet thee 'er never forgot beyin' locked ite."

Frozzen stiff an' clemmed death

"Snow's a grand thing when yer young, inna it?" said Jabez. "Sledgin' an' snowboin' an' slarrin' an' meekin' snowmen. But th'owder yer get th'less yer larke it. Dust know, sirree, ar've never felt th'seeme abite snow since that dee ar walked back from Betley in a blizzard. Ar was ony a youth at th'tarme.

It was one Satdee at th'back-end o' January. Ther was a scitterin' o' snow on th'grind but it was a neyce dee – just reyght fer a good walk rind. So, after ar'd 'ad me dinner ar laubed some dubbin' on me big shoes an' burrered me feyther's leather geeters.

Ar struck off dine th'feylds an' then went through Warton's Wood passed owd Johnny Collier's an' come ite on th'meen Nantwich road. Be that tarme th'sky 'ad clouded ower an' it began fer luk terrible black ower Bill's mothers. But ar wonna aw that bothered.

Ar went through Wrine'ill an' ar was just abite level with th'Black 'Oss in Betley when th'snow started. Ee! it didna 'afe come dine sirree, an' th'sky lukked full o' snow. Ar thowght ter mesel': Jabez lad, theydst better meeke tracks fer wom'.

So ar turned up be th'Church an' set off across th'feylds fer Wilmer Hills. Ar oughta known better – ther inna much shelter up theer. Th'wind was gettin' strunger an' strunger, an' it was blowin' th'snow reyght in me feece. It was larke tryin' walk ferrerds when somebody was tryin' pull thee backerds.

Ar reckoned fer know th'path across them feylds larke th'back o' me 'and, but it wonna many cracks afoer ar was lost. Th'trouble was ar couldna sey wheer ar was goin' fer th'snow in me eyes, an' ar couldna get me breath fer th'wind. Ar was in a reyght pittle, ar tell thee.

Ar kept blunderin' inter snowdrifts an' foin' dine. Thee cost soon exhaust theesel' in th'snow, costna? Ar remember thinkin' abite that lad in Good King Wenceslas wot felt ey couldna go now lunger. Mind thee, ey'd got footsteps fer foller, 'adna 'e?

Ar musta done a lot o' wanderin' abite 'cos instead o' comin' ite at th'fer end o' Cradduck's Moss ar funt mesel' at th'back o' Yelly Castle. Ar'd still got a lung wee fer go but ar was reyght glad fer know wheer ar was.

Dust know wot bucked me up moer than owt else? Ar kept thinkin' abite that greet big fire thee'd 'ave at wom, an' ar decided ar was going' sit reyght on top on it fer thaw ite, an' ar was goin' meeke mesel' rinds an' rinds o' thick drippin' toast.

But wot dust think, sirree? When ar got wom th'back doer was weyde open an' smoke was pourin' ite on it. It lukked as though th'ice 'ad ketched fire or summat. But it 'adna. Th'snow 'ad blocked th'chimney-pot an' me feyther was just takkin' th'fire ite o' th'greete on a shovel. Th'ice was full o' smoke an' sut, an' it was as cowd as charity.

An' theer ar was – frozzen stiff an' clemmed death. Ar coulda blarted me eyes up!"

Owd Jock in a quandary

"Talkin' abite snow reminds me o' th'tarme thee funt owd Jock at th'bottom o' th'leene," said Jabez. "Thee wouldstna remember Jock wouldst?

Ey was a big red-yedded Scotchman wot come fer live in th'village fer a wheyle. Ey 'ad a biggish family fer feyd but ey managed find enough money from somewheer fer 'is drinkin'.

As soon as ey got a bit merry ey awwees got th'bag-pipes ite. Ey'd march up an' dine iteside th'ice pleein' theyse pipes fer aw ey was woth.

Come fer think on it ar've never seyn anybody plee bag-pipes sittin' dine, 'ast they?

Every so offen Jock an' is missus 'ud 'ave an awmighty row ower summat or other. Theyse red-yeds are mostly a bit 'ot-tempered, anna thee? But 'is missus could 'owd 'er own when it come ter a bit o' argufyin'.

Th'neeghbours reckoned yer could awwees tell when 'er'd bested Jock in th'argument 'cos thee'd 'ear th'pipes start up. If ey couldna beat 'er with 'is tungue ey could still 'ave th'last word with 'is bagpipes.

Mind thee, some o' th'neeghbours didna exactly enjoy owd Jock's pleein'. Them bagpipes anna everybody's cup o' tea, are thee? One o' th'neeghbours once upset 'im be tellin' 'im ey could get better music ite o' their tum-cat. An' ey give Jock a demonstreetion. Ey tucked th'cat under 'is arm with its yed feecin' backerds an' then marched up an' dine bitin' th'end o' its teele an' pressin' on its bally with 'is elber. Owd Jock come nigh ter doin' murder that dee.

But anyroad, ar started tellin' thee abite th'tarme thee funt Jock dine th'leene, didna ar? It was a perishin' cowd winter's neyght when ther was a lot o' snow on th'grind. Two colliers from Silverdeele were goin' wom from Leycitt pit when thee come across Jock with 'is arms clasped teyght rind one o' th'posts o' them toll-geetes wot used bey at th'bottom o' th'leene.

Thee didna recognise 'im at fost so thee just said goodneyght an' walked passed 'im. But Jock shyted 'em back. It was many a wheyle afoer thee could meeke ite wot ey was tryin' tell 'em. Thee talk a bit funny at th'best o' tarmes theyse Scotchmen do, dunna thee? But with owd Jock beyin' full o' whisky an' 'is teyth chatterin' gether with cowd ey tuk a bit o' understandin'.

It turned ite as ey was tryin' tell 'em ey was in a bit of a quandary. Ey said if ey let go o' this post ey'd fo' dine in th'snow an' wouldna bey eeble get up aggen. On th'other 'and, if ey didna let go o' th'post ey'd freyze death.

So thee tuk 'im from rind th'post an' 'elped 'im walk up th'leene. Owd Jock was that glad fer get wom ey promised 'em if ever ey seyd 'em in a pub ey'd pee fer aw th'liquor thee could drink.

Theyse two Silverdeele men used chuckle every tarme thee towd this teele abite this Scotchman's promise. Th'joke was thee were both teytotallers."

When granfeyther packed 'is traps

Me granfeyther on me mother's side once went America, thee knowst," said Jabez. "Ey was in 'is twenties at th'tarme an' was workin' at them iron-works at Furnace Bonk.

One dee ey 'ad a letter from a mate o' 'is wot'd gone ter America. This letter said wot a grand pleece it was, an' ther was some reyght good jobs fer anybody wot knew owt abite meekin' iron.

Me granfeyther was aw fer goin' but ey 'adna bin married aw that lung an' ey didna larke th'idea o' takkin' a young weyfe aw that wee on spec. In th'end ey decided fer go 'imsel' an' sey wot it was larke. Then if ey decided fer stop ey'd send fer me granmother.

Thee cost imagine th'stir it musta meed in th'village in them dees. Ther'd bey a lot o' sheekin' o' yeds goin' on, wouldna ther? An' folks 'ud bey tellin' 'im abite aw th'terrible things wot could 'appen ter a village lad in them fereign parts.

But me granfeyther was a stubborn mon. If ey meede is mind up fer do summat there was now stoppin' 'im. So ey packed 'is traps an' off ey went.

'Course thee didna'ear owt on'im fer wiks an' wiks. Then one dee thee got a letter from 'im. Ey'd funt a good job in a rowlin' mill an' ey reckoned it wouldna bey lung afoer ey was foreman.

Ar reckon ey'da meede a rattlin' good foreman an' aw – ey was a good 'un fer dishin' orders ite.

But ey 'adna bin theer many months afoer me granmother was tuk bad. 'Er got woss and woss. Thee 'ad wreyte ter me granfeyther an' tell 'im if ey wanted sey 'er alive ey'd better come back. So ey 'ad fer pack 'is traps aggen, but be th'tarme ey got wom me granmother was gettin' better.

This mate o' 'is kept wreytin' ter 'im fer try 'tice 'im go back, but th'babbies started arrivin' pretty smartly, an' wot with one thing or another thee never got rind ter it. Ey got 'is owd job back at th'ironworks but ey never stopped talkin' abite America.

It musta bin abite 30 yeer or moer after me granfeyther come back when one dee this owd mate o' 'is turned up. Ey was back in th'owd country fer 'is 'olidees. Me granfeyther 'appened fer bey bad in bed at th'tarme so me granmother tuk 'im upsteers an' left , em 'gether fer 'ave a good natter. 'Er used see 'er didna know wot them two 'ad gotten up ter in America but th'pair on 'em did a lot o' laughin' an' shytin'.

Anyroad, when this bloke 'ad gone me granmother 'eerd some funny noises comin' from upsteers, so 'er went up. Me granfeyther was lyin' cross-roads on th'bed moanin' an' groanin' an' ey couldna speyk. 'Er sent fer th'doctor streeght awee – 'er was certin ey'd 'ad a stroke or summat. Ey seymed fer bey a bit better be th'tarme th'doctor come but ey give 'im a good examinin'.

Then ey turned ter me granmother an'said: Woman, yoer weestin' mar tarme an' yoer money. Smell at 'is breath – th'mon's dead drunk!'

Me granmother said 'er felt such a foo' – 'er coulda gone dine a mouse-'ole. It turned ite as this mate o' 'is 'ad brought a bottle o' whisky with 'im an' thee'd gotten threy part on it dine 'em."

Jabez paused for a while and then said: "Dust know, sirree. It's only just struck me. If me granfeyther 'ad gone back America ar mitta bin born a Yankee. Just fancy that nar!"

A teele o' two dogs

"Ar've offen wondered whey it is as thers awwees one or two folks yer conna get on with," said Jabez.

"Some o' th'neycest folks ar've ever come across awwees seymed fer 'ave somebody thee couldna stomach at any price. Ther wonna owt yer could put yer finger on – thee just seymed fer rub one another up th'wrung road. Funny thing, inna it?

It's just th'seeme with dogs thee knowst. Thee't get a dog wot'll bey as friendly as owt with aw th'dogs in th'village bar one.

Th'pair on 'em 'ave ony got ketch seyght o' one another an' it inna many cracks afoer th'blood's fleyin'.

One o' th'dogs wot used bey larke that was a black curly-'aired mongrel thee cawed Gyp. Ey just couldna stand th'seyght o' a little wheyte cross-bred terrier wot lived at th'other end o' th'village. Th'black un 'ud bey abite as big as a collie an' ey belonged ter th'youngest o' owd Tum's lads.

Mind thee, thee 'adst a job fer tell whether th'dog belonged ter th'lad or th'lad belonged ter th'dog.

If ever thee seydst that black dog thee couldst bet thee bottom dollar as th'lad wouldna bey fer awee. Thee were larke one another's shadders.

Anyroad, one dee this lad an' 'is dog were walkin' dine th'leene when thee spotted this wheyte terrier comin' up th'bonk. Th'black un's 'ackles went up, an' ey showed 'is teyth an' tuk off after th'terrier. Th'terrier spun rind an' belted off dine th'leene as fast as 'is little legs 'ud carry 'im.

If ar remember reyghtly it was abite th'tarme when th'fost busses started runnin' through th'village. Anyroad, this terrier was in that big a 'urry fer get awee ey never seyd this bus comin' up th'leene.

Ey went slap-bang betweyn th'front wheyls o' this bus an' come ite at th'back-end withite a scratch.

Th'black un musta thowght ey could do th'seeme, but ey was a bit too big. Th'poer thing got ketched with summat under th'bus an' ey was kilt stone jed.

Tum's lad brok 'is young 'art an' it was a lung wheyle afoer ey got ower it.

But, after a bit, a funny thing started 'appenin'.

This little wheyte terrier started follerin' th'lad abite! Ey used shyte at 'im, an' if ther was a brick 'andy ey'd slat it at 'im. Mind thee, it was ony natural fer th'lad bleeme this terrier fer wot 'ad 'appened, wonna it?

But ey couldna get shut on'im. Th'dog kept 'is distance but follered 'im everywheer. Whenever th'lad stopped fer tell 'im go awee ey'd stand theer with 'is yed on one seyde an' then ey'd give 'is little stump of a teele a wag or two.

Ar know it synds daft but it was fer aw th'world as though this terrier was tryin' meeke it up ter th'lad fer losin' 'is black dog.

An' th'little terrier won in th'end. Th'tarme come when th'lad tuk ter 'im, an' thee went everywheer 'gether just larke 'im an' th'black un used do.

It taks a bit o' reckonin' up, but ar wouldna bey surprised if th'black un 'adna sensed aw alung as th'terrier was attracted ter th'lad. It'd meeke 'im jealous enough fer go fer th'terrier wouldna it?"

Th'tum-cat rabbit-ketcher

"Funny creytures cats are, anna thee?" said Jabez. "One minute theen bey meekin' a greet big fuss on thee, an' th'next minute theen walk streeght past thee as if theen never set eyes on thee afoer. Mind thee, ar know some folks wotta a bit larke that, dustna they?

At one tarme ther used bey a big wheyte tum-cat in th'village wot thee cawed Fred. Leastroads, ey was supposed fer bey wheyte. Mostly, though, ey was a sote o' gree with red blotches. Ey lukked gree 'cos ey wonna ower fond o' weshin' 'imsel', an' th'red blotches were blood.

Ee! ey was a dinga fer feyghtin'. Dust know, sirree, ey wouldna let any other cat come within seyght o' th'cottage wheer ey lived – or dogs neether fer that matter. Th'ony tarme ey run awee from dogs was when thee ketched 'im unawares. Providin' ey seyd 'em comin' ey'd stand 'is grind.

Many a dog's put 'is teele betweyn 'is legs an' belted fer wom as soon as Fred put 'is back up an' started spittin'.

Ar've seyn that cat goin' wom in th'early mornin' covered in blood an' barely eeble drag one leg in front o' th'other. Th'folks ey belonged terreckoned ey used crawl in th'ice an' flop dine on th'hearth-rug an sleyp larke a jed un'till dinner-tarme.

When thee wanted sheeke th'rug, thee eether 'ad fer pick Fred up an' put 'im dine somewheer else, or pick th'rug up be one end an' rowl 'im off onter th'floer. When thee swept up thee could push 'im aw rind th'floer with th'brush an' ey'd never weeke up.

But come dinner-tarme ey'd rowst 'imsel', an' give 'imsel' a lick or two. Ey never ower-did th'lickin' though. Then ey'd start pesterin' 'em fer 'is dinner, an' ther wonna a bit o' peyce fer anybody'till ey'd 'ad it. Thee used get some leyghts fer 'im every wik from th'butcher, an' a two-threy yeds an' teeles from th'fish-mon wot used come rind.

But ey used go rabbitin' an'aw. Theedst think a rabbit 'ud bey eeble spot a wheyte cat a mile awee, wouldstna? Thee were ony part-grown uns wot ey ketched, but ey used bring 'em aw wom. Mind thee, thee wonna any good fer owt be th'tarme ey'd mauled 'em abite.

An' then one mornin' ey brought a full-grown un wom. It was too big fer 'im carry so ey was draggin' it up th'road. Th'folks wot seyd 'im with this rabbit said thee coulda kilt ther-sels with laughin'. Ey kept draggin' it a yard or two an' then gettin' dine at th'seyde on it an' 'avin a bit of a snooze. Then ey'd drag it a bit further an' get dine aggen. Ey was jiggered up, but ey was determined get it wom.

Th'folks ey belonged ter said thee funt Fred an' this rabbit lyin' 'gether on th'back-doer step. Fred was fast asleyp.

Ey didna weeke up'till dinner-tarme, an' ey lukked aw ower th'pleece fer this rabbit. But ey'd bin robbed. It was in th'stew-pot in th'oven an' ey 'ad fer bey content with a lump o' leyghts. Ar reckon Fred musta bin reyght sneaped abite 'em pinchin' 'is rabbit 'cos it was a lung tarme afoer ey brought another un wom."

A little pit dine th'back wood

"Dust remember me tellin' thee abite owd Tum's lad an' them two dogs?" asked Jabez. "Th'black un got run ower be a bus if thee rememberst, an' then that little wheyte terrier, wot th'black un was runnin' after started follerin' th'lad abite.

Anyroad, one dee this lad o'Tum's was dine th'back wood with this terrier when summat funny 'appened. It was in th'nineteyn twentysix strike, an' Tum an' a relative o' 'is cawed Dan 'ad gotten a little pit dine theer.

Thers a lot o' shaller seyms o' coal in that wood thee knowst, an' Tum an' Dan 'ad done a bit o' measurin' up, an' a bit o' cogitatin', an' thee'd figured ite as if thee dug in a certain spot thee oughta come across a good thick seym o' coal.

So thee set abite it. Th'spot wheer thee started diggin' was part wee up a bonk on th'fer side o' that little bruk in th'top corner o' th'wood. Thee expected strike coal abite ten foot dine, but thee didna.

It was rawngin' work throwin' shovelfulls o' clee up from that depth, an' thee 'ad fer keyp choppin' treys dine fer make props fer 'owd th'sides up. Thee were just abite ready fer jack it in.

An' then one mornin' Dan come trundlin' through th'wood with an owd mangle straddled across a wheyle-barrer. Tum said: 'What's up, sirree? Is it weshin' dee?' But Dan said ey'd gotten a good idea – it'd come ter 'im aw of a suddin in th'neyght.

Ey set this mangle up at th'bottom side o' th'ole an' 'eld it dine with some big stones. Then ey fastened a rope ter one o' th'rowlers an' tuk it ower a pulley-wheyle across th'top o' th'ole. Ey'd meede a rattlin' good winch! Tum's lad was in 'is element weyndin' a bucket up an' dine with this owd mangle.

On th'follerin' Satdee af'noon thee struck coal abite twenty foot dine. Tum was dine th'ole at th'tarme an' ey sent a bucket o' this coal up fer Dan an' th'lad 'ave a luk at.

Th'lad got that excited. Ey was dancin' abite, an' shytin' dine th'ole ter 'is feyther. Th'little terrier couldna understand wot aw th'commotion was abite an' ey started barkin' is yed off An' then th'lad spotted somebody comin'. A mon was runnin' full tilt dine th'bonk, an' ther was summat up with 'im.

Ey was meekin' some funny noises an' ey was blue in th'feece. An' wost of aw ey was yeddin' streeght fer th'ole. Th'lad shyted, an' Dan was just in tarme fer step rind th'top side o' th'ole an' push this bloke ite o' th'road. Ey went yed fost inter th'little bruk at th'bottom o' th'bonk an' summat shot ite o' 'is mythe.

Wot dust think it was, sirree? It was a peyce o' apple. It turned ite ey'd bin walkin' through th'wood bitin' this apple an' a peyce on it 'ad got stuck fast in 'is throat.

Ey said ey'd 'eerd th'noise wot Tum's lad an' th'dog meede when thee struck coal an' ey'd run ter wheer th'synd was comin' from.

Another minute or two with that apple in 'is throat an' ey'd bin a gonner. An' if it 'adna bin fer th'lad ey'da fell dine th'ole an' very larkly kilt 'imsel'.

But theydst never guess who ey was. It was th'dreyver o' that bus wot'd run ower th'lad's black dog! It's funny th'road things turn ite, inna it?"

"Wey used get aw excited when it was prize-dee at Sundee Schoo'," said Jabez. "Thee awwees dished theyse prizes ite in th'Chapel at th'af'noon service.

Th'books used bey in piles on a teeble at th'front, an' if thee cockst thee yed on one seyde thee couldst reyd some o' th'titles. Ar used try an' guess which on 'em was marn.

Everybody 'ad a prize thee knowst. It didna matter if theedst ony bin Sundee Schoo' threy or foer tarmes ther'd bey a book fer thee o' some sort. Mind thee, them with most marks got th'best uns. Ar've still got most o' marn but ar've lost one or two with lendin' 'em ite.

It reminds me o' th'teele abite that bloke wot towd folks ey'd decided ey wonna goin' lend any o' 'is books ite anymoer, but if anybody wanted reyd any on 'em thee could come rind ter 'is 'ice an' reyd 'em. But th'tarme come when this bloke with th'books wanted burrer some gardnin' tools off a mate o' 'is.

This mate towd 'im ey'd decided ey wonna lendin' 'is tools ite anymoer, but ey was welcome fer come rind an' use 'em in 'is gardin. Sarved 'im reyght, didna it?

Anyroad, ar was tellin' thee abite theyse prize-dees, wonna ar? Thee used try an' get a special preycher fer give theyse prizes ite. One yeer wey 'ad a professer! Ey was a local lad – born an' bred at Red Hall farm. Ey used walk Silverdeele an' back every dee fer ketch th'tram ter th'igh Schoo' in 'Castle. Tidy walk fer a lad, wonna it?

Us lads expected this professer fer preych one o' them ower-thee-yed sermons wot nowbody could understand. Wey reckoned wey were doomed fer suffer in silence fer abite 'afe-an-'our afoer us got us 'ands on us books. But wey didna.

Ar con remember ter this dee wot ey talked abite. Ey didna preych wot theedst caw a sermon – ey come dine ite o' th'pulpit an' just chatted ter us abite words.

Ey said thee'd gotten thysands o' books at this University wheer ey worked, an' theyse books 'ad gotten millions o' words in 'em. But ther were some words 'is mother used wot wonna in any o' theyse books. Ey reckoned it was a pity thee'd missed 'em ite 'cos some on 'em were reyght good uns.

Ey mentioned a lot o' theyse words – ar conna remember aw on 'em, but ey said ther was threy words 'is mother used wot ey'd larke us childer fer remember. One on 'em was nowce, one on 'em was gumption, an' th'other was stickability.

Ey said everybody 'ad got some nowce, but some 'ad gotten a bit moer than others. Th'folks as went ter 'is University 'ad gotten a fair 'elpin' o' nowce but some on 'em 'adna got any gumption at aw. Ey reckoned yer 'ad fer 'ave gumption as well as nowce.

But 'is mother 'ad towd 'im if ey wanted get ter th'top o' th'trey ey'd got 'ave stickability as well. 'Er said stickability was a bit larke a dog with a bone. Yer'd got fer keyp gnawin' at things 'til yer'd got aw th'meyt off 'em.

Wey never expected a professer use words larke them. But ar reckon ey knew wot ey was talkin' abite, dustna they?"

Me owd Anty Kitty

"Ar'm very partial ter a pittled onion," said Jabez. "But ar never 'ave a pittled onion withite thinkin' abite me owd Anty Kitty. Th'little cottage wheer 'er lived was pulled dine a lung wheyle back.

It stuck ite inter th'road an' when th'buses started runnin' ther was 'ardly room fer'em get passed. Er said 'er didna know wot thee'd got 'ave them greet lommerin' things on th'road fer. Thee tried shiftin' 'er ite a tarme or two so's thee could knock th'cottage dine, but 'er said: 'Ower mar jed body'. So thee 'ad fer leyve 'er alone 'til 'er did go jed.

Ar dunna know whether th'cottage 'ad sunk or th'road 'ad come up, but th'kitchin' floer was a good foot below grind level. Mind thee, th'owd cottage musta bin well-built 'cos ar've sut in theer when th'buses went passed th'doer an' thee couldstna feyl a tremor.

Me Anty Kitty didna go ite very offen, but ther wonna much goin' on in th'village wot 'er didna know abite. Ther was a little winda in th'parlour wot lukked dine th'village, an' another little winda in th'kitchen wot lukked up th'village. So one road or another 'er seyd a lot o' things wot went on. An' wot 'er didna sey 'er eksed abite.

When ar was a lad it wonna very offen ar could get passed th'cottage withite 'er spottin' me. 'Er'd bey at th'doer in a crack an' 'er'd see ter me: 'Wheer are yo' off to'? Fancy tryin' dodge passed withite me seyin' yer. Yoer a nowghty lad'.

An' 'er'd meeke me go in an' sit dine on th'owd settle an' talk ter 'er. 'Er'd give me a peyce o' treycle toffee, or an apple, or mebbe a stick o' rhubub with some sugar in a saucer fer dip it in. Sometarmes 'er'd see: 'Thers some cake in th'pantry – go an' get a peyce'. 'Er used meeke some grand seyd-cake but th'trouble was ar was frittened death o' that pantry.

It was as dark as a bag, an' ther was a well in th'floer. Funny pleece fer 'ave a well wonna it?

Mind thee, ar reckon it was neyce an' 'andy in th'bad weather. Me feyther 'ad towd me a teele abite a mon wot neyly got dryndcd in that well – th'trap-doer 'ad rotted.

So ar never trusted it. Ar used 'owd on ter one o' th'pantry shelves an' get a peyce a cake with me other 'and. 'Er meede me put a peyce o' news-peeper across me kneys so's th'cake-crumbs wouldna go on th'floer. Then th'questions 'ud start.

'Er'd see: 'Wots yer mother doin' terdee? Wheer did yer feyther go off ter last neyght? Wot tarme did ey come back? Wheer did yer get them new clogs from? Wot did yer mother pee fer 'em?' Ther was now end ter th'questions. 'Er was ever larkly know wot was goin' on in th'village.

But ar was tellin' thee abite pittled onions, wonna ar? When th'poer owd soul's teyth started droppin' ite thee tried fer persuade 'er 'ave a set o' fawce uns, but 'er wouldna. Th'tarme come when 'er'd ony got one tooth left in 'er yed. It was a front un on th'reyght-'and side goin' in. It musta bin a bit ockerd fer th'owd girl but 'er reckoned 'er could eat owt.

Somebody eksed 'er wot abite nuts, but 'er said 'er wonna a monkey. An' then somebody eksed 'er abite pittled onions, 'cos thee knew 'er was partial ter 'em. But 'er'd gotten an answer fer that an'aw. 'Er said it was simple – 'er just rowled 'em arind 'er mythe 'til 'er speared 'em with this tooth, an' then 'er just sat an' sucked em.

Ar awwees think abite me owd Anty Kitty when ar 'ave a pittled onion."

Kitty's Cottage 1939

Th'mystery o' owd Isaac's mutton chop

"Did ar ever tell thee abite owd Isaac's mutton chop?" asked Jabez. "Ey used dabble a bit with 'erbs thee knowst, an' one o' th'things ey used meeke was a concoction fer folks wot'd 'ad too much drink. Ey cawed it a yed-mender.

It was rattlin' good stuff be aw accynts. Folks used tell me as after a dose o' Owd Isaac's yed-mender, th'ommers stopped bangin' in ther yeds an' thee could stand th'dee-leyght in ther eyes aggen. Thee couldst eether 'ave a penn'orth or two-penn'orth depending on th'state o' thee yed.

Isaac's missus didna agrey with this yed-mender. 'Er was a big Chapel woman was Jane, an' 'er reckoned as Isaac was doin' th'devil's work 'cos it egged folks on fer drink. 'Er used see ter 'im: 'Let 'em suffer Isaac, let 'em suffer.'

Mind thee, owd Isaac larked a drop o' ale 'imsel'. Mostly, though, ey knew when ey'd 'ad enough. P'raps it was th'prospect o' 'avin' th'lenth o' Jane's tungue wot kept 'im sober. But nar an' aggen at 'olidee-tarmes ey'd 'ave a drop too much.

One Stoke Weekes Satdee mornin' ey went off ite an' towd Jane ey'd bey back fer 'is dinner. 'Er said 'er'd gotten a couple o' mutton chops so ey'd better not bey leete or else thee'd bey spoilt.

Jane got on with 'er cleynin' an' polishin' an' then put theyse two mutton chops in th'oven.

Thee were just done ter a turn abite one o'clock, but ther was now sign o' Isaac. 'Er weeted an' weeted fer 'im, but in th'end 'er decided fer 'ave 'er dinner withite 'im. 'Er put Isaac's chop betweyn two pleetes fer keyp warme on th'ob.

It musta bin gettin' on fer threy o'clock afoer ey showed up. Ey come 'urtlin' through th'doer as drunk as a fiddler. Ey meede fer th'sofa an' ey was fast asleyp afoer Jane 'ad a chance get 'er tungue unrowled. 'Er sat theer scowlin' at 'im sprawled across th'sofa with 'is mythe weyde open. Ee! 'er was mad.

'Er snatched 'is chop off th'ob an' was just goin' put it in th'pantry when 'er 'ad an idea. 'Er smiled ter 'ersel' an' then sut dine at th'teeble an' got owd Isaac's chop dine 'er.

But 'er left some o' th'dip on th'pleete an' tuk it across ter th'sofa. 'Er dipped 'er finger in this dip an' daubed it aw rind Isaac's mythe an' aw dine 'is chin. Ey was that fer gone ey never felt owt. Then 'er weshed-up an' sut 'ersel' dine fer a snooze.

It was gettin' on fer tey-tarme afoer ey wok up. Ey sut up an' lukked arind 'im an' said: 'Ee! ar'm famished. Ar'll 'ave that mutton chop nar.'

Jane jumped up an' said: 'Mutton chop? Wot on earth at talkin' abite? Theyt th'limit, they at. Thee sits theer with mutton fat aw rind thee mythe an' runnin off th'end o' thee chin, an' theest got th'nerve fer tell me thee 'astna 'ad thee mutton chop?'

Owd Isaac lukked at 'er a bit funny larke. Then ey licked 'is tungue aw rind 'is mythe an' ey could teeste this mutton fat. Ey said: 'Well ar'll bey jiggered. Fer th'leyfe on me ar conna remember eatin' that mutton chop.' Jane said: 'Ar anna surprised. They dustna even know wot dee it is when theyst 'ad drink.

Ar reckon it must addle thee breens or summat, but if they't still 'ungry thers a bit o' bread an' cheyse in th'pantry.'

But owd Isaac went an' 'got 'imsel' a double dose o' yed-mender. Ey was still a bit bothered abite that mutton chop."

Owd Whacker's besket o' weshin'

"Every Tuesdee neyght 'cept when it was reenin' or snowin' owd Whacker used set off fer 'Ommerend with a close-besket o' weshin' on 'is yed," said Jabez. "Whacker's missus did th'weshin fer one o' th'Ommerend pubs, an' 'er used wesh on th'Mondee an' iron on th'Tuesdee.

Ey used leyve th'basket at th'pub on th'Tuesdee neyght an' then go dine aggen on th'Satdee neyght fer collect th'next wik's weshin'.

One Satdee neyght ey got a mate o' 'is neemed Ezra fer go with 'im. When thee got ter th'pub Whacker bought 'im a pint o' ale, an' ey'd no sooner dined it than ey bought 'im another un. Ezra thowght ter 'imsel': 'That's funny – it inna larke Whacker fer splash 'is money arind that larke that. Ar wonder wot ey wants off me?'

Th'pair on 'em sat suppin' ther ale an' Ezra got th'feylin' as Whacker was up ter summat. Ey seymed fer bey weetin' fer summat 'appen.

Just nar th'landlord shyted across ter 'em as th'weshin' was ready. Whacker jumped up an' put some money on th'teeble an' towd Ezra get 'imsel' another pint.

Ey said ey was just going' ite ter th'back. Ezra thowght ter 'imsel': 'Ar dunna belave it. That's threy pints o' ale ey's bought me – it must bey a dreym ar'm 'avin'.'

Whacker 'adna bin back a couple o' minutes afoer ey was off aggen, an' ey kept poppin' in an' ite larke a dog at a fair. Ezra said: 'Wot's th'matter with thee sirree? At feylin' bad or summat'. Whacker said ey'd gotten th'trots, an' it musta bin summat ey'd etten.

But Ezra said: 'It inna th'trots theyst gotten – it's th'gallops. Every tarme thee comst back thee cost 'ardly get thee breath. Ar reckon theyt up ter summat'.

But owd Whacker said: 'Ar anna up ter nowt, but it's a good job ar brought thee with me. Ar feyl that bad ar dunna think ar con manage carry that besket o' weshin' wom on me own. Wut give us a 'and with it?'

So thee supped up an' got this besket o' weshin' ite o' th'back an' set off fer wom. But thee 'adna gone very fer afoer Ezra said: 'Bar gum Whacker, it's a tidy weeght this besket is. Dun thee awwees 'ave this much weshin?

‘ Whacker said: ‘Thee do. Theen gotten a biggish family thee knowst, an theer very cleyn folk. Thee cheenge ther clothes two or threy tarmes a wik’.

Ezra thowght abite this fer a bit an’ then ey said: ‘That dunna meeke sense. If thee ‘ave fer cheenge ther clothes as offen as that thee must bey dirty folk not cleyn folk’.

Instead o’ comin’ up through Augers Bonk thee tuk a short cut through th’Stone-’ole, an’ when thee were liftin’ this besket ower one o’ th’stiles Ezra pretended ey’d missed ‘is footin’ an’ dropped ‘is end o’ th’besket. Aw th’weshin’ rowled ite on ter th’grind but wot dust think was underneyth it sirree? Th’bottom o’ th’besket was full o’ jed fowls!

It turned ite as some o’ th’folks in them ‘ises top-side o’ th’pub kept a fowl or two at th’back. When Whacker ‘ad bin nippin’ in an’ ite o’ th’pub ey ‘adna bin bȧd at aw. Ey’d bin goin’ rind th’backs o’ theyse ‘ises knockin’ th’fowl off one be one an’ poppin’ ‘em in th’besket under th’weshin’.

Ey was a fawce un was owd Whacker! “

Joe's mother an' 'is weyfe

"Th'other dee," said Jabez, " 'ar was thinkin' abite a bloke ar used know, an' it reminded me o' that bit in th'owd Book wheer it says a good woman's woth moer than a lot o' rubies.

This bloke was neemed Joe an' ey lived with 'is widdered mother. 'Er used weet on 'im 'and an' foot. Stirred 'is tea an' weyped 'is nose, if thee knowst wot ar meyn. 'Er wouldna let 'im do owt fer 'imsel'. Ey didna 'ave lift a finger in th'ice, an' 'er wouldna let th'wind blow on 'im if 'er could 'elp it.

Ar reckon it's a big misteeke fer a woman molly-coddle a mon larke that, 'cos when 'is mother deyed ey was in a reyght mess. Ey'd bey in 'is thirties at th'tarme but ey'd bin that used ter 'avin' everythin' done fer 'im ey was as 'elpless as a new-born babby. Joe couldna boil a kettle let alone a egg.

'Course, some o' th'women felt surry fer 'im, an' betweyn 'em thee did 'is 'ice-work an' 'is weshin', an' one on 'em did 'is shoppin' an' got a bit o' dinner ready fer 'im. But ey wonna a bit greetful – ey tuk it aw fer granted. Ey treyted theyse women larke scivvies, grumblin' at 'em an' dishin' 'is orders ite. Folks wunna stand fer that sort o' treytment, wun thee?

It wonna lung afoer theyse women 'ad 'ad as much as thee could stomach, an' thee left 'im fer fend fer 'imsel.' Dust know sirree, ar've never seyn a mon go dine-bonk faster than Joe did.

Th'flesh seymed fer drop off 'im an' ey used go slouchin' rind th'village lukkin' larke a tramp. Folks wot'd bin ter th'ice said it was beginnin' luk larke a middin.

This musta gone on fer abite a twelve-month, an' then ey seymed fer smarten 'imsel' up. Ey started weshin' 'imsel' a bit offner, an' ey went dine th'Co-op an' got 'imsel' a new suit fer th'wik-ends. Then one dee somebody seyd 'im dine 'Castle with a good-lukkin' young woman on 'is arm. Joe was mashin'

Th'prophets o' doom in th'village said 'er'd never marry 'im, an' even if 'er did ey'd soon 'ave 'er runnin' arind after 'im larke 'is mother used do. But thee were wrung.

Thee 'adna bin wed very lung afoer one o' th'neeghbours seyd Joe with a apron on, weshin' up. 'Er couldna beleyve 'er eyes. An' then somebody else reckoned thee'd seyn 'im on 'is 'ands an' kneys scrubbin' th'kitchin floer. Joe's mother woulda turned in 'er greeve if 'er'd seyn 'im. Ther was now dite abite it though – ey was a cheenged mon.

Mind thee, ey tried fer stick ter some o' 'is owd 'abits, but this young weyfe soon cured 'im. Ar larke th'teele abite th'road 'er stopped 'im from reydin' th'peeper when ey was 'avin' 'is dinner. Ey'd bin used ter eatin' 'is dinner with th'peeper propped up in front on 'im. It used aggrevate 'er.

One dee 'er meede a jam-tart fer 'is puddin'. 'Er left it in th'oven 'til ey was ready fer it, an' then 'er whipped it ite an' put a peyce on it on 'is pleete.

Th'jam was still bubblin' but ey was that intent on reydin' th'peeper ey never lukked wot ey was eatin'. Ey picked 'is spoon up an' put a dollop o' this beylin' jam-tart in 'is mythe!

It tuk th'skin cleyn off 'is tunge, an' it was many a dee afoer ey could eat or smoke in comfort. 'Er'd cured 'im! It's larke th'owd Book says – thee costna put a price on a good woman, cost?"

A farmer, two lads an' a chonnuk

"It's a lung tarme since ar seyd a child with a bowler", said Jabez. "Th'wenches used 'ave wooden uns, but th'lads 'ad iron uns. Simple things wonna thee? Mind thee, them iron uns wonna as simple as thee lukked – thee 'adst fer get th'knack o' bowlin' 'em proper.

Ther were tarmes when ar never went anywheer withite me bowler. Ar remember when mey an' another lad neemed Lenny 'ad bin bowlin' us bowlers aw af'noon. Wey musta bin feylin' 'ungry 'cos wey decided wey'd 'ave a chonnuk. When wey got ter th'chonnuk feyld wey left us bowlers on th'path an' went alung th'rows o' chonnuks lukkin' fer a good un.

Th'big uns tended fer bey a bit pithy, if thee knowst wot ar meyn, an' th'little uns tended fer bey a bit 'ot. It was a nice middlin'-sized un wey were lukkin' fer.

Wey'd just yanked one ite when Lenny shyted: 'Eh up! th'farmer's comin'. Wey dropped dine inter th'furrer an' squinted ower th'top o' th'chonnuks. Wey could sey th'farmer at th'top end o' th'feyld. Ey musta seyn us an' aw, 'cos ey snatched 'is cap off 'is yed an' started runnin' dine th'path. Wey didna want lose us bowlers, but wey dostna go an' get 'em off th'path fear lest ey recognised us.

So wey 'ad fer leyve th'bowlers an' belt off across th'chonnuk feyld. When wey got ter th'edge-bonk wey struck off in different derections. Lenny went straight across th'next feyld but ar went dine th'edge-side. Th'farmer couldna very well foller both on us. Ey 'esitated fer a bit an' then decided fer go after Lenny. Lenny 'ad gotten a red ganzy on an' p'raps ey thowght ey could keyp track on 'im better. But th'last ar seyd o' Lenny ey was goin' larke th'wind across that feyld an' th'farmer was losin' grind.

It was goin' dusk afoer ar dost venture back wom. Ar wonna sure if th'farmer 'ad recognised me or not. Ar was in fer a good tankin' off me mother if ey 'ad. But ar neydna 'ave worried. Ar could tell me mother didna know owt abite it 'cos when ar walked in th'ice 'er didna reych fer th'walkin'-stick.

Lenny got off scot-frey an' aw. It turned ite as when th'farmer 'ad run ite o' puff Lenny 'ad doubled back wom. Ey'd tuk 'is red ganzy off an' then, bowd as brass, ey'd got 'is brother's bowler off th'closet wo' an' started pleein' with it in th'road.

When th'farmer come trudgin' back through th'village with us bowlers ey'd lukked at Lenny a bit queer larke, but ey 'adna said nowt. Ey musta decided Lenny couldna bey th'chonnuk- pincher 'cos ey 'adna got a red ganzy on, an' ey 'adna lost 'is bowler. Lenny 'ad used 'is yed, 'adna 'e?

Yeers after, when ar used go ter th'farm fer 'elp 'em ite at th'arvest, ar come across two cirtles o' rusty owd iron 'angin' up on a neel on th'shippon wo'. It was marn an' Lenny's bowlers!

Mey an' Lenny were a bit too owd fer bowlers be then, but ar brought 'em wom an' cleyned 'em up fer owd tarme's sake. Ar kept em in th'shed fer a bit an' then ar give 'em awee ter a couple o' lads in th'village.

Ar wonder if them two lads ever went chonnuk-pinchin' with 'em larke wey did?"

Sam's mother-in-law an' 'er aspidestra

"Folks tell me as aspidestras are comin' back inter fashion aggen," said Jabez. "Thee anna much fer luk at, are thee? It inna as though thee'd gotten a nice flower or owt. Mind thee, some o' th'owd folks used bey reyght pryde o' ther aspidestras.

Did ar ever tell thee abite that one owd Sam's mother-in-law 'ad? It was reckoned fer bey th'biggest in th'village.

Poer owd Sam never got on with 'is mother-in-law, thee knowst. Th'pair on 'em were awwees at daggers-drawn. Th'trouble was 'er didna think Sam was good enough fer marry 'er dowghter, an' 'er never stopped tellin' 'im.

Anyroad, when Sam used do 'is courtin' in th'parlour this aspidestra stood in a greet big Wedgwood pot on a little rind teeble with a wheyte leece cloth on it. Ey didna tak much notice on it in them dees 'cos 'is mind was on other things, if thee seyst wot ar meyn.

But Sam 'adna bin wed ter this wench fer very lung afoer th'mother-in-law deyd. Straight after th'funeral, Sam's missus come dingin' wom with this aspidestra an' th'little rind teeble.

Sam said ey wonna goin' 'ave it in th'ice, but 'er said 'er'd promised 'er mother 'er'd tak care on it, an' 'er couldna breek a death-bed promise. So inter Sam's front room it went.

Sam couldna abide it. Th'moer ey lukked at it, th'moer it reminded 'im o' 'is mother-in-law. 'Im 'an 'is missus 'ad many a row abite it. It was as though th'flippin thing was comin' betweyn 'em.

Sam swore ey could sey 'is mother-in-law scowlin' at 'im from betweyn th'leyves. Ey funt 'imsel' meekin' feeces at it an' cawin' it neemes.

In th'end, it got on 'is nerves that much ey stopped goin' in th'front-room if ey could 'elp it.

So ey meede 'is mind up ey'd got get rid on it one road or another. Ther was a bloke ey worked with from Silverdeele wot was a good gardner, an' ey remembered 'im talkin' abite weyd-killers. So ey 'ad a word with 'im.

Mind thee, ey dostna tell this bloke wot ey wanted it fer, fear lest word got back ter 'is missus. Anyroad, this Silverdeele mon browght 'im some stuff larke sugar in a peeper bag, an' towd 'im dissolve it in some weyter an' pour it aw ower th'weyds.

But ey couldna very well pour it aw ower th'aspidestra 'cos if 'is missus seyd weyter on th'leyves 'er mit twig summat. Ey didna know wot do fer a bit, an' then ey 'ad a breen-weeve. Ey'd noticed as nar an' aggen 'is missus used weyter it with cowd tea an' wesh th'leyves in it an' aw. It was supposed for bey good fer'em.

So th'next tarme ey seyd 'er gettin' ready fer do th'aspidestra ey spied 'is chance an' put a good dollop o' this weyd-killer in th'cowd tea when 'er wonna lukkin'. That was on th'Satdee.

On th'Mondee neyght when ey come wom from work 'er was weetin' fer 'im at th'doer. 'Er lukked proper upset – 'er couldna weet fer 'im get in th'ice. 'Er said: 'Summat's 'appened ter me mother's aspidestra – aw th'leyves are turnin' bryne.'

Sam was reyght chuffed but ey dostna show it.

Ey just said: 'Fancy that nar – p'raps wey're going' 'ave a early Autumn.'

Be th'end o' th'wik th'owd aspidestra 'ad shrivelled up ter nowt. Sam's missus said: 'Dust think summat's gotten at th'roots?'

Sam said ey wouldna bey surprised an' ey'd tak it iteside an' 'ave a luk at it. When ey firked it ite o' th'pot, it lukked as jed as mutton, but just fer meeke sure ther wouldna bey a resurrection, ey chopped it up in little peyces with 'is shovel.

That neyght Sam sut in th'front-room for th'fost tarme in months. Th'next mornin', 'is missus said: 'Sam, ar've bin thinkin'.

Sam said: 'Thee shouldstna – it inna good fer thee.' But 'er said: 'Ar'm still upset abite me mother's aspidestra. Dust think that tea ar weytered it with was a bit too strung fer it?'

Sam chuckled ter 'imsel' an'then said: 'Ar reckon theyst just abite 'it th'neel reyght on th'yed.' But ey dostna tell 'er wot ey was chucklin' abite."

" 'Ast noticed as everybody seyms fer 'ave dees when everythin' goes aggen 'em?" said Jabez.

"It seyms as though it dunna matter wot yer do yer conna do reyght fer doin' wrung. It's a pity wey dunna know when them sort o' dees are comin', inna it? Wey could stop in bed aw dee an' keyp ite o' th'road.

Ar remember 'avin' one o' them sort o' dees when ar was a lad. In a manner o' speykin' it aw started afoer ar even got up – ar fell ite o' bed onter th'floer!

Ar reckon it musta bin one o' them omens, or whatever thee cawst 'em, 'cos nowt went reyght fer th'rest o' th'dee.

Ar dunna remember whether it was a Satdee or whether it was in th'schoo' 'ollidees – it was one or th'other. Anyroad, ar was in me mother's bad books afoer ar'd finished me bit o' breakfast.

Ar went an' knocked me cup o' tea flyin' aw ower th'teeble-cloth. An' then things went from bad ter woss. Afoer ar went ite plee me mother wanted me go th'shop. 'Er'd given me a ten-bob note, an' on th'road back ar'd got me cheenge clutched in me fist.

Ar dunna know whether it was me shadder ar fell ower or wot, but 'afe-wee dine th'leene ar come a reyght cropper.

It ony scrawped me kneys an' elbers a bit but when ar got wom me cheenge was 'afe-a-dollar short! 'Afe-a-dollar was a lot o' money in them dees, wonna it?

Dust know, sirree, ar dunna think ter this dee as that 'afe-dollar got ite o' me fist, but th'shop-woman swore 'er 'adna short-cheenged me. So ar was in 'ot-weyter aggen off me mother.

When ar went fer caw on me mates wey decided fer go an' plee dine th'back wood. Ther used bey a bruk wot run through th'wood. It's mostly dried up nar but in them dees ther was a middlin' lot o' weyter in it, an' it was a grand pleece fer plee.

This perticler dee, wey were goin' try an' dam this bruk up. Ther was one pleece wheer th'bonk-sides were abite threy foot 'igh. If wey built th'dam theer wey could meeke a nice little poo'.

But th'fost thing wey'd got do was dig a bit of a trench further up th'bruck fer turn th'weyter off its course'till wey'd finished th'dam. Ar remember takkin' me shoes off an' puttin' 'em in a seefe pleece so's thee wouldna get wet – ar didna want blot me copybook with me mother aggen.

Be th'tarme wey'd carried bricks an' stones an' clods fer this dam, an' then plastered it aw up with clee, wey were rowelled up. Ar managed weype some o' th'wost on it off with gress an' ferns, but wet clee taks a bit o' shiftin' off thee clothes, dunna it?

When ar come fer luk rind fer me shoes ar couldna find 'em anywheer. Ar thowght thee mitta bin weshed dine th'bruk inter th'poo' wot wey'd meede. But yer couldna sey owt in th'poo' wey'd churned th'weyter up that much it lukked larke bryne soup.

Th'other lads wouldna let me meeke a 'ole in th'dam fer let th'weyter ite, so ar 'ad fer weede inter it an' feyl fer me shoes with me feyt. Ar never funt em. It was as though thee'd vanished off th'feece o' th'earth.

Thee cost imagine wot a mess ar musta lukked when ar got wom. Ar was soppin' wet an' covered in bryne clee, an' ar'd lost me shoes.

Fer meeke matters woss, one o' me Anties 'ad turned up fer th'dee – th'oity-toity un. 'Er lukked at me as though ar'd just crawled ite from under a brick.

Me mother give me a reyght good tankin' an' packed me off bed withite any snappin'. P'raps 'er thowght it was th'seefest pleece fer me. Mind thee, it wouldnera surprised me if th'ceylin' 'ad fell in on me.

It was one o' them dees."

"When ar luk back", said Jabez, "ar remember some folks moer fer wot thee said than fer wot thee did. Tak me owd Ant Hannah fr'instance. Ar conna remember much abite wot 'er did, but ar keyp bringin' ter mind a lot o' things 'er said.

'Er seymed fer 'ave an owd seein' fer everythin' wot 'appened. Mind thee, ar reckon 'er invented some on 'em 'ersel'.

One o' th'things 'er couldna abide was grumblers, perticly them wot sut on ther backsides an' grumbled abite wot other folks were doin'. 'Er used tell 'em: Th'ony folks wot dunna do owt wrung are them wot dunna do owt.'

Owd Ant Hannah 'ad moer than 'er fair share o' trouble in 'er tarme but 'er never let things get 'er dine. If anybody tried sympathise with 'er 'er'd see ter 'em: 'Them as anna bin in th'valleys dunna appreciate th'myntains.'

An' if ar fell dine when ar was a little lad 'er'd see ter me: Dunna blart. If thee never fawst dine thee't never know th'road fer get up.' Thers a lot o' good sense in that thee knowst.

But talkin' abite rememberin' folks fer wot thee said, ther used come a woman fer sey me mother nar an' aggen. 'Er was a nice woman but 'er 'ad a funny road o' puttin' things. As soon as 'er got in th'ice 'er eyes 'ud bey everywhere. After 'er'd 'ad a good luk rind 'er'd see ter me mother: 'Anna them bin good curtins?' or 'Anna that bin a good frock yer'n gotten on?' or 'Anna this bin a good bit o' carpet?'

Th'woman didna meyn any 'arm thee knowst, but th'road 'er said it used aggravate me mother now end. Fer yeers me mother just grinned at 'er, but th'dee come when 'er couldna stand it any lunger. 'Er turned on this woman an' said: 'If thee meynst it's abite tarme ar'ad some new curtins, or a new frock, or a new carpet, whey on earth dustna see so instead o' tellin' me wot good uns theen bin!'

'Er didna come aggen fer a lung wheyle but ever after that wey used mimic this woman. If me feyther thowght it was abite tarme ey 'ad a new pair o' trysers ey'd luk dine at th'pair ey'd got on an' ey'd see: 'Anna theyse bin good trysers?'

An' if any on us brok owt wey'd see: 'Anna this bin a good cup?' or 'anna this bin a good winda?' It seeved me from many a good 'idin', 'cos me mother couldna 'elp smilin' whenever ar said it.

But it was me feyther wot tuk th'biscuit. Ey was up on th'roof one dee doin' a bit o' bodgin'-up rind th'chimney-pot. Ey'd practically finished when ey missed 'is footin'.

Ey musta clutched at th'chimney-pot fer try an' seeve 'imsel' but it come off in is 'ands, 'an 'im 'an th'pot come slitherin' dine th'roof an' dropped in th'gardin'. Me mother rushed ite expectin' 'im fer bey crippled fer life. But ey wonna.

Ey adna even brokken a bone, but it'd given 'im a reyght good sheekin' up.

Ey lee theer groanin' amongst th'rows o' taters with th'smashed-up chimney-pot aw arind 'im. Ey felt 'imsel' aw ower an' then ey lukked up at me mother an' said: 'Anna that bin a good chimney-pot?'

Me mother didna know whether laugh or blart.

Fanny's 'erb beer

"Folks dunna seym fer meeke 'erb-beer nar-a-dees, dun thee?" said Jabez. "Yeers ago ther was awwees somebody in th'village wot meede it. Rattlin' good stuff it was an' aw.

Ther was nowt larke it fer quenchin' thee thirst. It was a lot better than lemonade or owt larke that on a ot'-dee. Mind thee, wey dunna seym fer 'ave many 'ot-dees leetly, dun we?

Owd Fanny used brew a drop o' good. Ar con sey 'er nar, goin' rind th'feyds with a basket an' a pair o' scissors getherin' 'erbs. 'Er awwees wore a pair o' owd gloves fer stop th'nettles stingin' 'er. 'Er used do a good treede in th'summer, perticly at th'wik-ends when ther was a cricket match on. Threy a'pence a bottle 'er used charge fer it. Thee were threy-afe-pint bottles thee knowst, with th'corks fastened dine with string.

Some o' th'village youths used bet one another thee couldna drink a bottleful withite takkin' ther mythes awee. Ar ony knowed one bloke wot could do it reglar – a pint an' 'afe at one gollup blew thee up larke a balloon thee knowst.

Us lads used 'ave a bottle betweyn threy on us – that was a'penny apeyce. Th'one wot fetched it an' tuk th'empty bottle back could drink th'beer in th'neck fer 'is trouble. Wey marked th'rest o' th'bottle off in threy parts so's everybody knowed wheer drink to.

Ar remember owd Danny's missus tellin' me abite th'tarme Danny 'ad a go at meekin' 'is own 'erb-beer. Ey reckoned as Fanny's wonna strung enough for 'im. Ey got Fanny's recipe off 'er, an' then ey put in a extra fistful o' yarrer an' some errif an' a two-threy moer 'erbs wot come into 'is yed. Ey brewed it up in 'is missus's big fish-kettle.

Ar dunna know whether ey put too much yeyst in it or whether it was th'-extra 'erbs, but Danny an' 'is missus didna 'ave a wink o' sleyp that neyght. After ey'd tied th'corks dine ey'd put th'bottles on th'pantry floer. Thee 'adna bin in bed very lung afoer thee 'eerd a noise larke a gun goin' off.

It was one o' th'bottles blowin' its cork. Thee 'eerd th'cork go rattlin' rind th'pantry shelves.

An' then fost one an' then another o' theyse bottles went off, an' after Danny 'ad bin dine-steers threy or foer tarmes 'is missus got up an' meede a pot o' tea.

'Er reckoned 'er'd never seyn owt ser funny in 'er life as Danny in 'is neyght-shirt with a candle paddlin' rind in th'spilt beer on th'pantry-floer tryin' find theyse blown-off corks fer put 'em back in th'bottles.

In th'end ther was ony threy or foer bottles wot 'adna blown-off so ey tuk 'em upsteers with 'im so's ey wouldna 'ave get up aggen.

Ey put 'em under th'bed but thee adna got off sleyp afoer ther was another explosion under th'bed an' a cork thumped inter th'mattress under Danny's missus. 'Er said 'er wonna goin' lie theer fer bey shot at, an' 'er got up an' got th'breakfast ready. An' th'rest o' th'bottles went off afoer Danny went work an' ther wonna 'afe a mess on th'bedroom floer.

Ey awwees reckoned as Fanny 'ad codded 'im when 'er'd give 'im th'recipe but ar dunna think 'er would – 'er wonna that sort. But one thing was certain – 'er never 'ad any competition from Danny when it come ter meekin' 'erb-beer."

A customer for Fanny's 'erb beer

Th'cantankerous big ginger mare

"Cost remember me tellin' thee abite that greet big ginger mare wot was frittened with that steym-injin an' welly kilt me?" said Jabez. "Well, ar was thinkin' abite that mare th'other dee an' ar remembered as 'er once brok a bloke's leg an' then seeved 'is leyfe.

This bloke was leebourin' at th'farm at th'tarme, an' when ey wanted 'er ey used go ter th'fer end o' th'farmyard an' whistle ite.

But this mare was a bit cantankerous – sometimes 'er'd come ter 'im an' sometarmes 'er wouldna. It aw depended on wot sort o' mood 'er was in. Just larke a woman, wonna it?

Anyroad, on this perticler dee 'er was actin' a bit 'ard-earin', an' 'er tuk not a scrap o' notice on 'im. Ey neyley blew 'is front teyth ite with whistlin' but it was now good. 'Er just wonna in th'mood fer workin' that dee.

So ey 'ad fer go reyght dine th'feyld ter 'er an' fetch 'er. Ey grabbed 'owd o' a fistfull o' meene wot was angin' dine betweyn 'er ears an' dragged 'er off towards th'farm.

But thee'd ony got abite 'afe-wee across th'feyld when aw of a suddin this mare reared up in th'air on 'er back legs. Afoer this bloke could let go 'er'd flung 'er yed rind an' slat 'im dine on th'grind.

Then 'er galloped off rind th'feyld larke a mad thing. Th'bloke landed with one leg underneyth 'im an' 'is leg-bone snapped larke a twig.

Theedst never guess wot 'ad upset 'er sirree. It was one o' them theer greet airship things goin' ower. Thee cawed it th'R-100 or th'R-101 – ar conna remember which.

Th'owd mare musta 'eerd it or seyd it goin' ower, an' it'd frittened 'er death.

This leebourer lee 'elpless in agony on th'grind. Ey shyted an' shyted but nowbody in th'village 'eerd 'im 'cos o' th'excitement o' this air-ship goin' ower. Ey managed drag 'imsel' across th'feyld a bit, but ey was bleydin' larke a stuck pig an' ey was gettin' weyker an' weyker.

Th'mare was still beltin' rind th'feyld aw of a lather, but just afoer ey past ite ey remembered whistlin' th'mare an' seyin' er comin' towards 'im. Ey couldna remember owt else after that'till ey funt 'imsel' in th'Infirmary.

It turned ite as when this mare 'ad calmed dine a bit 'er musta come inter th'farmyard. Th'farm-woman was busy in th'dairy an' 'er 'eerd summat thud inter th'back-doer. When 'er opened th'doer th'ginger mare was standin' theer.

'Er shyted fer th'leebourer but when 'er got now answer 'er knew summat was up. 'Er went aw rind th'farmyard, an' then 'er spotted 'im lyin' in th'feyld. 'Er got some men ite o' th'village fer carry 'im up ter th'ice, an' it wonna lung afoer ey was on 'is road th'Infirmary.

Ey was off work fer months but if it 'adna bin fer th'mare bangin' on th'doer it coulda bin napoo with 'im. Funny thing, wonna it?"

Weather foercastin'

"Ther inna much sense in grumblin' abite things wey conna alter, is ther?" said Jabez. "Tak th'weather fr'instance. Folk moan abite th'weather moer than thee moan abite owt else, an' yet wey anna got a earthly chance o' alterin' it.

Funny thing, inna it? 'Course it must bey disappointin' when folks go on 'olidee an' th'weather turns bad on 'em.

Dust remember when th'weyerless fost started givin' weather foercasts? Somebody once towd owd Sarah Jane as this weyerless mon reckoned it was goin' poer dine with reen th'next dee. Th'owd lass knew a thing or two abite th'weather thee knowst, an' 'er said: 'Wot does ey know abite th'sort o' weather wey're goin' 'ave rind this road?

Ey's miles awee in London, inna 'ee? Ey conna sey th'sky let alone th'clouds or th'ills from wheer ey is. Who does ey think ey's coddin? If wey get moer than two spots o' reen termurrer ar'll eat me straw bonnet.

Theest ony got luk arind thee an' thee't sey plenty o' signs o' wot th'weather's goin' bey larke fer th'next hour or two.

Th'swallers an' th'gnats an' th'speyders an' th'toads seym fer 'ave th'knack o' knowin' when thers goin' bey a cheenge in th'weather.

An' then thers that owd rhyme wot says:

'If Beystin's pleen,
it's goin' reen.'

It meyns if thee cost sey Beystin Castle standin' ite nice an' clear thee cost bet thee bottom dollar it wunna bey lung afoer wey get some reen.

Mind thee, some owd joker added a couple o' lines ter th'rhyme, so's it went:

'If Beystin's pleen, it's goin' reen,
If Beystin's gone, it's reenin.'

Some folk reckon fer bey eeble tell wot sort o' summer or winter wey're goin' have, but ar reckon ey's a breeve mon wot sticks 'is neck ite as fer as that.

It reminds me o' th'teel abite that farmer wot towd a mate o' 'is it was goin' bey a champion summer cos th'rooks were buildin' 'igh up in th'treys.

It turned ite fer bey one o' th'wettest summers wey'n ever 'ad, so when this bloke seyd this farmer in th'autumn ey said ter 'im: 'Ar thowght thee saidst it was goin' bey a good summer. Ar reckon theyst got that thing abite th'rooks aw wrung. Them rooks musta bin buildin' ther neysts in th'top o' th'treys so's thee wouldna get flooded ite.'

An' talkin' abite weather prophets, ar was reydin' in th'peeper th'other dee abite some brids wot theen got in one o' theyse fereign countries. Thee caw 'em reen brids 'cos thee ony whistle just before it's goin' reen. At any other tarme thee just keyp ther big mythes shut.

Ar reckon thers folks wot ought tak a lesson or two off them brids, dustna they?"

Napoleon's second Weyterloo

" 'Ast noticed as when yer gettin' on a bit yer con remember things wot 'appened when yer were a child but yer conna remember wot yer 'ad fer yer dinner yesterdee?" said Jabez.

"Ar seyd in th'peeper th'other dee wheer a bloke ar went schoo' with 'ad gone jed aw of a suddin', an' it set me thinkin' abite some o' th'things wey got up ter at schoo'.

On wet dees thee used let us plee in th'class-room at dinner-tarme, but wey wonna allowed plee with a bo' fear lest wey brok owt. One dee this lad ar went schoo' with browght a big bo' with 'im. It wonna queyte as big as a footbo' but it was gettin' on that road.

It was reenin' cats an' dogs at dinner-tarme so wey couldna plee iteside with this bo', but wey reckoned it wouldna do any 'arm if wey just pleed ketchin' with it in th'class-room.

Aw th'teychers used go inter another room fer ther dinners, so wey got one o' th'wenches fer keyp a luk-ite at th'doer so's 'er could tip us th'wink when th'teychers were comin' back. Wey pushed aw th'desks up aggenst th'wo' an' then started pleein' nice an' gentle with this big bo'.

But it wonna lung afoer things got a bit rough, an' some o' th'lads started kickin' th'bo' an' yeddin' it instead o' throwin' it.

Ther was a big picture o' Napoleon on th'wo' at th'back o' th'class-room. Ey was standin' on th'deck o' a ship with one arm tucked in 'is jacket an' a funny-lukkin' 'at on 'is yed. Ey awwees lukked reyght miserable. Ar think thee were takkin' 'im ter one o' theyse deserted islands somewheer, so's ey wouldna bey eeble kick-up anymoer bother.

Anyroad, owd Napoleon met 'is second Weyterloo that dee 'cos somebody kicked this bo' straight inter th'picture. Th'glass smashed ter smithereyns an' Napoleon come crashin' dine off th'wo an' landed behind th'ot-weyter pipes.

Wey didna know wot do abite this picture – th'teycher couldna 'elp but notice it was missin'. An' then one o' th'lads 'ad a breen-weeve. Ey said if wey tuk every bit o' glass ite o' th'freeme p'raps nowbody 'ud notice as th'glass was missin'.

Be th'tarme th'teycher come back from 'is dinner weyd gethered up aw th'brokken glass off th'floer, an' owd Napoleon was back on th'wo' as good as new, 'cept ey 'adna got any glass fer luk through.

Th'teycher never spotted ther was owt wrung with this picture, an' ar think wey'da gotten awwee with it if it 'adna bin fer one o' th'wenches. Wey 'appened fer bey tormentin' this wench one dee an' 'er went an' blabbed on us.

Th'yed-master give every lad in th'class six o' th'best across 'is backside – threy fer pleein' with a bo' in th'class-room an' threy fer breekin' owd Napoleon's picture.

Ar reckon it was us lads wot met us Weyterloo that dee, dustna they?"

When th'queyn toppled off th'throne

"Did ar ever tell thee abite th'tarme when th'throne toppled?" asked Jabez. "It was in th'dees when wey used 'ave a carnival every yeer fer th'Infirmry.

Ar didna 'afe enjoy them carnivals when ar was a lad. Whey aw dressed up as summat or other an' wey eether walked in th'procession or else wey rid on one o' th'farm-wagons.

Th'osses were groomed 'til thee shone, an' ther teels an' meenes were done up with fancy ribbons. Th'oss-brasses were polished 'til thee lukked larke gowd, an' th'wagons were peented an' decorated with coloured peeper. Thee were a grand seyght.

One o' th'wagons was awees meede up fer luk larke a ward in th'Infirmry. Thee'd 'ave somebody in a bed an' ther'd bey folks dressed up as nosses an' doctors fer luk after 'em.

Ar remember thee 'ad a lad wey cawed Fatty in this bed one yeer, but ey didna suit th'part 'cos ey 'ad a feece larke a big rosy apple wot'd just bin polished. Th'nosses 'ad fer keyp daubin' Fatty's feece with flour fer meek 'im luk bad.

But ar was tellin' thee abite th'throne topplin' wonna ar? Thee used pick a Carnival Queyn from amongst th'village wenches. Mind thee, it awwees caused a bit o' bother amongst th'wenches mothers. Ther wonna 'afe some back-beytin' behind th'sceynes.

Anyroad, one yeer th'Queyn was sittin' on 'er throne on th'wagon at th'side o' th'owd village greyn. This throne was somebody's owd arm-cheer wot'd bin titivated up a bit.

Th'procession was formin' up but it was takkin' a lung wheyle an' th'Queyn's 'oss was gettin' a bit restless. Ey'd seyn some nice-lukkin' gress on th'fer side o' th'greyn an' afoer anybody could stop 'im ey'd set off across th'greyn fer get it. Th'trouble was ther was awwees a 'ole or two in th'greyn wot us lads 'ad dug, an' th'wagon 'adna gone very fer afoer one o' th'front wheyles dropped in one o' theyse 'oles.

Thee'd forgotten fasten th'throne dine an' it come 'urtlin' across th'wagon an' tipped th'Queyn yed fost onter th'greyn! Aw 'er clothes come up ower 'er yed an' th'cryn went rowlin' off dine th'leene' 'Er didna luk much larke a Queyn be th'tarme thee'd gethered 'er up, but thee dusted 'er dine a bit an' put 'er back on th'throne an' off wey aw went.

That was th'seeme yeer as ar went dressed up as a shepherd lad. Wey 'ad a big curly-'aired mongrel at th'tarme an' ey was supposed fer bey me sheyp-dog. Mind thee, ey didna luk much lark a sheyp-dog, an' ey was that owd an' fat ey couldnera ketched a sheyp if yer'd given 'im ten yards start.

Me feyther 'ad funt me a proper shepherd's crook from somewheer but ar reckon it musta bin meede for a ten foot shepherd! Ar was only a bit of a lad at th'tarme an' th'bottom end o' this greet lung crook kept gettin' mixed up with me feyt an' leggin' me dine.

Ar dunna know whether th'judges thowght ar was a comic turn or whether thee felt surry fer me, but thee give me th'third prize. It was ony 'afe-a-dollar but ar felt larke th'richest shepherd lad in th'world."

Carnival Queen at Scott Hay

Wey anna gotten th'nowce

"Ar've awwees reckoned as thers things goin' on arind us wey anna got th'nowce fer understand," said Jabez. "It strikes mey us 'umans are gettin' a bit too big-yedded. Now matter wot 'appens wey awwees try an'expleen it dunna we?

An' if wey conna expleen it we cod 'ersels it eether anna 'appened or else it inna true. Ar caw that big-yedded, dustna they?

Ar meyn fer see, practically everybody's 'ad summat 'appen ter 'em wot thee conna expleen. Tak that dee me feyther cawed fer sey owd Joe an' 'is missus dine th'bottom 'o 'Ommerend. It was at th'back-end o' th'yeer an' ey'd bin fer a walk rind Shraley Bruk.

Th'weather 'ad turned terrible cowd aw of a suddin', an' Joe 'ad meede a rattlin' good fire 'afe-wee up th'chimney. Me feyther pulled a cheer up an' th'threy on 'em sut rind th'fire-pleece natterin' abite this an' that an' nowt in perticler.

Just nar me feyther thowght ey 'eerd somebody moving' abite in th'bedroom ower th'top on 'em. Ey could 'ear th'floer-boerds creykin' as if somebody 'ad just got ite o' bed an' was comin' ter th'top o' th'steers. Ey thowght ter 'imsel'; 'That's funny – ar didna know thee'd gotten anybody livin' with 'em.'

An' then th'steers started creykin' one after th'other an' ey lukked rind at th'stair-foot doer expectin' sey it open. But it didna!

Ey lukked across at Joe an' 'is missus but thee didna seym fer bey takkin' any nowtice So ey said: 'Ar coulda sworn ar 'eerd somebody comin' dine steers but ar must bey misteeken'.

Th'pair on 'em lukked at one another an' then Joe said it was nowt – it was ony th'owd timbers movin' abite a bit with th'cheenge in th'weather. But me feyther could tell ther was moer ter it than that be th'road ey said it.

Ey 'ad it on th'tip o' 'is tungue fer esk Joe who ey thowght ey was coddin', but ey thowght ey'd better keyp 'is nose ite. It wonna any o' 'is business if thee'd gotten somebody upsteers wot thee didna want 'im know abite.

Ey didna let on ter anybody abite it, an' ey'd practically forgotten abite it 'til ey 'appened fer bump inter owd Joe's youngest brother dine 'Castle one dee. Be this tarme Joe an' 'is missus were jed an' gone, an' that row o' cottages wheer thee lived 'ad aw bin knocked dine.

Me feyther got talkin' ter this brother o' Joe's abite th'owd tarmes, an' ey mentioned that dee when ey'd bin in th'cottage an' fancied ey'd 'eerd somebody comin' dinesteers. This brother said ey'd 'eerd it an' aw, but Joe an' 'is missus never talked abite it fear lest thee ever wanted sell th'cottage.

Thee didna want word get arind as thee'd gotten a ghost or summat.

An' then ey said ter me feyther: 'Dust 'appen fer remember wot tarme it was when thee cawdst at th'cottage?' Me feyther said it'd bey five o'clock as near as meede now difference. An' wot dust think Joe's brother said, sirree? Ey said: 'That's th'funny part abite it – it didna 'appen very offen but when it did it was awwees rind abite five o'clock'.

Try an' expleen that if thee cost."

Rough Justice

"Thers a lot fer bey said fer rough justice, if thee knowst wot ar meyn," said Jabez. "Thee 'eerst a lot o' talk theyse dees abite it beyin' bad fer a child fer bey punished when ey's bin nowghty. But ar reckon yer con owerdo this sparin' o' th'rod.

When ar was a lad ar 'ad me fair share o' wot me owd yedmaster used caw 'instant retribution'. Th'fost tarme ey said it ar didna know wot ey meant, but when ey come up behind me an' rapped me across th'knuckles with 'is ruler fer doin' a funny drawin' on 'im in me sum book, ar knew exactly wot ey meant.

Mind thee, th'owd yedmaster wonna th'ony one wot could dish ite this 'instant retribution'. Me mother was pretty good at it an' aw. 'Er didna tell me fer weet 'til me feyther come wom - 'er used give me one theer an' then. Ar dunna reckon it did me any 'arm though, dust they?

An' then ther was that bobby dine Silverdeele. Ey didna beleyve in weestin' folks's tarme an' money in summonses if ey could deyl with it on th'spot. Ar remember one Sundee neyght when wey were up th'Monkey-run. That's wot thee cawed that road up th'bonk from Silverdeele bridge. It used bey thronged of a Sundee neyght with youths an' wenches walkin' up an' dine an' standin' talkin'.

Thers many a good bloke wot met 'is Weyterloo on th'Monkey-run thee knowst.

Anyroad, this perticler Sundee neyght ther were threy on us walkin' 'gether. Wey'd just gotten us fost pair o' lung trysers an' wey didna 'afe fancy us chances with th'wenches. An' wey musta bin feylin' a bit cocky an' aw 'cos this Silverdeele bobby was walkin' up th'bonk in front on us an' wey were takkin' 'im off

Ey was a biggish bloke an' ey was ploddin' up th'bonk larke an owd cart-'oss, gruntin' an' blowin'. Wey started fer mimic 'im an' laugh at 'im behind 'is back.

Ey didna seym fer tak any nowtice fer a bit, but aw of a suddin' ey whipped 'is cape off 'is showder an' swung it rind at us. Two on us went dine on th'grind larke nine-pins, an' aw th'wenches started laughin' at us. It knocked some o' th'cockiness ite on us.

Th'owd bobby never spok a word – ey just swung 'is cape back on 'is showder an' went ploddin' up th'Monkey-run aggen. Ar reckon that bobby did us lads a power o' good.

An' then wey got some rough justice from Big 'Arry one dee. Ey 'ad a grand bed o' strawberries in one o' them gardins dine th'leene – beauties thee were!

Us lads 'ad meede a gap in th'bottom o' th'edge on th'feyld-side, an' wey could get ter theyse strawberries withite anybody seyin' us. Wey used go an' get a 'andful or two practically every dee fer as lung as thee lasted. Anyroad, one dee wey were crawlin' through this gap on us ballies one behind th'other. Ar was just abite 'afe-wee through this gap when th'two lads wot'd gone through in front on me started meekin' some funny noises. It synded as if thee were both goin' bey sick.

Wot dust think Big 'Arry 'ad done on us, sirree? Ey'd gone an' emptied th'closet-pon in th'bottom o' th'gap an' put a bit o' gress on top so's wey wouldna sey it. Wey'd got it aw up th'front o' us gansies. Wey sort o' lost interest in th'strawberries.

Come fer think on it, it wonna exactly 'instant retribution', was it? It was moer larke crime prevention, wonna it?"

Emma's fortune

"Ast ever 'ad thee fortune towd?" asked Jabez. "Ar've never ad much feeth in it mesel'. Mind thee, a lot o' women seym fer beleyve in it, dunna thee?

Wey used get gypsies goin' rind th'village at one tarme, an' it was surprisin' th'number o' women wot'd cross theyse gypsies' palms with silver fer 'ave ther fortune towd. Some on 'em were big Chapel-women an' aw!

Me mother wouldna 'ave any truck with 'em though. 'Er used see: 'Ar reckon ar shall 'ave tak wot comes. If it's goin' bey bad ar dunna want know abite it, an' if it's goin' bey good ar con weet fer it.'

Some folks reckon thee con tell th'future in th'stars or th'cards, or in th'tey-leyves in thee cup. Me mother used tell th'teele abite th'tarme a relative o' 'ers come visit 'er. Ar think 'er was me mother's second cousin on me feyther's side – or summat larke that.

Anyroad up, th'pair on 'em sut 'avin' a cup o' tey after ther dinners when owd Emma walked in wot lived dine th'leene. 'Er was a regular tey-bally was Emma, so me mother got another cup ite an' Emma sut 'ersel' dine.

Theyse women were natterin' abite this an' that, an' it turned ite as this relative o' me mothers reckoned 'er could reyd th'cups. 'Course me mother wouldna 'ave owt do with it, but Emma said 'er didna mind avin 'er cup read as lung as it was good news.

So Emma supped up an' give this woman 'er cup fer reyd. After 'er'd 'ad a good luk at Emma's cup 'er said 'er could sey an umbrella in it. 'Er was just goin' tell Emma wot this umbrella meant when me mother went 'ave a luk at it. 'Er said: 'Umbrella me foot! It dunna luk larke an umbrella at aw. It's too pointed at th'top, an' it anna got a 'andle fer ketch owd on it with.' Me mother said it looked moer larke one o' them big Chinamon's 'ats wot yer sey 'em wearin' in pictures.

Me mother 'ad 'ardly got th'words ite o' 'er mythe when Emma jumped up off 'er cheer as if 'er'd bin shot. 'Er feece dropped a mile an' 'er said: 'Oh mar lors' and went through th'door an' off dine th'yard larke a ship in full seel.

Thee couldna think wot'd struck Emma fer meeke 'er rush off larke that. But 'er was back aggen in abite ten minutes, puffin' an' blowing. 'Er was a big woman was Emma an' 'er 'ad fer let 'er corsets ite a bit afoer 'er could speyk proper.

As soon as 'er'd got 'er breath back 'er said it was me mother wot'd done it. 'Er said: 'Ar reckon ther must bey summat in this cup-reydin' 'cos as soon as yo mentioned th'word Chinamon ar remembered that big rice puddin' ar'd put in th'oven fost thing this mornin'.

'Er said 'er was ony just in tarme fer ketch it afoer it burnt dry, an' 'er owd mon couldna abide burnt puddin'. Me mother 'ad a good laugh at Emma an' 'er rice puddin', an' then 'er said ter this relative: 'It luks as though ar'm better than yo at this cup-reydin'. Dun yer think ar ought tak it up?'

But 'er was ony coddin'."

A dee fer accidents

"Dust remember me tellin' thee abite Emma 'avin' 'er fortune towd in a tey-cup?" asked Jabez.

"Well, ar 'appened fer bump inter one o' owd Tum's sons th'other dee. Thee knowst who ar meyn, dustna? – owd Tum wot used do a lot o' local preychin'.

Ar was tellin' this son o' Tum's abite owd Emma, an' ey started tellin' me abite a bloke ey used work with neemed Jim.

This Jim towd folks's fortunes be th'stars. Ey meede a reyght good job on it be aw accynts. It wonna enough fer 'im know wot dee thee wast born on, ey 'ad fer know th'exact spot an' th'exact tarme.

Then ey'd meeke a big drawin' fer show wheer aw th'stars were at th'very minute thee wast born. Musta 'ad a good yed on 'is showders, mustna 'e?

Ey reckoned as thee character an' aw thee future depended wheer theyse stars were when thee tukst thee fost breath.

An' ey said ther were certin dees when theyse stars got a bit cross-omical an' theyse perticler dees were awwees bad fer summat or other.

Ther were dees wot were bad fer accidents, an' dees wot were bad fer fo'in' ite, an' dees when yer shouldna start owt or go anywheer. It awwees seymed fer bey a bad dee fer summat.

Tum's son said ter 'im one dee: 'Theyt awwees tellin' us abite th'bad dees. Wot abite th'good dees? Thee never tellst us owt abite them. Dunna wey get any good dees?'

Anyroad, theyse men decided plee a trick on owd Jim. Thee started collectin' owd bottles an' jamjars an' tin-cans, an' thee put 'em in a cupboard 'til thee'd gotten it full. Then thee weeted 'til th'next tarme ey said it was a bad dee fer accidents.

Sure enough, it wonna lung afoer th'stars 'ad gotten thersels cross-omical aggen, an' Jim said: 'It's a dee fer accidents terdee, lads. Bey careful wot yer doin'.'

Jim worked with 'is back ter theyse other men an' just nar one on 'em sidled up ter th'cupboard an' put 'is arm in it an' swept aw theyse bottles an' jars an' tins onto th'floer.

Thee meede an awmighty crash, an' Jim spun rind shytin': 'Ar towd yer! Ar towd yer it was a bad dee fer accidents. P'raps yer'll beleyve me nar.'

Course, aw theyse men bost ite laughin' at 'im, an' when Jim seyd th'trick thee'd pleed on 'im ey went reevin' mad. Ey cawed 'em aw th'neemes under th'sun an' stormed ite through th'doer.

But wot dust think ey did, sirree? As ey went through th'doer ey tripped up ower th'step an' come a cropper on th'yard iteside. Ey didna breek any bones but ey knocked 'imsel' abite that much ey 'ad fer go on th'club. It musta bin a dee fer accidents after aw."

Th'charabang weddin'

"It's surprisin' th'road some women flock fer gawp at a weddin', inna it?" said Jabez.

"An' thee't awwees sey some on 'em bartin' ther eyes up. Ar've offen wondered wot thee blart fer. Dust think it's because theer wishin' it was their turn aw ower aggen, or because th'poer bride dunna know wot 'ers lettin' 'ersel' in fer?

Mind thee, ar've awwees bin partial ter a good weddin'. 'Ast noticed as some weddin's seym fer go larke clockwork, an' some on 'em seym fer bey a reyght muddle-up?

Th'wost weddin' ar ever 'eerd abite was at a little church th'other side o' Leyk. Ar 'appened fer meyt th'owd parson wot'd tied this couple 'gether an' ey was tellin' me aw abite it.

This weddin' was supposed fer kick-off at 11 o'clock but it'd gone 'afe-past an' nowbody 'ad turned up bar th'parson an' a clutch o' women standin' in th'road.

Th'parson began think ther'd bin a misunderstandin' abite th'tarme. 'Course, theyse women in th'road were gabblin' awee at twenty ter th'dozen. Thee'd aw decided ther'd bin a last-minute jiltin', an' it was bound fer bey th'mon's fawt. Thee were tellin' one another wot a cryin' sheeme it was, an' men were aw th'seeme – yer couldna trust 'em, an' th'poer lass must bey 'eart-brokken.

But just nar, th'parson 'eerd some singin' in th'distance, an' ey towd theyse women fer shut up a bit. This singin' seymed fer bey gettin' closer an' closer, an' then a big charabang come 'urtlin' rind th'corner. It was full o' folks singin' ther yeds off

Dust know who thee were, sirree? Thee were th'weddin' guesses – thee'd aw come 'gether. This charabang 'ad bin goin' rind th'countryside collectin' 'em aw up, an' thee'd gotten th'bride on th'back seyt.

It pulled up at th'church-doer an' th'fost one fer get ite was a bloke wot was blindfolded with a red 'enkerchief! Somebody 'elped 'im dine an' led 'im inter th'church pretty smart.

Ar bet them women's tungues didna 'afe start clackin' aggen. Then aw th'rest on 'em got ite o' th'charabang an' th'bride follered 'em inter th'church.

It turned ite as this blindfolded mon was th'bridegroom. Ey wonna supposed fer bey in th'charabang. Ey was supposed fer meeke 'is own road ter th'church, but 'im an' th'family 'ad 'ad a bit o' a boozy do th'neyght afoer, an' nowbody 'ad wok up 'til th'charabang come fer pick 'em up.

Then thee couldna find th'best mon. It wouldnera mattered aw that much ony ey'd got th'ring. Thee remembered ey'd bin at this do with 'em th'neyght afoer but thee couldna find 'im 'igh nor low. It was many a wheyle afore thee come across 'im – somebody fell ower a couple o' feyt stickin' ite from under th'end o' th'sofa, an' theer ey was.

It was too leete fer th'bridegroom get ter th'church on 'is own – ey'd 'ave go in th'charabang. But th'bride's mother turned ockerd. 'Er said it was bad luck fer th'bridegroom set eyes on th'bride afoer thee got church.

So thee were flummoxed fer a bit. An then somebody 'ad a bright idea – if thee blindfolded 'im ey wouldna bey eeble sey th'bride. So that's wot thee did.

Ar've 'eerd abite shot-gun weddin's – but ar've never 'eerd abite a bridegroom beyin' tuk ter th'church blindfolded afoer, 'ast they?"

"Ar think ar towd thee a bite abite owd Charlie wot used come preychin', didna ar?" said Jabez.

"Somebody mentioned 'im th'other dee an' tuk me mind back ter some o' th'sermons ey preyched. Ey was ony a miner thee knowst, an' ey 'adna 'ad much schoolin', but dust know, sirree, ar'd as lief listen ter owd Charlie as any parson ar've ever 'eerd.

It was aw good gress-root stuff – none o' thee 'igh-falutin' theology, or whatever thee cawst it. One minute ey'd 'ave yer chucklin' ter yersel'. an' th'next minute ey'd 'ave tears in yer eyes. But yer didna ferget wot ey said.

When ey got warmed up, th'pulpit wonna big enough fer 'im. Ey'd come dine ter th'front an' pather back-an'-to across th'full width o' th'Chapel. An' ey 'ad th'knack o' meekin' yer think abite wot ey was tellin' yer.

Ey'd see summat larke. 'Us wot come Chapel anna any better than them as dunna – wey are ony tryin' fer bey.' Then ey'd leyve yer fer think abite it fer a minute or two wheyle ey 'ad another bit of a pather across th'Chapel. Then aw of a suddin ey'd stop in 'is tracks an' stare at th'congregation an' shyte ite: 'It's true, inna it?' Ey 'ad a rattlin' good pair o' lungs did Charlie, an' nowbody nodded off when Charlie was preychin.'

An' thee shouldsta 'eerd 'im sing! It was now use th'organist thinkin' ey could dictate th'road th'hymns were goin' bey sung. As soon as Charlie started up, th'organist 'adna got an earthly. Ey could pull as many stops ite as ey larked, an' ey could pedal 'til ey bost th'bellers, but ey wouldna meeke any impression on Charlie. An' if Charlie tuk a fancy ter one o' th'verses, or ter th'chorus, ey'd start singin' it aggen after th'organist 'ad finished pleein'.

One dee th'organist started pleein' a different tune ter one o' Charlie's feevourite hymns. Ar reckon ey thowght ey was goin' 'ave it aw 'is own road fer a cheenge. But ey 'adna got very fer with it afoer Charlie shyted: ' 'Owd on! 'Owd on! Ar dunna want any o' thee new-fangled tunes – th'owd un's good enough fer mey.'

Ar con still remember th'gist o' some o' 'is sermons. One in perticler was abite beyin' kind ter other folks. Ey tuk 'is text from th'Owd Testament. It was: 'Cast thy bread upon the waters; for thou shalt find it after many days.'

Ey started this sermon off with a teele abite a little lad wot tuk some o' 'is mother's fresh-beeked bread fer feyd th'ducks with on th'pond. 'Course, it wonna lung afoer some o' th'ducks started doing' th'bottoms-up fer get this bread ite o' th-weyter. Th'little lad run back wom shytin: 'Come quick, mother – that bread o' yoers is sinkin' th'ducks!'

Then owd Charlie went on fer tell us as if yer cast enough o' th'bread o' 'uman kindness on th'weyter o' life some on it comes back ter yer two- or threy-fold.

But ey didna put it larke that. Wot ey said was: 'Ar've dished ite many a lot o' th'bread o' kindness in me tarme. Some on it was weested, an' some on it sunk larke a brick. But, praise the Lord, some on it come back ter me with a greet big dollop o' jam on it!'

Owd Charlie awwees seymed fer 'ave th'knack o' puttin' things so's yer'd remember 'em."

Crab-apple jelly

"Dust larke crab-apple jelly?" asked Jabez. "Ar 'ad a jar given me off owd Martha th'other dee. 'Er said 'er knowed it was good stuff 'cos it was meede with Siberian crabs wot 'er'd gethered 'ersel'.

Ar towd 'er ar didna know 'er'd bin gallivantin' off ter fereign parts, but 'er didna seyme fer sey th'funny side on it. Mind thee, 'er was awwees a bit of a sober-sides was Martha.

Me mother used meeke a bit 'o crab-apple jelly every yeer. Thers threy or foer treys dine th'feylds, but me mother reckoned as th'best uns were ite o' owd Joe's copse dine in th'valley. Joe an' 'is missus lived in a little cottage at th'side o' this copse. Ar dunna think it reyghtly belonged th'cottage, but owd Joe soon kicked anybody ite if ey seyd 'em in it.

Just inside th'copse was a biggish crab trey, an' me feyther used go an' get a basketful when ey reckoned owd Joe 'ud bey ite. Theyse crabs were that sour thee set yer teyth on edge just fer luk at em, but thee meede rattlin' good jelly.

One yeer me feyther was off work bad, an' ey couldna go an' get any crabs. Ar was ony a bit o' a lad at th'tarme but ar towd me mother ar'd go an' get some fer 'er. 'Er didna relish th'idea – 'er said owd Joe ud ketch me an' ther'd bey trouble. But ar talked 'er into it in th'end.

Ar tuk th'big shoppin' basket an' sneyked inter th'copse rind th'back road. But somebody 'ad kayled me sirree – ther was 'ardly a crab left on th'trey. Ther was ony them at th'fer end o' th'branches wot yer couldna reych. Th'ony road ar could get any crabs was be climbin' up th'trey an' sheekin' 'em dine.

But now sooner 'ad ar got up th'trey when ar'eerd somebody comin' through th'copse. Ar jumped dine an' grabbed me empty basket an' skidaddled inter th'bushes.

It was owd Joe, an' wot dust think sirree? Ey'd got a basket in one 'and an' a ladder in t'other. Ey'd come pickin' crabs an' aw! Wey'd both bin pipped ter th'post.

When ey lukked up inter th'trey an' seyd thee'd practically aw bin tuk ey swore summat terrible. Then ey got up th'trey on th'ladder an' started sheekin' th'branches just larke ar was goin' do. Ar dostna move fear lest ey spotted me. Ar'd got stee theer an' wetch 'im get aw th'crabs. Ar was reyght sneaped.

When ey'd shuk 'em aw dine ey didna gether 'em up straight awee – ey sut 'imsel' dine with 'is back ter th'trey an' lit is pipe up. It seymed larke 'ours afoer ar 'eerd somebody start shytin': 'Joseph! Joseph! Come here!'

It was 'is missus. Ey muttered summat under 'is breath an' knocked 'is pipe ite. Ey didna stop fer pick th'crabs up – ey left 'is basket an' th'ladder an' went off at th'double. Joe's missus wore th'trysers be aw accynts, an' when 'er cawed th'tune owd Joe danced.

Nar was me chance! Mind thee, ar felt a bit guilty abite pickin' aw theyse crabs up wot Joe 'ad knocked dine, but ar didna larke th'idea o' disappointin' me mother. An', any road, ar was theer fost, wonna ar?

Ther was barely a basketful an' ar've offen wondered wot Joe said when ey come back an' funt 'is crabs 'ad vanished. An' ar bet ey copped it when ey went back ter 'is missus with a empty basket.

Poer owd Joe – it was a bit rough on 'im, wonna it? It's a funny thing but ar dunna think th'crab-apple jelly teested queyte as good that yeer."

"Ar anna a bettin' mon. At they?" said Jabez. "Some folks'll bet on owt though, wunna thee?

Th'wost un ar ever 'eerd abite was a bloke neemed Ephraim thee cawed 'im Eeph fer short. Ey never bet on 'osses or owt larke that, but ey was awwees 'avin' bets with 'is mates, an' folks in pubs.

Ey did a lot o' reydin', an' if ey come across summat unusual or summat as synded impossible ey'd remember it, an' then sooner or leeter ey'd bey eeble 'ave a bet abite it. Ey wouldna come ter th'point straight awee though.

Fr'instance, if ey'd read summat abite ships wot was 'ard fer beleyve ey'd start up a conversation abite fishin', an' then bit be bit ey'd bring th'talk rind ter boats an' ships. Ey was a cunnin' beggar was Eeph.

One dee at work ey started talkin' abite wot tarme ey got up in a mornin' an' wot tarme ey went bed. An' then ey gradually turned th'talk rind ter clocks an' wetches.

After a bit, one o' 'is workmates neemed Alfie said ey'd got a good wetch at wom. It was a gowd 'unter wot'd belonged 'is feyther. Ey said it was a champion tarme-keyper.

It ony lost a minute a dee an' ey put it reyght every Satdee neyght. Eeph smiled ter 'imsel' – Alfie 'ad fell yed fost inter th'trap!

Eeph let 'im sing th'preeses a' this wetch fer a bit, an' then ey said: 'Ar've gotten a wetch wot'll beat that. Ar bought it off a bloke on th'Stones dine 'Castle.'

Alfie said: 'Who dust think thee't coddin'? They dustna 'afe come ite with some corkers. Dust meyn fer tell us as a wetch thee 'adst off th'Stones is better than me feyther's gowd 'unter?' So Eeph said: 'Ar'm just tellin' thee it keyps better tarme than thee feyther's gowd 'unter, an' it ony cost me 'afe-a-dollar. It anna lost or geened a minute in nigh on ten yeer.'

Alfie said ey didna beleyve a word on it, an' ey dost bet as Eeph couldna show 'em this wetch. Eeph said ey larked a mon whose pocket was as big as 'is mythe, an' if Alfie was prepared fer bet a quid on it ey'd bring this wetch in an' prove it.

Th'other blokes egged Alfie on fer 'ave this bet with Eeph. Thee said ther wonna such a thing as 'afe-dollar wetch wot didna neyd alterin' in ten yeer. So Alfie said. 'Awreyght – ar bet thee a quid.'

One on 'em went an' fetched th'foreman fer 'owd th'money, an' th'next mornin' Eeph turns up with this 'afe-dollar wetch an' plonks it dine on th'bench.

Aw theyse workmen cryded rind fer 'ave a luk at it, an' then one on 'em said: 'Th'flippin' thing inna goin'!' Eeph said: 'Ar know it inna – it anna gone fer nigh on ten yeer. Ar towd yer it neether lost nor geened.' Alfie bost ite laughin' an' said: 'Theyst lost thee bet this tarme me owd soul.' An' ey went fetch th'foreman so's ey could get th'money.

But just as th'foreman was goin' give Alfie th'money Eeph said ter 'im: 'Owd thee whip a bit sirree. That money belongs ter mey, an' ar'll prove it ter thee.'

Ey said: 'Ar bet Alfie a quid as mar wetch was a better tarme-keyper than 'is feyther's gowd 'unter, didna ar? Alfie says as th'gowd 'unter loses a minute a dee, an' ey puts it reyght every Satdee neyght.

So, Alfie's wetch ony shows th'reyght tarme on Satdee neyghts – that's once a wik. Aw th'rest o' th'wik it's tellin' th'wrung tarme.

Nar, mar wetch stopped at 'afe-past threy neyley ten yeer ago. But at 'afe-past threy in a mornin' an' at 'afe-past threy in th'afternoon mar wetch shows th'reyght tarme – that's tweyce a dee.

Theyst got fer admit as a wetch wot shows th'reyght tarme tweyce a dee is a better tarme-keyper than one wot ony shows th'reyght tarme once a wik. So give me th'money.'

Ar reckoned owd Eeph desarved fer win that quid, dustna they?"

Th'owd gardners

"Ar've offen wondered if some o' theyse new-fangled things wot folks use in ther gardins are as good as some o' th'owd fashioned uns," said Jabez. "Th'owd gardners used get up ter aw sorts o' dodges thee knowst.

Ar used wetch owd Danny strike 'is prize carnations. Ey'd cut th'shoots off just below a joint an' stick a redish seyd up th'bit o' 'oller stem, an' then plant it. Ey reckoned as when th'redish seyd sprouted it'd feyd th'carnation cuttin' 'til it growed roots o' its own. It worked an' aw – ar've awwees done marn larke that ever since ey showed me th'knack.

Danny was a greet beleyver in leyf-mowld an' mosses, but ey'd ony 'ave leyf-mowld from under oak treys or beych treys. An' ey knew wheer ey could drop on different sorts o' mosses. Thers nowt larke a bit o' good moss fer keypin' things moist thee knowst.

An' ar've seyn 'im grow cuttin's off bushes an' treys in owd brids' neysts. Ey larked throstles' neysts best 'cos thee'r lined with mud, an' thee dunna come ter peyces aw that easy. Ey'd fill th'neyst with a bit o' leyfe mowld an' sand an' moss. An' then after ey'd planted th'cuttin' in it ey'd bury aw th'lot in th'gardin wheer ey wanted it grow.

An' then ther was owd Minty. Ey sowed be th'moon. Some things 'ad fer bey sowed when th'moon was weenin', an' some when th'moon was waxin'. When ey fost towd 'is missus ey was goin' sow be th'moon 'er got th'wrung idea. 'Er thowght ey was goin' do 'is gardin' at neyght. 'Er said: 'Yo must bey mad! Yer conna go plunderin' arind th'gardin in th'middle o' th'neyght sowin' seyds. Wot would th'neeghbours think?'

But ar reckon th'bloke wot capped th'lot was owd Isaac. Ey was a cow-flop an' 'oss-droppin's mon. Ey used roam rind th'feylds getherin' dried-up cow-flops on a lung stick with a pointed end. Ey reckoned as if yer mixed a bit o' good soil with theyse dried-up cow-flops it was th'best compost yer could lee yer lands on.

But 'oss-droppin's was 'is feevourite. Ey 'ad an owd beer-barrel in th'gardin wot ey kept full o' weyter ite o' th'well. Ther was awwees a bag-full o' fresh 'oss-droppin's danglin' in it from a stick across th'top o' th'barrel. Ey kept it well stirred, an' used th'juice fer weyterin' 'is gardin with. Ey used tell folks it meede plants shoot up that quick it was best fer stand well back when yer started weyterin' with it.

Ey kept a little bucket an' shovel just inside th'gardin gate, an' as soon as ey 'eerd a 'oss comin' up th'leene ey was ite larke a shot with this bucket an' shovel. Ar've known 'im foller 'osses rind th'village, an' ey was reyght sneaped if th'oss didna oblige 'im.

Mind thee, ey never 'ad any luck with th'rag-an'-bone mon's 'oss. Th'poer thing was nowt but skin an' greyf. One dee ey said ter this rag-an'-bone mon: 'Ar dunna reckon thee feydst that owd nag o' thine – ey'll bey droppin' jed betweyn th'shafts one o' theyse dees.'

But th'rag-mon 'ad got 'is answer ready. Ey said: 'If this 'oss 'ad relied on th'rags theyst given me fer buy 'is oats ey'da clemmed death yeers ago. If thee atna prepared fer put owt in 'im thee costna expect fer get owt ite, cost?'

Ar dunna think Isaac bothered follerin' th'rag-an-bone mon's 'oss after that."

Th'little Chapel

"It's nigh on 100 yeers since th'Chapel was built, inna it?" said Jabez. "Th'owd folks musta 'ad a lot o' feeth fer put a buildin' larke that up, mustna thee? Me feyther could remember it beyin' built.

Th'land was bought off owd Captin Ethcote fer 50 quid. Thers a 'ole in that stone at th'reyght-'and corner, an' me feyther remembered seyin' 'em put a bottle in this 'ole with aw sorts o' peepers an' things in it. Ar reckon somebody 'ull come across it one o' theyse dees when wey're aw jed an' gone.

After th'stone-leein' thee 'ad a bun-feyght in a tent in that feyld behind wheer th'owd farm cart-shed used bey.

Th'buildin' cost 'em 550 quid. That was a lot o' money in them dees, wonna it? Me feyther used tell me abite aw th'trouble thee 'ad for find this money. Thee managed fer burrer it from different pleeces, but th'poer souls couldna reese enough money fer pee th'interest.

Thee 'ad fer burrer moer money fer pee th'interest on th'money thee'd burrered. Afoer thee'd finished thee'd peed moer money in interest than aw th'money thee'd burrered.

An' then abite 7 yeer after it was opened, th'back-'afe o' th'chapel started fer sink inter th'grind an' th'side-wo's split open. If thee lukst dine th'side o' th'chapel thee cost still sey wheer th'back-end bends dine.

Thee were still up ter the ear-'oles in debt, an' nar thee'd gotten find some moer money fer 'ave th'back-end built up aggen. But afoer thee could do that thee 'ad fer 'ave th'vestry pulled dine so's thee could get at th'trouble. It was enough fer breek ther 'earts, wonna it?

Th'owd folks musta bin in a reyght pickle, 'cos thee couldna 'owd tea-meytins or seeles o' work in th'Chapel fer reese money fear lest it fell in on 'em. Thee tried aw sorts o' dodges fer meeke a copper or two. Thee 'ad tea-meytins dine Silverdeele an' dine 'Ommerend, an' thee 'ad one in a barn at th'farm.

Mind thee, thee didna stint thersels at theyse tea-meytins. Ar once seyd an owd minute book, an' at one o' theyse tea-meytins thee decided fer 'ave wot thee cawed a 'plain' tea. Thee'd ordered curran-bread, seyd-bread, wheyte-bread, bryne-bread, groceries, celery, an' 18 pynds o' best 'am!

If that's wot thee cawed a 'plain' tea ar'd larke fer know wot thee 'ad fer a good tea, wouldstna they?

Ar think thee musta got a bit fed up with 'am though, 'cos at th'next tea-meytin thee decided fer 'ave fresh salmon instead. Th'owd souls musta bin fond o' ther bellies, munna thee?

It was a good many yeers afoer thee got ite o' debt, but ar reckon thee built one o' th'nicest little Chapels rind this road, dustna they?"

Hill Top Methodist Church Scott Hay

A Glossary of North Staffordshire Dialect

Compiled from the Jabez Stories by Ian K Bloor

Dialect	Meaning	Context	Meaning
Abite	About	Messin' abite in weyter	Messing about in water
Accynt	Account	Be aw accynts	By all accounts
Adna	Had not	Wey adna got a steeble fer put it in	We had not got a stable to put it in
Adst	Had	Thee 'adst fer bey careful	You had to be careful
Afe	Half	'Afe a mile awee	Half a mile away
Af'noon	Afternoon	One Satdee afnoon	One Saturday afternoon
Afoer	Before	Afoer dark	Before dark
Aggen	Again	Nar an' aggen	Now and again
Agrey	Agree	Isaac's missus didna agrey	Isaac's wife did not agree
Aimer tote	Nearer to something	Dunna get aimer tote yon thresher	Do not get closer to that thresher
Akses	Ask	They akses t'many questions	You ask too many questions
'Andicapped	Handicapped		

Dialect	Meaning	Context	Meaning
Anna	Have not	Ar anna got a 'oss fer put thee on	I have not got a horse to put you on
Anythin'	Anything		
Anywheer	Anywhere		
'Appened	Happened		
Ar	I	Ar coulda towd 'im that	I could have told him that
Ar'ad	I had	Ar remember th'fost bike ar'ad	I remember the first bicycle I had
Ar'd	I would (or I'd)	Ar'd never 'ave guessed it	I would never have guessed it
'Ard	Hard	'Er'd bin a bit 'ard on 'him	She had been a bit hard on him
'Ardly	Hardly		
Ar'eerd	I heard	Ar 'eered somebody comin'	I heard somebody coming
Ar'll	I will	Ar'll come an' sey yer aggen	I'll come and see you again
Ar'm	I am	Wot ar'm tryin' fer tell thee	What I am trying to tell you
Ar've	I have (or I've)	Ar've 'eerd tell	I have heard tell

Dialect	Meaning	Context	Meaning
Arind	Around	Th'feylds arind th'village	The fields around the village
Asker	A newt	Amphibian of the Salamandridae	Family
As'll	That will	Summat as'll put that reyght	Something that will put that right
'Ast	Have you	'Ast ever etten cuttle-fish bone	Have you ever eaten cuttle-fish bone
'astna	(You) have not	Pretend thee 'astna seyn 'im	Pretend you have not seen him
Atna	(You) are not	They atna a sparrer	You are not a sparrow
'ave	have	Mowles 'ave fer 'ave weyter	
'avin'	having	'avin' a good luk dine this trench	Having a good look down this trench
Aw	all	Thee were aw sittin' dine	They were all sitting down
Awee	away	Yone get blowed awee	You will get blown away
Awwees	always		

Dialect	Meaning	Context	Meaning
Backerd(s)	backward(s)	Backerds 'an fererds / forrerds?	Backwards and forwards
Ballyful	Belly full	Get a ballyful o' lobby q.v.	Get a belly full of lobby
Bank(ed)-up		To heap fuel and ashes onto a fire	To make it burn slowly overnight
Basselow		Spoil-heap from mining activity	
Be	By	Be th'tarme ar got iteside	By the time I got outside
Beestin	Beestings		The first milk after a cow gives birth
Beleyve	believe		
Beleyver	believer		
Betweyn	between		
Bey	Be	Bey queyet	Be quiet
Beyf	beef	Beyf tey	Beef tea – made by boiling lean beef
Beyin	being	Me feyther beyin a collier	My father being a collier
Beylin'	Boiling		

Dialect	Meaning	Context	Meaning
Beym	Beam	A throstle's neyst on a beym	A thrush's nest on a beam
Bezzler	Drunkard		
Biddle Moer	Biddulph Moor	A high and wild part of Staffordshire	
Blartin'	Crying / Weeping	One o' th'wenches started blartin'	One of the girls started weeping
Bletherer			One who talks too much and too long
Bonk	bank or hill	'edge-bonk Up th'bonk Augers Bonk	hedge-bank = raised bank with bushes Up the hill Alsagers Bank is a village in Staffordshire
Bowd	Bold	Bowd as brass	Bold as Brass
Bowler		An iron hoop, used as a toy	
Breekes	Brakes		As in brakes on a bicycle
Brid	Bird		
Bryne	Brown		

Dialect	Meaning	Context	Meaning
Brynin'	Browning	Greevy brynin'	Gravy browning
Bucked		Brought to a halt	
Butties	Sandwiches	Butties an' cakes	Sandwiches and cakes
Cannonbo'	Cannonball		
Cawd	Called	'er cawd me Jabez	She called me Jabez
Childer	Children		
Chonnuck	Turnip		
Chuntering			Grumbling monotonously
Cirtle	circle		
Cleyn	clean	Cleyn weyter	Clean water
Cleyned	cleaned		
Clockin'	To hit with a fist	Ar felt larke clockin' 'im one	I felt like hitting him
Comin'	coming		
Comst	Comest	If thee ever comst across 'im . . .	If you ever come across him . . .
Con	can	Ar con remember . . .	I can remember
Concreyte	concrete		

Dialect	Meaning	Context	Meaning
Conna	Cannot (can't)	Ar conna find owt ar want	I cannot find anything I want
Cos	because		
Costna	Cannot (with thee / 'thou')	Thee costna put a price on a good woman	You can't put a price on a good woman
Coulda	Could have	Ar coulda towd 'im that	I could have told him that
Couldna	Could not	Ey couldna stand up	He couldn't stand up
Cowd	cold	Cowd weyter / Cowd in th'yed	Cold water / Cold in the head
Crack	An instant or short space of time		
Crowline	A straight line	Mixture of As the crow flies, and a bee-line	
Cuttin'	Cutting		Cutting a hedge / plant / hair / grass / railway
Dee	Day	Mondee, Tuesdee, Freydee	
Dees	Days	Satdees. 'olidays	Saturdays, Holidays

Dialect	Meaning	Context	Meaning
Didna	Did not / Didn't	Wey didna know wot fer do	We didn't know what to do
Dite	Doubt To extinguish	Ther were now dite abite it Costna dite 'it?	There was no doubt about it Can't you put it out?
Dockleyf	Dock leaf	Leaf of Rumex obtusifolius	Rubbed on to relieve nettle stings
Doer	Door	Pronounced doh-er	
Dostna	Dared not		
Dresser			Welsh dresser or China Hutch (US)
Dunna	Do not	Dunna owerfill them bags	Don't over-fill those bags
Dustna	Don't with thee and they	Thee knowst wot ar meyn, dustna? Dustna they reyd thee Bible?	You know what I mean, don't you? Don't you read your Bible?
'eathen	heathen	They atna queyte such a 'eathen as ar thowght thee wost	You are not quite such a heathen as I thought you were.
Eatin'	eating		

Dialect	Meaning	Context	Meaning
'eerd	heard		
Een	eyes		
'elp	help		
'em	them		
Enjoyin	enjoying		
Er	She		
Er'd	She had or She'd		
Errif	Local name for 'Cleavers"	Galium aparine, a herb with possible medically beneficial attributes	
Eringe	Orange	An eringe-box	An orange-box
'ers	She is	Er inna a bad sort	She is not a bad sort
Ersel's	Our selves	Wey hurt ersel's	We hurt ourselves
Esking	asking	Ar'm esking thee	I'm asking you
Esses	Ashes (from a fire)		
Essole	fireplace		
Etten	eaten		
Everythin	everything		

Dialect	Meaning	Context	Meaning
everywheer	everywhere		
Ey	he		
Ey'd	He had / he'd		
Ey'll	He will		
Ey's	He is /he's		
Fawse	false		
Fawt	fault	it wonna 'er fawt	it asn't her fault
Fer	For To	Fer a wik or moer Thee 'adst fer bey quick	For a week or more You had to be quick
Fererd(s) Forrerd(s)	forward(s)	Backerds 'an fererds Backerds comin' forrerds	Backwards and forwards Backwards at coming forwards
Fergotten	Forgotten		
Fermentin'	fermenting		
Feyd	Feed		
Feyl	Feel		
Feyld	Field		
Feyther	Father		

Dialect	Meaning	Context	Meaning
Finishin'	finishing		
Firmatree	frumenty		Cooked wheat grain with raisins etc.
Fithers	feathers		
Fleys	fleas		
Flippin'	flipping	an 'intensifier' or mild expletive	
Floer	floor		
Fo'	fall	A fo' o' sut	A fall of soot
Foer	four	Foer o'clock in th'mornin'	Four o'clock in the morning
Foller	follow		
Foo'	fool		
Footbo'	football		
Forrerd	Forward		
Fost	First		
Foty	Forty		
Fritten	Frighten		
Frum	From		
Fryin'	Frying		

Dialect	Meaning	Context	Meaning
Funt	Found	'Ast funt it?	Have you found it?
Gain	Gainly / nimble	Ey didna seym bey aw that gain	He didn't seem to be very gainly
Gansy	Sweater or Cardigan		
Gathered	Gathered		
Getst	Get (with Thee)	When thee getst owd	When you get old
Gettin'	Getting		
Gimme	gave me	Ey gimme a pair fer shut me up	He gave me a pair to shut me up
Givin'	giving		
Goin'	going		
Gorra	Got to (= must)	Theen gorra get snappin' . . .	They've got to get food . . .
Gotst	Got (with Thee)	When thee gotst theer . . .	When you got there . . .
Greet	great or grate	greet big box Fire-greet	great big box Fire grate
Greevy	gravy		

Dialect	Meaning	Context	Meaning
Greyhind	greyhound		The dog rather than the coach service
Grun	Ground (=powdered)	Grun-up oyster shells	Ground up oyster shells
Guessin’	guessing		
Ha’penny	Half penny		
i’	In	A cowd i’ th’yed	A cold in the head
‘ice	House (plural ‘ises) However th’ice	eyd come terth’wrung ‘ice could be the house or the ice	He’d come to the wrong house
‘im	Him		
‘imsel’	Himself		
‘inged	Hinged		
Inna	Is not	It inna as ‘ot as aw that	It isn’t as hot as all that
‘ises	Houses		
Ite	Out		
Iteside	Outside		
Jack-stuns	Jack-stones	The game of Jacks	Played with five pebbles or ‘stones’

Dialect	Meaning	Context	Meaning
Jed	dead		
Joey		Silver threepenny piece	
Jonnuck	Fair / correct	'er was jonnuck with 'im	She dealt fairly with him
Jowl	Large bowl		
Jynt	joint	Wik-end jynt	Weekend joint (of meat)
Jynts	Joints	Screws in me jynts	Screws in my joints (arthritis)
Keggy-handed		Left-handed	
Ketched	Caught		
Keyper	Keeper	Th'Geeme-keyper	The Game-keeper
Keypin'	Keeping		
Killin'	Killing		
Kitchin	Kitchen		
Knacker's	Knacker's man	Knacker – disposer of dead farm animals	
Kneyves	Knives		

Dialect	Meaning	Context	Meaning
Knowed	Knew	Ar ony knowed one bloke as 'ud . .	I only knew one man who would . .
Knowst	Know (with Thee)	Thee knowst	You know
Kynt	Count	Since th'last kynt	Since the last count
Lapped	Wrapped	Ey wouldna 'ave it lapped up	He would not have it wrapped up
'lastic	Elastic		
Larke	Like	Larke a fish ite o' weyter	Like a fish out of water
Lee ite on	Lay hold of	Wey leede ite on 'im	We laid hold of him
Leece	Lace – shoelace or material		
Leene	Lane	Dine th'leene	Down (along) the lane
Lettin'	letting		
Leyghtnin'	lightning		Thunder and . . . .
Leyghts	Lights = Offal		

Dialect	Meaning	Context	Meaning
Leyk	Leek	Town in Staffordshire Moorlands	
Leyves	leaves	Leyves on th'treys	Leaves on the trees
Lide	Loud	It was that lide	It was so loud
Linseyd	Linseed		
Lobby		North Staffs beef or lamb stew	Lots of different 'original' recipes !
Locusses	Locusts		Voracious insects
Lors		Variant of 'Lawks' or 'Lord'	Expression of surprise
Luk	Look		
Lyin'	Lying		
Macheyne	Machine		
Maggies	Magpies		Birds of the crow family Pica Pica
Maggy Ann	Margarine		
Mak	Make		
Marrer	Marrow	Gourd family Cucurbitaceae	

Dialect	Meaning	Context	Meaning
Mashin'	Mashing	Courting.	Dating is the modern word.
Maxim		A lottery. A number of workers pay a certain sum for a certain time. Lots are drawn who shall take the whole of the 1st week's subscription, who the second, etc.	
Me	My or me (see Mey)	Me feyther used tell me abite	My father used to tell me about
Meede	made	wey must 'ave meede a lot o' noise	We must have made a lot of noise
Meeke	Make		
Meekin'	Making		
Meller	Mellow		
Mentionin'	Mentioning		
Mesel'	Myself		
Mey	Me (See Me)	Used as an emphatic ME	Give it ter mey! But Dance wi'me.
Meyce	mice		
Meyl	meal		
Meyn	mean		
Meyt	meat		

Dialect	Meaning	Context	Meaning
Meythered	Mithered		mither = to make a persistent fuss
Miaowin'	Meowing		noise made by a cat
Migratin'	Migrating		
Mit	Might	Ar mit as well . . .	I might as well
Mithe	Mouth		
Mithefuls	Mouthfulls		
Mitta	Might have	Ar mitta known . . .	I might have knowm
Moer	More	Con ar 'av some moer	Can I have some more
Mon	Man	Th'magic-lantern mon	The magic-lantern (epidiascope) man
Mornin'	Morning		
Mowles	moles		Mammals of the Family Talpidae
Murderin'	murdering		
Musta	Must have	Ar musta dozed off	I must have dozed off
Nar	now	Nar an' aggen	Now and again

Dialect	Meaning	Context	Meaning
Neeghbours	neighbours		
Neeme	name		
Neemes	names		
Neyght	night		
Neyst	nest		
Neysts	nests		
Nickneemes	nicknames		
Noss	nurse		
Now	No	It were now use.	It was no use
Nowt	Nothing Naughty child	Nowt in perticler Ey were a bit o' a nowt	Nothing in particular He was a bit of a naughty child
Nowtice	Notice	Tek now nowtice	Take no notice
Nowty	Naughty / Peevish	Yer a pair o' nowty lads	You are a pair of naughty lads
'ob	Hob	top of a stove	
Ockerd	Awkward		
Oky	Hokey-pokey	Cowd as oky	As cold as ice-cream

Dialect	Meaning	Context	Meaning
‘olly	Holly		
‘ommer	Hammer		
On’em	Of them / on them	One on’em / ey sat one on’em	One of them / he sat on one of them
On spec.	Speculatively	With no certainty of success	
Ony	only		
Openin’	opening		
‘oss	horse		
Ot	Hot		
Owd	old		
‘owd	hold		
‘owdin’	holding		
Ower	over	Yed ower ‘ales	Head over heals
Owerdid	overdid		
Owerfill	overfill		
Owt	anything	‘Ast they ‘ad owt do wi’ this?	Have you had anything to do with this?
P’raps	perhaps		

Dialect	Meaning	Context	Meaning
Peyce	Piece / peace	A worm on a peyce o' string. A 'peyce' Th'seyson o' peyce an' goodwill	A worm on a piece of string A thick slice of bread The season of peace and good will
Peyces	Pieces		
Peys	Peas		
Pickin'	Picking		
Picotees		Types of carnation having petals with darker edges	
Pittle	Pickle		
Plee	Play	Game / trick / instrument	
Pleece	Place	Th'place were as black as a bag	
pleeces	Places		
Pobs		Bread or toast in warm milk or tea	
Poer	poor		
Pokin'	poking		

Dialect	Meaning	Context Meaning
Pon	pan	Eg Saucepan / Frying pan
Poo	pool	pond
Poppin’	popping	Popping out = appearing (suddenly) Popping in = placing in (suddenly)
Pottry	pottery	
Powltice	poultice	Hot moist mass used to relieve pain or swelling
Powlticin’	poulticing	Applying a poultice
Pree	pray	
Preed	prayed	
Preein’	Praying	
Pullin’	Pulling	
Puthery	Humid / oppresive	
Quarries		Thick, plain,hard-wearing floor tiles
Queyet	Quiet	

Dialect	Meaning	Context Meaning
Queyte	Quite	
Rattlin’	Rattling	Making a noise by shaking something like a rattle Talking quickly or incessantly
Rattlin’ good		Very good
Rawngin’	Physically stressful	Eg Rawngin’ work
Redish	Radish	Raphanus sativus
Reen	Rain	
Reyched	reached	
Reyd	read	
Reyder	reader	
Reydin’	reading	
Reyght	Right / write	Numerous meanings of right
Rhubub	rhubarb	Rheum rhabarbarum
Rindin’ on	Rounding on	Suddenly attack (verbally or physically)

Dialect	Meaning	Context	Meaning
Road	Can be way or method	Shifted it ite o' th'road A road ey'd read abite	Moved it out of the way A way/method he'd read about
Roarin' trade	Roaring trade	Selling a lot of things quickly	
Rowst	Rouse	To get up / arise / wake up	
Ruck	Heap	An untidy heap / a lot	
Runnin'	Running		
Salary	Celery	Apium graveolens var. dulce	
Sarved	Served	It sarved 'im reyght	It served him right. He deserved it.
Sarves	Serves	It sarves 'im reyght	
Sawt	salt		
Schoo'	School		
Scoer	Score – 20 items		
Scrapin'	Scraping		
Screymed	Screamed		

Dialect	Meaning	Context	Meaning
Scuft		To strike a glancing blow	
Scuftin’	Scufting		
Sedst	Said Would say	Thee sedst it were mar fawt Afoer thee sedst it were mar fawt	You said it was my fault before you would say it was my fault
Seeme	same		
Settin’	setting	Set seeds / set fire to	
Sey	see	Wey can sey wot’s ‘appened.	We can see what has happened
Seyd	Noun - seed noun - side	Redish seyd foer lads on each seyd	Radish seed four lads on each side
Seyd	Verb - saw	If ey seyd a ‘ole	If he saw a hole
Seyds	seeds		
Seyn	seen	Pretend thee astna seyn ‘im	Pretend you haven’t seen him
Seyson	season		
Seyst	See (with thee)	If thee seyst ‘im	If you see him

Dialect	Meaning	Context	Meaning
Shan	Shall	Wey shan bey threshin' aw neyght	We shall be thrashing all night
Sheepe	Shape	It were th'wrung sheepe	It was the wrong shape
Shifty	Tricky	Ey's a bit shifty in th'een	Looks untrustworthy about the eyes
Shillin'	Shilling	One twentieth of One Pound Sterling pre-decimalisation	Twelve pennies made One shilling. 240 pennies / pence to the Pound
Shippon	Cattle shed		
Shoulda	Should have	Ey shoulds sowd it ter th'cobbler	He should have sold it to the cobbler
Sin'	Since		
Singin'	singing		
Sirree	Sir – as intensifier	Dust know wot, sirree?	Do you know . . .
Slarrin'	Sliding – on ice		
Sleck	Slack – fine coal		

Dialect	Meaning	Context	Meaning
Sledgin’	Sledging – on snow		
Sleyp	sleep		
Snappin’	Snapping	Snappin’ tin = lunch box	Food eaten whilst at work
Snive	Swarm / be full of	Snived wi’ little shaller pits	Teeming with small shallow mines
Soakies	See pobs		
Soce-pan	saucepan		
Somewheer	somewhere		
Sowd	sold		
Sparrers	Sparrows	Family of small passerine birds, **Passeridae**	
Speyd	speed		
Speyke	Speak	Er could ‘ardly speyke	She could hardly speak
Summat	Something		
Summat’s	Something has		
Surry	Sorry		
Sut	Soot		

Dialect	Meaning	Context	Meaning
Swaller	Swallow	Bird in the family Hirundinidae	
Sweatin'	Sweating		
Sweypin'	Sweeping		
Sweyt	Sweet		
Synd	Sound		
T'many	Too many		
T'other	The other		
Tak	take		
Taks	takes		
Talkin'	talking		
Taller	tallow	Rendered beef or mutton fat	
Tankin'	Spanking	Ey 'ad a reyght good tankin'	He had a very severe spanking
Tarme	time		
Tarme	time	'Arvest tarme	Harvest time
Teeble	table		
Teeblespoon	tablespoon		
Tellin'	telling		
Ter	to		

Dialect	Meaning	Context	Meaning
Terneyght	tonight		
Th’	the		
Th’air	the hair or the air	th’air growin’ ointment Up in th’air	the hair-growing ointment Up in the air
Th’een	The eyes	Ey’s a bit shifty in th’een	He looks a little furtive in the eyes
Th’entry floer	The entry floor	The floor of the passage between adjacent terraced houses	
Th’luk	The look	Ar didna larke th’luk o’ this box	I did not like the look of this box
Th’wrong	The wrong		
Th’year	The year		
Th’yed	The head		
Thar	You or your	Thar greet babby / It’s thar fawt	You big baby / It’s your fault
Thee’ad	They had	Thee’ad fer leyve ‘er alone	They had to leave her alone
Thee’adst	You (one) had	Thee’adst a job fer tell	You (one) had difficulty to discern

Dialect	Meaning	Context	Meaning
Thee'd	They had, or would		
Thee'da	They would have		
Thee't	You (one) are (is)	Thee't ready fer owt	You are ready for anything
Theer	There		
Theer's	There is	Theer's nowt like people	There is nothing like people
Theesen	Yourself		
Theest	You have	Theest got me wrong aggen	You have me wrong again
Thee't	You are / will		
Ther	There / their		
Ther'll	There will	Ther'll always bey summat wey dunna know	There will always be something that we do not know
Thers	There is / has	Thers sut everywheer Thers bin a fo' o' sut	There is soot everywhere There has been a fall of soot
Theydst (1)	You have	Theydst got 'im guessin'	You have got him guessing
Theydst (2)	You would	Theydst 'ave push me work	You would have to push me to work

Dialect	Meaning	Context	Meaning
Theyse	These	Ar used plee with some o' theyse childer	I used to play with some of these children
Theyst (1)	You have	They's kilt 'im fer sure	You have (surely) killed him
Theyst (2)	You had	Theyst better come dine	You had better come down
Theyt	You will / You are	Theyt no dite manage fer get wom Theyt th'answer ter me prayer	You will no doubt manage to get home You are the answer to my prayer
Theyts (1)	You would	If theyts do that ter thar thumb	If you would do that to your (own) thumb
Theyts (2)	You had (should)	Theytst better stop wheer thee at	You had better stop where you are
Thinkin'	Thinking		
Tho'	Though		
Thowght	Thought	Ar thowght me number were up	I thought my number was up
Thrashin'	Thrashing	Wey shan be thrashing' aw neyght	We shall be thrashing all night

Dialect	Meaning	Context	Meaning
Threy	Three		
Throstle	Thrush	Song Thrush - Turdus philomelos	
Tine	Town	Dine th'tine	Down the town – Down = at
Tote	Towards	Wey kept goin' tote this charabang	We kept going towards the charabang
Towd	Told	Ar towd 'er ar didna know	I told her that I did not know
Treede	Trade	Er used do a good treede in th'summer, perticly at th'wik-ends	She used to do a good trade in the summer, particularly at the week-ends
Treen	Train	Th'treen-fare	The Train-fare
Tryin'	Trying		
Trysers	Trousers		
Tuk	Took	Ar tuk th'key wi' me be mistake	I took the key with me by mistake
Tongue	Tongue		
Tweyce	Twice		
Two-threy	Two or three	Not many	

Dialect	Meaning	Context	Meaning
‘ud	Would	Nowbody ‘ud notice	Nobody would notice
‘ull	Will	Th’redish seyd ‘ull throw ite roots	The radish seed will throw out roots
Underclose	Under-clothes		
‘ungrier	Hungrier		
‘uns	Ones	Thee wonna as good as bought ‘uns	They were not as good as bought ones
Upsteers	Upstairs		
Uptychuck		To bowl a cricket ball using an elevated trajectory	
Voss	Verse (of poem or hymn)		
Walk rind	A walk around	A leasurely stroll perhaps	
Wantst	(You) want	Thee wantst plant it wi’taters	You want/should plant it with potatoes
Wee	Way	‘afe-wee through	Half-way through

Dialect	Meaning	Context	Meaning
Weekes	Wakes	Local workers' holiday period	
Weest	Waist		
Weet	Wait	Left 'im fer weet for th'treen	Left him to wait for the train
Welly	Nearly	'air welly dine ter 'er weest	Hair nearly down to her waist
Wench	Girl		
Weshed	Washed		
Wetch	Watch	To observe or a time-piece	
Wey	We	Wey shall bey stuck 'ere aw dee	We shall be stuck here all day
Wey'd	We would, or we had	We'd try it this idea After wey'd put worm's on th'ooks	We would try out this idea After we had put worms on the hooks
Weyer	wire	A can with a weyer 'andle	A can with a wire handle
Weyn	wine We have	wayter inter weyn Weyn 'ad a bit ter drink	water into wine We've had a little to drink
Weyn (1)	Wine		

Dialect	Meaning	Context	Meaning
Weyn (2)	We will	Weyn 'ave some roasted taters fer us suppers	We will have some roasted potatoes for our suppers
Weynd	Wind	weynd th'clock up	wind the clock up
Weyter	Water		
Wheer	Where		
Wheyle	While		
Wi'	With		
Wik	Week	Th'fost wik ey did fer me doer-mat	The first week he did for my door-mat
Withite	Without		
Wo'	Wall	Ar used get up on th'pig-sty wo'	I used to get up on the pig-sty wall
Wom	Home	He went wom an' blarted	He went home and cried
Wonna	Was not	It wonna moer than 'afe a mile	It wasn't more than half a mile
Woodpidgins	Wood pigeons		
Workin'	Working		

Dialect	Meaning	Context	Meaning
Woss	worse	from bad ter woss	From bad to worse
Wost	Were	They wost lucky	You were lucky
Wot (1)	What	Wot 'appened last wik?	What happened last week?
Wot (2)	That	Clee wot meede reyght good 'uns	Clay that made right (really) good ones
Wot'll	That will	A dog wot'll bey friendly	A dog that will be friendly
Wot's	What is / That is		
Woth	Worth	It wonna woth me goin'	It was not worth me (my) going
Wots	What have	Wots bin up ternar?	What have (you) been up to now?
Wouldna	Would not	'Er wouldna rest	She would not rest
Wrobble	A tangle	Theyt be getting' thee tungue in a wrobble	You will be getting your tongue in a tangle.
Wun	Wound	Ey wun up th'clock	He wound up the clock

Dialect	Meaning	Context	Meaning
Wunna	Will not	Ey wunna come anywheer near it	He will not come anywhere near it
Wutna	Will not (with You)	They wutna lose thee thumb	You will not lose your thumb
Wutsna	Would not	Thee wutsna remember owd Tum	You would not remember old Tom
Wutstna	Would not		
Yed	Head		
Yeds	Heads		
Yeer	Year		
Yer	You	It'll thrash yer inter little peyces	It will thrash you into little pieces
Yersels	Yourselves		
Yeyst	Yeast		
Yo	You	Nar yo childer	Now, you children
Yoer	Your		

A Pronunciation Guide

QR codes and short URL links to audio files of Wilfred Bloor reading selected phrases from his stories

"QR Code" a registered trademark of DENSO WAVE

"ter" - "to"
"If thee wentst dine ter th'surgery ey'd lance thee a boil"
(If you went down to the surgery he would lance you a boil)

https://bit.ly/36yyV36

"two" - "two"
"Thee kept ite o' Martha's road fer a dee or two"
(They kept out of Martha's road for a day or two)

https://bit.ly/36wy4jn

"moer" – "more"
"Mind thee, considerin' ey were moer used ter andlin a pick an' shovel…"
(Mind you, considering he was more used to handling a pick and shovel…)

https://bit.ly/37L6Shv

"Lee" – "lay"
"But th'owd feller just lee theer"
(But the old fellow just lay there)

https://bit.ly/3CRFWrC

"beyf" – "beef"
" 'er'd forgotten tell me abite th'beyf-tea"
(She had forgotten to tell me about the beef tea)

https://bit.ly/3ilrsXH

"doer" – "door"
"When Fanny opened th'doer…."
(When Fanny opened the door…)

https://bit.ly/3CPtTv2

"lukkin" – "looking"
"Ar remember an owd widower 'er was lukkin' after"
(I remember an old widower she was looking after)

https://bit.ly/3tlYQ6S

"peentin" – "painting"
"Me mother at do aw the'rest o' th'peentin' an' peeperin' 'ersel' "
(My mother had to do all the painting and papering herself)

https://bit.ly/3tlYQ6S

Resources

QR and short URL links to resources

Google Map of Scott Hay

http://bit.ly/Scott_Hay

http://bit.ly/keelewab

Keele University Archives of Wilfred Alan Bloor's papers

http://bit.ly/keelewab

Wilfred Bloor's Obituary

https://bit.ly/3JmDqvT

http://bloor.org/

The Bl(o)or(e) One Name Society

http://bloor.org/

Alphabetical Table of Contents

V

W

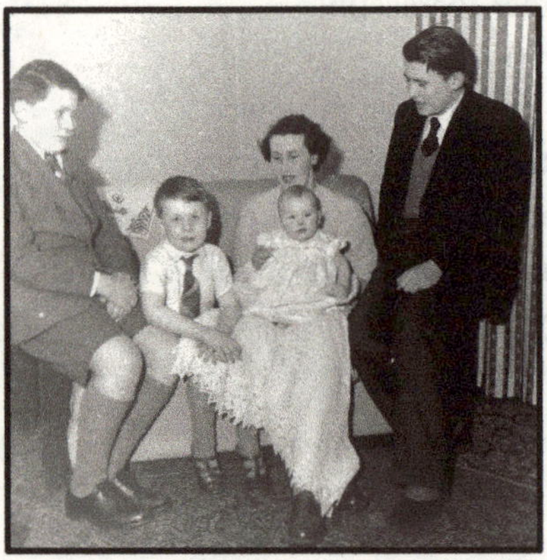

The Bloor family

Ian, Roger, David & Irene, Alan

photograph by W.A.Bloor

The Jabez Stories Album's on CD

If you enjoyed the Jabez stories then you can listen to Wilfred Bloor narrating the stories in dialect buy purchasing the albums which were recorded and sold on tape in 1980 and 1989 and are now available again on CD.

Copies are for sale of the following CD's

Jabez Album II, written and narrated by Wilfred Bloor in 1989

Jabez Album I, live at the Audley Theatre on 19th June 1980

To purchase the albums please phone the Keele University Archives on 01782 733237.

The CD's are priced at £10.00 each (plus postage)

The Archive Web Page for the Wilfred Bloor Papers is:

http://www.keele.ac.uk/library/specarc/collections/wilfredbloor/

The Digitised Jabez Stories

Following Keele University's participation in the British Library's 'Unlocking Our Sound Heritage' project, Wilfred Bloor's 'Jabez' recordings have now been digitally preserved and catalogued.

To mark 50 years since Wilfred Bloor first published his 'Jabez' tales in book form, Keele University are making some of the recordings freely available online. All stories are written and performed by Wilfred Bloor, in North Staffordshire dialect, in the character of 'Jabez'.

The digitised stories

The following stories are available in the digitised collection

The Wilfred Bloor Collection is held in Keele's Special Collections and Archives. Material dates from the 1960s to the 1990s and comprises manuscript and typescript articles, cuttings, correspondence and numerous audio recordings
https://www.keele.ac.uk/library/specialcollections/wilfredbloor/

Lightning Source UK Ltd.
Milton Keynes UK
UKHW040608101222
413690UK00001B/3

9 781739 800765